# Innovation (Bid'ah) in Islam

## Dr. Aminul Islam Laskar

INDIA • SINGAPORE • MALAYSIA

# Contents


Preface — iv

Chapter 1  Tawheed and Shirk — 1

1.1  Tawhid — 1

1.2  Shirk — 10

1.3  Major and Minor Sins — 14

1.4  Boundary/Limit of Islam — 21

1.5  Mushrikun say, "Allah has a begotten son, Glory to Him" — 23

1.6  The disbeliever seeking ransom on the Day of Judgement — 26

1.7  The disbeliever is rewarded for his good deeds in this world — 27

1.8  Minor Shirk — 27

1.9  Riya (Show off) is a hidden Shirk — 28

1.10  Superstition, Astrologer and Fortune teller — 31

1.11  Shirk is the biggest sin — 38

1.12  Consequence of Shirk — 40

1.13  People often commit shirk while mentioning the Creator and creations — 41

1.14  Warning by Allah SWT against Shirk — 46

1.15  We have to seek only from Allah, nobody else — 46

1.16  Intermediation — 57

1.17  Swearing by something other than Allah SWT is a         67
      Shirk

Chapter 2   Innovation (Bid'ah)                                69
2.1   Characterization of Bid'at                               69
2.2   Negligence and Bid'ah                                    75
2.3   Why should not there be any innovation?                  80
2.4   Why is the last prophethood important?                   87
2.5   Treatment with innovators                                89
2.6   Examples often quoted by innovators for                  90
      misguidance
2.7   Warning against Bid'at in the Qur'an                     92
2.8   Warning against Bid'at by the Prophet (ﷺ)               93
2.9   Who is responsible for introducing Bid'at?              94
2.10  Whom to follow in case of Bid'at                         97
2.11  Sunnah of Righty guided Khalifas                        101
2.12  Who are Khulafa ar-Rashideen?                           103
2.13  Whoever obeys the Prophet (ﷺ) will enter Paradise       105
2.14  Whom to follow if there is no righteous group of        106
      Muslims
2.15  Consequence of Bid'ats                                  107
2.16  The grant is from Allah SWT only                        109
2.17  Graves                                                  111
2.18  Part of the Head is Shaved and Other Parts are          113
      Left Long
2.19  Not to narrate from tampered Torah and Bible            114
2.20  Why does Bid'at exist?                                  115
2.21  Good Practices and Bid'at                               119

Contents


2.22  Night Prayer during Ramadan in congregation   121

2.23  Congregational coexistent Bid'ah in Masjid   123

2.24  Mid Sha'ban/Lailatul Barat Prayer   130

2.25  Bid'at has made Islam bulky   133

2.26  Sects (Firqa) in Islam   135

2.27  Islamic Brotherhood   139

2.28  Mujaddid (Revivalist)   144

Chapter 3  Knowledge of Unseen (Ilmul Gaib)   147

3.1  Ilmul gaib of the Prophet (ﷺ)   149

3.2  Does the Prophet (ﷺ) know about the happenings on earth after death?   159

3.3  Companions had no knowledge of unseen   164

3.4  Knowing another person's mind   174

3.5  Guess, Intuition, Inspiration, Karamaah and Mu'jiza   176

3.6  Jinns have no Ilmul gaib   202

3.7  Seeing (virtuous) dead persons when awake   203

3.8  Seeing the Prophet (ﷺ) when awake   205

3.9  The Prophet (ﷺ) is the last   224

3.10  Wali of Allah   226

3.11  Can anyone see Allah SWT in dreams and when awake?   231

3.12  Glorification by inanimate objects   236

3.13  Mubasshirat   240

Epilogue   247

# Preface

بِسْمِ ٱللَّهِ ٱلرَّحْمَـٰنِ ٱلرَّحِيمِ

And all praise is due to Allah, the Lord of all creation. May Allah, the Exalted bestows His peace and Blessings upon Prophet Muhammad (ﷺ), upon the family and Companions of the Prophet (ﷺ). Allah says in the Qur'an (that means): *Certainly, Allah's only Way is Islam* (Ch 3:19). The Prophet of Allah (ﷺ) said, "Whosoever introduces a new belief in our religion which contradicts with it is rejected." After the demise of the Prophet (ﷺ), many rituals penetrated into Islam which were non-existent during the Prophet (ﷺ) and his companions. Those rituals now are so firmly rooted that anybody objecting to those is considered to be out-numbered and is humiliated. Further, misuse of knowledge of unseen led to many innovations over the years. In view of above, an attempt has been made to disseminate the teachings of the Quran and Sunnah in this regard to the Muslim Ummah. Clear concept about innovation and knowledge of unseen will help to refrain from polytheism. May Allah guide us to understand the essence of Islam.

Tafseer Ibn Kasir (abridged) and transliteration of the Verses of the Qur'an are reproduced from online version available at www.quran.com. Most of the Hadiths are reproduced from the websites www.hadithunlock. com, www.sunnah.com, and www.abuaminaelias.com. Many Hadiths, comments, definitions and explanations included in the book have been taken from www.islamqa.info/en. The lecture videos and research papers from the website ahlesunnatpak.com were of tremendous help in preparing the manuscript. I gratefully acknowledge my sincere gratitude to these websites. May Allah grant the efforts of these websites towards spreading of Islam. Suggestion for rectification of mistakes if any will be highly appreciated. May Almighty grant us the best life here and Jannat-ul-Firdous hereafter. Ameen.

Aminul Islam Laskar, 2025

# Chapter 1

# Tawheed and Shirk

Bid'ah in Islam refers to introducing a new practice or belief that has no basis in the teachings or actions of the Prophet Muhammad (ﷺ) and his Companions. It represents an innovation in religious matters that was neither known nor practiced during their time. To properly understand Bid'ah, one must also grasp the concepts of Tawheed (the oneness of Allah) and Shirk (associating partners or ascribing rivals with Allah). For this reason, Chapter 1 provides a brief introduction to both Tawheed and Shirk.

Another key topic discussed in this book is the Knowledge of the Unseen ('Ilm al-Ghayb), which holds a special place in Islamic theology. Sometimes, the misuse or false claims related to this knowledge can lead to the introduction of Bid'ah. Hence, the concepts of Bid'ah and the claim to possess knowledge of the unseen are closely linked and can lead to deviation from the true path of Islam.

## 1.1 Tawheed

Tawheed (تَوْحِيد) is derived from the verb *wahhada*, which means 'to make something singular'. Tawheed means uniqueness of Allah سُبْحَانَهُ وَتَعَالَى (abbreviated as SWT, meaning May He be Praised and Exalted or the most Glorified, the most High). In Islam, Tawheed is to single out Allah 'alone' and to worship none but Him and to obey Muhammad (ﷺ) as the Messenger of Allah and that Allah will not accept any religion except Islam. The person who believes in these by heart is a believer or Mu'min. Allah SWT lists the qualities of a beliver in the Qur'an in many places and some of these are as follows (interpretation of meaning):

- *The believers are only the ones who have believed in Allah and His Messenger and then doubt not but strive with their wealth and their lives in the cause of Allah. It is those who are the truthful. (Al-Hujurat Ch 49:15)*

- *Alif, Lam, Meem. This is the Book about which there is no doubt, a guidance for those conscious of Allah, who believe in the unseen, establish prayer, and spend out of what We have provided for them. (Al-Baqarah Ch 2:1-3)*

- *The true believers are only those whose hearts tremble at the remembrance of Allah, whose faith increases when His revelations are recited to them, and who put their trust in their Lord. They are those who establish prayer and donate from what We have provided for them. (Al-Anfal Ch 8: 2-3)*

Allah SWT commands us for Tawheed in the Holy Book (interpretation of meaning):

- *And your devotion will be entirely to Allah; (Al-Anfal Ch 8:39)*

- *I did not create jinn and humans except to worship Me. (Az-Zariat Ch 56 :51)*

- *Worship Allah alone and associate none with Him. (An-Nisa Ch 4:36)*

- *So call upon Allah with sincere devotion, even to the dismay of the disbelievers. (Surah Ghafir Ch 40:14)*

Tawheed is the very purpose of the sending of the Messengers from the first to the last of them. Allah SWT said in the Qur'an:

- *We never sent a messenger before you 'O Prophet' without revealing to him: "There is no God 'worthy of worship' except Me, so worship Me 'alone." (Al-Anbiya Ch 21: 25; interpretation of meaning)*

The Prophet Muhammad (ﷺ) was sent to affirm this Tawheed with a complete affirmation and he (ﷺ) prohibited people from associating partners with Allah. According to the Islamic scholars, Tawheed includes all the three types which are interconnected and are as follows:

The first is **Lordship of Allah** or Tawheed ar-Rububiyyah. It is to believe that *only* Allah SWT is the Creator of everything, and is the Disposer of Affairs of everything, and He has no partners besides Him in that. It also means attributing Governance and Legislation *only* to Allah, through sending His Messengers and revelation of His Books. Allah says (interpretation of meaning):

- *Surely, His is the Creation and Commandment. Blessed is Allah, the Lord of the 'Alamin (mankind, jinn and all that exists)! (Al-A'raf Ch 7: 54)*

- *The Lord of the Heavens and the earth and everything in between, the Most Compassionate. No one will dare speak to Him. (An-Naba Ch 78:37)*

The second is **His worship** or Tawheed al-Uloohiyyah. It is to believe that Allah SWT is the One worshipped in truth, and He has no partners besides Him in that. So, all the acts of worship from Salat (prayer), Sawm (fasting), and other acts **must be done sincerely for Allah alone and it is not permissible to associate, anything from these acts of worship, with anyone other than Allah.** Lordship is Allah's action that show control over His creation while Worship is our action towards Allah SWT. Allah SWT says in the Quran (interpretation of meaning):

- *He is the Lord of the Heavens, and the earth, and everything in between. So worship Him 'alone', and be steadfast in His worship. Do you know of anyone equal to Him in His attributes? (Surah Maryam Ch 19:65)*

- *It is truly I. I am Allah! There is no god 'worthy of worship' except Me. So worship Me 'alone', and establish prayer for My remembrance. (Surah Taha Ch 20:14)*

The third is **His Names and Attributes** or Tawheed al-Asmaa was-Sifaat. It is that we do not name Allah SWT except by what He has named Himself with or with what the Messenger (ﷺ) has named Him, and we do not describe Him except by what He has described Himself with or what the Messenger (ﷺ) has described Him. In His saying (interpretation of meaning):

- *There is nothing like Him, for He 'alone' is the All-Hearing, All-Seeing. (Ash-Shuraa Ch 42:11)*

- *Do you know of anyone equal to Him 'in His attributes'?" (Surah Maryam Ch 19:65)*

Every approach and intercession believed by the disbelievers who call upon others alongside Allah will be in vain on the Day of Judgement. Allah SWT says (interpretation of meaning):

- *He merges the night into the day and the day into the night, and has subjected the sun and the moon, each orbiting for an appointed term. That is Allah—your Lord! All authority belongs to Him. But those ˹idols˺ you invoke besides Him do not possess even the skin of a date stone. (Surah Fatir Ch 35:13)*

- *And who could be more astray than those who call upon others besides Allah—˹others˺ that cannot respond to them until the Day of Judgment, and are ˹even˺ unaware of their calls? (Al-Ahqaf Ch 46:5)*

There are verses in the Qur'an that prove that the polytheists of Makkah also believed in the Lordship of Allah (interpretation of meaning):

- <u>*And if you ask them (polytheists) who created the Heavens and the earth, they will definitely say, "Allah!" Say, "Praise be to Allah!" In fact, most of them do not know. (Surah Luqman Ch 31:25)*</u>

However, mushrikhs (disbelievers) denied worship of Allah SWT. They believed that responsibilities and powers were assigned to idols namely Laat, Uzza and Manaat, Hubal, Isaaf and Naa'ilah etc. This belief would not benefit them due to the fact that they considered idols as partners of Allah whereas Allah SWT deserves exclusive worship and submission. Allah SWT says: *Remember, Allah alone deserves the exclusive submission. As for those who have adopted guardians other than Him (saying), "We worship them for no other reason but because they would bring us near to Allah closely". (Az-Zumar Ch 39:3; interpretation of meaning)*

## His Throne was on the water

Narrated Imran bin Hussain (ra): While I was with the Prophet (ﷺ), some people from Bani Tamim came to him. The Prophet (ﷺ) said, "O Bani Tamim! Accept the good news!" They said, "You have given us the good news; now give us (something)." (After a while) some Yemenites entered, and he said to them, "O the people of Yemen! Accept the good news, as Bani Tamim have refused it." They said, "We accept it, for we have come to you to learn the Religion. So, we ask you what the beginning of this universe was." The Prophet (ﷺ) said "There was Allah and nothing else before Him and His Throne was over the water, and He then created the Heavens and the Earth and wrote everything in the Book." Then a man came to me and said: O `Imran! Follow your she-camel for it has run away! So, I set out seeking it, and behold, it was beyond the mirage! By Allah, I wished that it (my she-camel) had gone but that I had not left (the gathering). [Bukhari]

Note: For the companions of the Prophet (ﷺ), the abbreviation of *ra*, a short form of Radeyallahu 'Anhu (رضي الله عنه) is used which translates as "May Allah be pleased with him". For female companions, the Arabic phrase is Radeyallhu 'Anha (رضي الله عنها) which means "May Allah be pleased with her".

## Knowledge is with Allah SWT

Narrated Abdullah ibn Mas`ud (ra): While I was walking in company with the Prophet (ﷺ) in one of the fields of Madinah, the Prophet (ﷺ) was reclining on a palm leave stalk which he (ﷺ) carried with him. We passed by a group of Jews. Some of them said to the others, "Ask him about the spirit." The others said, "Do not ask him, lest he would say something that you hate." Some of them said, "We will ask him." So, a man from among them stood up and said: O Abal-Qasim (ﷺ)! What is the spirit (ruh)? The Prophet (ﷺ) kept quiet and I knew that he (ﷺ) was being divinely inspired. Then he (ﷺ) said: وَيَسْـَٔلُونَكَ عَنِ ٱلرُّوحِ ۖ قُلِ ٱلرُّوحُ مِنْ أَمْرِ رَبِّى وَمَآ أُوتِيتُم مِّنَ ٱلْعِلْمِ إِلَّا قَلِيلًا

*"They ask you concerning the Spirit, Say: The Spirit; its knowledge is with my Lord. And of knowledge you (mankind) have been given only a little."* (Ch 17:85) [Bukhari]

**Rights of His slaves upon Allah SWT**

Narrated Mu'az bin Jabal (ra): The Prophet (ﷺ) said, "O Mu'az! Do you know what Allah's Right upon His slaves is?" I said, "Allah and His Apostle (ﷺ) know the best." The Prophet (ﷺ) said, "To worship Him (Allah) Alone and to join none in worship with Him (Allah). Do you know what their right upon Him is?" I replied, "Allah and His Apostle (ﷺ) know the best." The Prophet (ﷺ) said, "Not to punish them (if they do so)." [Bukhari, Muslim]

**A person who believes in Tawheed will die as Muslim**

Narrated Al-Bara' bin Azib (ra): Allah's Messenger (ﷺ) said: O so-and-so, whenever you go to your bed (for sleeping) say, 'O Allah! I have surrendered myself over to you and have turned my face towards You, and leave all my affairs to You and depend on You and put my trust in You expecting Your reward and fearing Your punishment. There is neither fleeing from You nor refuge but with You. I believe in the Book

(Qur'an) which You have revealed and, in Your Prophet, [Muhammad ﷺ] whom You have sent.' If you then die on that night, then you will die as a Muslim, and if you wake alive in the morning then you will receive the reward. [Bukhari]. In Arabic:

اللَّهُمَّ أَسْلَمْتُ نَفْسِي إِلَيْكَ، وَوَجَّهْتُ وَجْهِي إِلَيْكَ وَفَوَّضْتُ أَمْرِي إِلَيْكَ، وَأَلْجَأْتُ ظَهْرِي إِلَيْكَ، رَغْبَةً وَرَهْبَةً إِلَيْكَ، لاَ مَلْجَأَ وَلاَ مَنْجَا مِنْكَ إِلاَّ إِلَيْكَ، آمَنْتُ بِكِتَابِكَ الَّذِي أَنْزَلْتَ، وَبِنَبِيِّكَ الَّذِي أَرْسَلْتَ

Narrated 'Aisha (ra): Allah's Messenger (ﷺ) died while Abu Bakr (ra) was at a place called As-Sunah (Al-Aliya). 'Umar (ra) stood up and said, "By Allah! Allah's Messenger (ﷺ) is not dead!" 'Umar (later on) said, "By Allah! Nothing occurred to my mind except that." He said, "Verily! Allah will resurrect him and he will cut the hands and legs of some men." Then Abu Bakr (ra) came and uncovered the face of Allah's Messenger (ﷺ), kissed him and said, "Let my mother and father be sacrificed for you, (O Allah's Messenger ﷺ), you are good in life and in death. By Allah in Whose Hands my life is, Allah will never make you taste death twice." Then he went out and said, "O oath-taker! Don't be hasty." When Abu Bakr (ra) spoke, 'Umar (ra) sat down. Abu Bakr (ra) praised and glorified Allah and said, "No doubt! Whoever worshipped Muhammad (ﷺ), then Muhammad (ﷺ) is dead, but whoever worshipped Allah, then Allah is Alive and shall never die." Then he recited Allah's Statement: *"(O Muhammad) Verily you will die, and they also will die."* (Az-Zumar Ch 39:30) He also recited: *"Muhammad is no more than an Apostle; and indeed, many Apostles have passed away, before him, if he dies or is killed, will you then turn back on your heels? And he who turns back on his heels, not the least harm will he do to Allah and Allah will give reward to those who are grateful."* (Surah Ali- Imran Ch 3:144)

The people wept loudly, and the Ansar were assembled with Sad bin 'Ubada (ra) in the shed of Bani Saida. They said (to the emigrants), "There should be one 'Amir from us and one from you." Then Abu Bakr (ra), Umar bin Al-Khattab (ra) and Abu 'Baida bin Al-Jarrah (ra) went to them. 'Umar (ra) wanted to speak but Abu Bakr (ra) stopped him. 'Umar (ra) later on used to say, "By Allah, I intended only to say something that appealed to me and I was afraid that Abu Bakr (ra) would not speak so well. Then Abu Bakr (ra) spoke and his speech was very eloquent. He said in his statement, "We are the rulers and you (Ansars) are the ministers (i.e. advisers)." Hubab bin Al-Mundhir said, "No, by Allah we won't accept this. But there must be a ruler from us and a ruler from you." Abu Bakr (ra) said, "No, we will be the rulers and you will be the ministers, for they (i.e. Quarish) are the best family amongst the 'Arabs and of the best origin. So, you should elect either 'Umar or Abu 'Ubaida bin Al-Jarrah as your ruler." 'Umar said (to Abu Bakr), "No but we elect you, for you are our chief and the best amongst us and the most beloved of all of us to Allah's Messenger (ﷺ)." So 'Umar (ra) took Abu Bakr's (ra) hand and gave the pledge of allegiance and the people too gave the pledge of allegiance to Abu Bakr (ra). Someone said, "You have killed Sad bin Ubada." 'Umar (ra) said, "Allah has killed him." [Bukhari]

Note the saying of Abu Bakr (ra): *"Whoever worshipped Muhammad (ﷺ), then Muhammad ﷺ is **dead**, but whoever worshipped Allah, then Allah is Alive and shall never die."* And the saying *"If he dies or is killed, will you then turn back on your heels? And he who turns back on his heels, not the least harm will he do to Allah and Allah will give reward to those Who are grateful."* The Companions of the Prophet (ﷺ) were the best in all respect among the Ummah and there is no question of worshipping the Prophet (ﷺ) [Abu Bakr (ra) knew it well]. It was actually a strong message of Tawheed sent to all mankind till the Last Day. In fact, that was the need of the hour as the Companions suddenly missed the Prophet (ﷺ). They were in a fix due to shocking and grieved mental state. But Abu Bakr (ra) was a wise man and by Allah SWT, he could control the situation of the great loss of the Companions. Abu Bakr (ra) knew that previous nations used to worship their apostles and their grave whenever the apostles died. Abu Huraira (ra) reported: The Messenger of Allah (ﷺ) said: Let there be curse of Allah upon the Jews and the Christians for they have taken the graves of their apostles as places of worship. [Muslim]

Also note "Allah will never make you taste death twice."  The Prophet (ﷺ) died and left for Heaven where life is eternal.

The topic of Tawheed and Shirk is incomplete without the beautiful Surah 'Al-Ikhlas'. The Surah is reproduced here with transliteration:

*Say, "The truth is that Allah is One. Allah is Besought of all, needing none. He has never had offspring, nor was He born. And there is none comparable to Him." (Ch 112; interpretation of meaning)*

## 1.2 Shirk

Shirk (شرك) is the direct opposite of Tawheed. It refers to associating partners or rivals with Allah in His Lordship, Worship, or in His names and Attributes. Allah SWT says in His Book:

- He is the One Who has made the earth a place of settlement for you and the sky a canopy; and sends down rain from the sky, causing fruits to grow as a provision for you. So, do not knowingly set up equals to Allah in worship'. (Al- Baqarah Ch 2:22; interpretation of the meaning)

Abdullah ibn Mas'ud (ra) reported: The Messenger of Allah (ﷺ) said, "Whoever dies while associating partners with Allah will enter Hellfire." And I said in his presence, "Whoever dies without associating partners with Allah will enter Paradise." [Bukhari and Muslim] Allah SWT says (interpretation of meaning):

- *Surely, Allah does not forgive that a partner is ascribed to Him, and He forgives anything short of that for whomsoever He wills. Whoever ascribes a partner to Allah commits a terrible sin. (An-Nisa Ch 4:48)*

Islamic scholars have categorized *shirk* into two types: minor *shirk* and major *shirk*. Various definitions of minor *shirk* have been provided by scholars, one of which states that it refers to anything that leads to major *shirk* or serves as a means to commit it. When a Muslim commits minor *shirk*, they remain within the fold of Islam but are in serious danger, as it is considered a major sin. On the other hand, major *shirk* occurs when acts of worship are directed to anyone or anything other than Allah SWT. Minor shirk is discussed separately in **Section 1.3**. The most evident form of major *shirk* is idolatry, and the Prophets were sent by Allah SWT to warn humanity against committing *shirk*. The Qur'an says:

- *"Surely, we have sent to every nation a messenger saying, worship Allah and avoid taghut..." (Al-Nahl Ch 36 :16; interpretation of meaning)*

Taghut means anything which is worshipped along with Allah or instead of Allah. Major Shirk is the worst act of rebellion against the Almighty

Lord and it is the ultimate and the greatest sin. It cancels out all activities whatever good it is and the destination is the Hell.

Another form of Shirk is 'sin of allowing what Allah The Almighty has forbidden and forbidding what Allah The Almighty has allowed, or believing that anyone has the right to do so except Allah The Almighty, or referring matters for judgment to *Jaahili* (non-Islaamic) courts freely and voluntarily, and believing that this is permissible.' [*Ref: **Prohibitions that are taken too lightly**, written by Sheikh Muhammed Salih Al-Munajjid*] This form of Shirk is mentioned in the Qur'an. Allah says:

- *They have taken their rabbis and monks as well as the Messiah, son of Mary, as lords besides Allah, even though they were commanded to worship none but One Allah. There is no God worthy of worship except Him. Glorified is He above what they associate with Him! (At-Tawbah, Ch 9:31; interpretation of the meaning)*

Ibn Kasir writes: Imam Ahmad, Tirmizi and Ibn Jarir At-Tabari recorded a Hadith via several chains of narration, from Adi bin Hatim, may Allah be pleased with him, who became Christian during the time of Jahiliyyah. When the call of the Messenger of Allah (ﷺ) reached his area, Adi ran away to Ash-Sham, and his sister and several of his people were captured. The Messenger of Allah (ﷺ) freed his sister and gave her gifts. So, she went to her brother and encouraged him to become Muslim and to go to the Messenger of Allah (ﷺ). `Adi, who was one of the chiefs of his people (the tribe of Tai') and whose father, Hatim At-Ta'i, was known for his generosity, went to Al-Madinah. When the people announced his arrival, `Adi went to the Messenger of Allah (ﷺ) wearing a silver cross around his neck. The Messenger of Allah (ﷺ) recited this Ayah: اتَّخَذُواْ أَحْبَـٰرَهُمْ وَرُهْبَـٰنَهُمْ أَرْبَاباً مِّن دُونِ اللَّهِ (They took their rabbis and their monks to be their lords besides Allah). `Adi commented, I said, "They did not worship them." The Prophet (ﷺ) said, "Yes they did. They (rabbis and monks) prohibited the allowed for them (Christians and Jews) and allowed the prohibited, and they obeyed them. This is how they worshipped them." The Messenger of Allah (ﷺ) said to `Adi, "O `Adi what do you say did you run away (to Ash-Sham) so that 'Allahu Akbar' (Allah is the Great) is not pronounced? Do you know of anything greater than Allah? What made you run away? Did you run away so that 'La ilaha illallah' is not pronounced? Do you know of any deity worthy of worship except Allah?" The Messenger (ﷺ) invited `Adi (ra) to embrace Islam, and he embraced Islam and pronounced the Testimony of Truth. The face of the Messenger of Allah (ﷺ) beamed with pleasure and he said to `Adi (ra), "Verily, the Jews have earned the anger (of Allah) and the Christians are misguided." Huzayfah bin Al-Yaman (ra), `Abdullah bin `Abbas (ra) and several others said about the explanation of 'They took their rabbis and their monks to be their lords besides Allah...' that the Christians and Jews obeyed their monks and rabbis in whatever they allowed or prohibited for them. This is why Allah said: While they were commanded to worship none but One God, Who, whatever He renders prohibited is the prohibited, whatever He allowed is the allowed, whatever He legislates, is to be the law followed, and whatever He decides is to be adhered to. "None has the right to be worshipped but He, Hallowed be He above what they associate (with Him)": Meaning, exalted, sanctified, hallowed above partners, equals, aids, rivals or children, there is no deity or Lord worthy of worship except Him.'

## How shirk came into practice?

Shirk came into practice before the Prophet Nuh (as). The incident is mentioned in the Qur'an. Allah SWT Says (interpretation of meaning):

- *And they said: Do not abandon your gods: do not abandon Wadd, nor Suwa', nor Yaghuth and Ya'uq and Nasr. (Surah Nuh 71:23)*

This is considered the first act of shirk on Earth. It began after the death of righteous people mentioned in 71:23, when their memory was preserved through statues — a seemingly innocent act that later transformed into idol worship under Satan's deception.

Narrated Ibn `Abbas (ra): All the idols which were worshiped by the people of Nuh (as) were worshiped by the Arabs later on. As for the idol Wadd, it was worshiped by the tribe of Kalb at Daumat-al-Jandal; Suwa` was the idol of (the tribe of) Hudhail; Yaghouth was worshiped by (the tribe of) Murad and then by Bani Ghutaif at Al-Jurf near Saba; Ya`uq was the idol of Hamdan, and Nasr was the idol of Himyar, the branch of Dhi-al-Kala`. The names (of the idols) formerly belonged to some pious men of the people of Nuh (as), and when they died, Satan inspired their people to prepare and place idols at the places where they used to sit, and to call those idols by their names. The people did so, but the idols were not worshiped till those people (who initiated them) had died and the origin of the idols had become obscure, whereupon people began worshiping them. [Bukhari]

## 1.3 Major and Minor sins

Sin is the result of actions committed by human beings that are disliked by Allah (SWT). Major and minor forms of Shirk are examples of such actions, and the sins that follow are the consequences of these violations. Al-Nawwas ibn Sam'an (ra) reported: The Messenger of Allah (ﷺ) said, "Righteousness is good character, and sin is what disturbs your heart and you hate for people to find out about it." [Muslim]

Wabisah ibn Ma'bad (ra) reported: The Messenger of Allah (ﷺ) said to me, "Have you come to ask about righteousness and sin?" I said yes. The Prophet (ﷺ) clenched his fist and struck his chest, saying, "Consult your soul, consult your heart, O Wabisah. Righteousness is what reassures your soul and your heart, and sin is what wavers in your soul and puts tension in your chest, even if people approve it in their judgments again and again." [Sunan ad-Darimi]

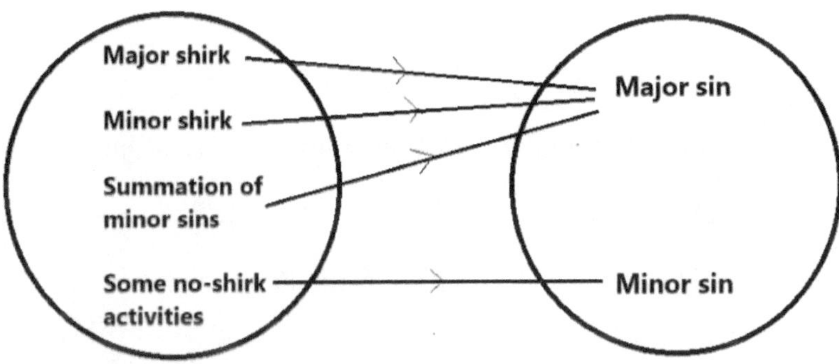


**Fig 1**: Mapping beween Shirk and sin

Major Shirk, minor Shirk and continuation of minor sins are related to major sin by 'many-to-one' and some non-Shirk activities are related to minor sin by 'one-to-one' mappings respectively. The relationship is depicted in Fig 1.

However, inverse mapping in Fig 1 is not always true. For example, eating pork is strictly forbidden (haram) in Islam, as clearly stated in the Qur'an: Ch 2:173. Violating a clear ḥaram command is considered a major sin. However, this act—while serious—does not amount to shirk, nor does it expel a person from the fold of Islam. The individual remains a Muslim but becomes a sinner in need of repentance.

Abu Bakrah (ra) reported: The Prophet (ﷺ) said: "Shall I inform you of the severest of the major sins?" He (ﷺ) repeated these three times, and then said: "Associating partners with Allah, mistreatment of parents." He (ﷺ) was reclining, and then sat up and said: "And indeed the false statement and the false testimony." He kept repeating this so many times that we wished he (ﷺ) should be quiet. [Bukhari, Muslim]

Narrated Abu Huraira (ra): The Prophet (ﷺ) said: Avoid the seven great destructive sins. The people enquired: O Allah's Messenger (ﷺ)! What are they? He (ﷺ) said:

i.     To join others in worship along with Allah (i.e Shirk),

ii.    to practice witchcraft,

iii.   to kill the life which Allah has forbidden except for a just cause, (according to Islamic law),

iv.    to eat up Riba (usury or interest),

v.     to eat up an orphan's wealth,

vi.    to give back to the enemy and fleeing from the battlefield at the time of fighting, and

vii.   to accuse, chaste women, who never even think of anything touching chastity and are good believers." [Bukhari]

Scholars are of the opinion that consequence associated with warning of punishment and mention of a curse is a major sin. Following are some examples:

- *But they were succeeded by generations who neglected prayer and followed their lusts and so will soon face the evil consequences. (Ch 19:59; interpretation of meaning)*

- *In it are clear signs and the standing-place of Ibrahim. Whoever enters it should be safe. Pilgrimage to this House is an obligation by Allah upon whoever is able among the people. And whoever disbelieves, then surely Allah is not in need of ˈany of Hisˈ creation. (Ch 3:97; interpretation of meaning)*

Detail description about major sins based on the Qur'an and Sunnah is available in the book titled **'The 70 Major Sins in Islam'**, written by Imam Sams Uddeen Zahnawi (1274-1348 AD).

Minor sins are those sins where no punishment is specified. Minor sins are forgiven by Allah SWT by day-to-day religious practices, provided one is safe from major sins. Allah SWT says (interpretation of meaning):

- *"If you avoid the great sins which you are forbidden to do, We shall remit from you your (small) sins, and admit you to a Noble Entrance (i.e. Paradise)" (An-Nisa Ch 4:31)*

There are many hadiths on forgiveness of minor sins and one such is presented here.

**Hadith**: It was narrated that Humran said: When 'Usman (ra) performed wudu, he said: 'By Allah, I am going to tell you a Hadith which, by Allah, were it not for a Verse in the Book of Allah, I would not tell it to you. I heard the Messenger of Allah (ﷺ) say: "No man performs wudu and does it well, then performs Salat, but he will be forgiven for whatever (sins) come between that and the Salat which follows it." [Muslim]

It is not permissible to take minor sins lightly, because summation of minor sins is a major sin. It was narrated from Abdullah ibn Mas'ud (ra) that the Messenger of Allah (ﷺ) said: "Beware of these sins that are regarded as insignificant, for they will accumulate until they destroy a man." [Musnad Ahmad]

Sahl ibn Sa'd (ra) reported: The Messenger of Allah (ﷺ) said, "Beware of minor sins like people who descend into the bottom of a valley. One comes with a stick and another with a stick until they fire to cook their bread. Verily, when the one who persistently committed minor sins is taken to account for them, they will ruin him." [Musnad Ahmad]

There is no specific list available for minor sins. Examples of minor sins can be daily activities such as saying bad words, making fun of people, bad behavior, bad treatment of people, keeping an eye on others' fault, being rude to elder and harsh on children, looking at something prohibited etc.

Allah SWT accepts the slave's repentance for sins. Allah SWT says (interpretation of meaning):

- *As for those who repent, believe, and do good deeds, they are the ones whose evil deeds Allah will change into good deeds. For Allah is All-Forgiving, Most Merciful. (Al-Furqan Ch 25:70)*

There are indications in the Qur'an and hadiths that Allah SWT forgives major Shirk if a person repents and his/her repentance is accepted. Allah SWT says (interpretation of meaning):

- *Say, O Prophet, that Allah says, "O My servants who have exceeded the limits against their souls! Do not lose hope in Allah's mercy, for Allah certainly forgives all sins. He is indeed the All-Forgiving, Most Merciful. (Az-Zumar Ch 39:53)*

Ibn Kasir writes: "Therefore, the outcome of the subject taken up in the verse (Ch 39:53) comes to be that, well before death arrives, the repentance made from sins, no matter how serious, even from kufr (disbelief) and Shirk (ascribing of partners to Allah), gets to be accepted. And by virtue of a genuine taubah (repentance), all sins will be forgiven, therefore, no one should lose hope in the mercy of Allah.

Sayyidna Abdullah Ibn Umar (ra) said that, out of all verses of the Qur'an, this verse (i.e. 39:53) brings the strongest message of hope for sinners. But, Sayyidna Ibn Abbas (ra) said that the strongest such verse is: وَإِنَّ رَبَّكَ لَذُو مَغْفِرَةٍ لِّلنَّاسِ عَلَىٰ ظُلْمِهِمْ

*(And surely, your Lord is the lord of forgiveness for the people against their wrongdoings. Ar-Ra'd, Ch 13:6; interpretation of meaning)"*

**Hadith**: Narrated by Anas ibn Malik (ra): The Prophet (ﷺ) said: Allah, the Exalted, has said: "O son of Adam! Certainly, I shall continue to pardon you so long as you supplicate Me and hope (for My forgiveness), whatever may be your faults and sins, I don't care. O son of Adam, even if your sins pile up as high as the sky, and you ask for My forgiveness, I will forgive you. O son of Adam, if you come to Me with an earth-full of defaults and meet Me, not associating anything with Me, I will come to you, with an earth-full of forgiveness." [Tirmizi]

People will be given different kinds of punishment according to their sins. Narrated Samurah (ra): The Prophet Muhammad (ﷺ) said, "There are some whom the Fire will take up to their ankles, others up to their knees, others up to their waists, and yet others up to their collarbones." [Muslim]

Narrated An-Nu'man ibn Bashir (ra): I heard the Prophet (ﷺ) saying, "The person who will have the least punishment from amongst the Hell Fire people on the Day of Resurrection, will be a man under whose arch of the feet a smouldering ember will be placed so that his brain will boil because of it." [Bukhari]

The following considerations are important in relation to sins:

1.  Minor sins are forgiven through other righteous deeds, provided a person refrains from committing major sins.

2.  Allah is Al-Ghaffar (The Most Forgiving) and Ar-Rahim (The Most Merciful). If a person sincerely repents, even major sins may be forgiven.

3.  However, if someone dies committing shirk (associating partners with Allah) without repentance, Allah may not forgive them.

4.  There is a specific case where a person avoids shirk and dies having repented, he may still not be forgiven by Allah SWT: if he has assumed the rights of others—such as occupying another's land or unlawfully taking their wealth—unless those rights are returned or the victims forgive them.

Narrated Abu Hurairah (ra): The Messenger of Allah (ﷺ) said: "Allah's Messenger (ﷺ) said, "Whoever has wronged his brother, should ask for his pardon (before his death), as (in the Hereafter) there will be neither a Dinar nor a Dirham. (He should secure pardon in this life) before some of his good deeds are taken and paid to his brother, or, if he has done no good deeds, some of the bad deeds of his brother are taken to be loaded on him (in the Hereafter)." [Sahih al-Bukhari]

## 1.4 Boundary/Limit of Islam

Boundary or limit of Islam is mentioned in the Qur'an several times. Allah SWT says (interpretation of meaning):

- *And those are the limits [set by] Allah. And whoever transgresses the limits of Allah has certainly wronged himself. (Surah At-Talaq Ch 65:1)*

- *And whoever disobeys Allah and His Messenger and transgresses His limits - He will put him into the Fire to abide eternally therein, and he will have a humiliating punishment. (Surah An-Nisa Ch 4:14)*

Islam is complete through the Qur'an and the Sunnah. For a Muslim, there are permissions, prohibitions and concessions from Allah SWT that constitute the universal set $U$. The subset $I$ is the Islam that has a clear-cut boundary. Forbidden elements are in the complement set (shaded area) that comprise haram, shirks and innovations and it is a danger zone of major sin. Thus, boundary is the barrier or wall between $I$ and. Crossing the boundary of $I$ is a transgression and is a major sin, since Allah SWT warned against such acts. Innovation is presented in Section 1.7 and

Shirk is elaborated in Section 1.2. Prohibitions, permissions, concessions, Halaal (lawful) and Haraam (unlawful) are prescribed in the Qura'an and Sunnah.

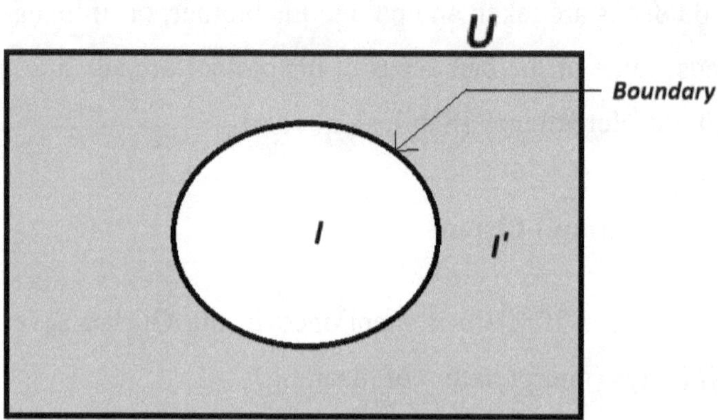


**Fig 2**: Boundary of Islam explained

The boundary shown above represents a general guideline. In reality, boundaries can vary depending on the specific context. For instance, the boundaries related to **food** are different from those related to **income**. Allah SWT says (interpretation of the meaning):

- *Forbidden to you [for food] are: al-Maytah [the dead animals - cattle-beast not slaughtered], blood, the flesh of swine, and the meat of that which has been slaughtered as a sacrifice for others than Allaah, or has been slaughtered for idols, etc., or on which Allaah's name has not been mentioned while slaughtering, and that which has been killed by strangling, or by a violent blow, or by a headlong fall, or by the goring of horns - and that which has been (partly) eaten by a wild animal - unless you are able to slaughter it [before its death] - and that which is sacrificed [slaughtered] on an-Nusub [stone altars]. (Ch 5:3)*

When it comes to **income**, crossing the boundary may involve earning through **riba (interest)** or **accepting bribes**. In **trade and business**, actions that go beyond permissible limits include **selling pork, distributing alcohol, deliberate under-measurement, adulteration of goods,** and similar unethical practices. Allah SWT says (interpretation of meaning):

- *But Allah has permitted trade and has forbidden interest. (Ch 2:275)*

- *They ask you about wine and gambling. Say, "In them is great sin and [yet, some] benefit for people. But their sin is greater than their benefit." (Ch 2: 219)*

## 1.5 Mushrikun say 'Allah has begotten a son, Glory is to Him'

The Christian doctrine of the Trinity refers to the belief in one God who exists in three distinct persons: the Father, the Son (Jesus), and the Holy Spirit—a concept often described as "one being in three ways of existence."

However, the Qur'anic references to the Trinity differ from the formal Christian understanding established by the Church since the 3rd century AD. In the Qur'an, the Trinity is portrayed as a belief held by disbelievers in three separate deities: Allah, Jesus ('Isa), and Mary (Maryam)—a concept of three independent gods, which the Qur'an firmly rejects. Allah SWT says:

- *Those who say, "Allah is one in a Trinity," have certainly fallen into disbelief. There is only One God. If they do not stop saying this, those who disbelieve among them will be afflicted with a painful punishment. (Al-Mai'dah Ch 5:73; interpretation of meaning)*

As-Suddi and others said: This was revealed concerning their making the Messiah and his mother into two gods with Allah, thus making Allah the third of three, according to this concept. As-Suddi said: This is like what Allah, may He be exalted, says at the end of al-Ma'idah (interpretation of the meaning):

- *And ˹on Judgment Day˺ Allah will say, "O Issa, son of Mary! Did you ever ask the people to worship you and your mother as gods besides Allah?" He will answer, "Glory be to You! How could I ever say what I had no right to say? If I had said such a thing, you would have certainly known it. You know what is ˹hidden˺ within me, but I do not know what is within You. Indeed, You ˹alone˺ are the Knower of all unseen.*

- *I never told them anything except what You ordered me to say: "Worship Allah—my Lord and your Lord!" And I was witness over them as long as I remained among them. But when You took me, You were the Witness over them—and You are a Witness over all things. [Al-Ma'idah Ch 5:116-117].*

[As-Suddi: His actual name was Isma'il ibn Abdur-Rahman Ibn Abu Karimah, and his nick name was Abu Muhammad Al-Hijazi, from Kufah, the interpreter of the meaning of the Quran. Among his teachers were: Anas Ibn Malik (ra), Ibn 'Abbas (ra), and others. It is said that he saw Abu Hurairah (ra) and Al-Hassan Ibn 'Ali (ra). He died in 127 A.H.]

Allah SWT condemned such concept of Shirk in the Qur'an (interpretation of meaning):

- *People of the Book! Do not go to extremes regarding your faith; say nothing about Allah except the truth. The Messiah, Issa, son of Mary, was no more than a messenger of Allah and the fulfilment of His Word through Mary and a spirit ˹created by a command˺ from Him. So believe in Allah and His messengers and do not say, "Trinity." Stop! for your own good. Allah is only One God. Glory be to Him! He is far above having a son! To Him belongs whatever is in the heavens and whatever is on the earth. And Allah is sufficient as a Trustee of Affairs. (An-Nisa Ch 4: 171)*

The Qur'an clarifies that Issa (as) never called for people to worship him and he is not responsible for the Shirk activities of the Christians. Allah SWT says (interpretation of meaning):

- *When Issa came with clear proofs, he declared, "I have come to you with wisdom, and to clarify to you some of what you differ about. So fear Allah, and obey me. Surely Allah ˹alone˺ is my Lord and your Lord, so worship Him ˹alone˺. This is the Straight Path." Yet their ˹various˺ groups have differed among themselves ˹about him˺, so woe to the wrongdoers when they face the torment of a painful Day! (Az-Zukhruf Ch 43:63-65)*

**Hadith**: Narrated Ibn ˋAbbas (ra): The Prophet (ﷺ) said: Allah said, "The son of Adam tells a against Me though he has no right to do so, and he abuses Me though he has no right to do so. As for his telling a lie against Me, it is that he claims that I cannot recreate him as I created him before; and as for his abusing Me, it is his statement that I have offspring. No! Glorified be Me! I am far from taking a wife or offspring." [Bukhari]

**Hadith**: Abu Musa (ra) reported that Allah's Messenger (ﷺ) said: There is none to show more patience at listening to the most irksome things than Allah, the Exalted and Glorious. 'Partnership is associated to Him (polytheism), and (fatherhood) of a child is attributed to Him, but in spite of this, He protects them (people) and provides them sustenance.' This hadith has been transmitted on the authority of Abu Musa (ra) with a slight variation of wording. [Muslim]

## 1.6 The disbeliever seeking ransom on the Judgement Day

Anas bin Malik (ra) reported Allah's Messenger (ﷺ) as saying: Allah, the Exalted and High, would say to one who shall have to undergo the least torture (on the Day of Resurrection): "Would you like to go as ransom if you had all worldly riches?" He would say: Yes. Allah would say to him, "When you were in the loins of Adam, I demanded from you something easier than this that you should not associate anything with Me." (The narrator says): I think He also said: "I would not cause you to enter Hell-Fire but you defied and attributed Divinity (to others besides Me)." [Muslim]

Anas bin Malik (ra) reported that a person said: "Allah's Messenger (ﷺ), how the non-believers be made to assemble on the Day of Resurrection (by crawling) on their faces?" Thereupon he (ﷺ) said: "Is He Who is powerful to make them walk on their feet not powerful enough to make them (crawl) upon their faces on the Day of Resurrection?" Qatada said: Of course, it is so. (He adjured): By the might of our Lord. [Muslim]

## 1.7 The disbeliever is rewarded for his good deeds in this world

Anas bin Malik (ra) reported that Allah's Messenger (ﷺ) said: "Verily, Allah does not treat a believer unjustly in regard to his virtues. He would confer upon him (His blessing) in this world and would give him reward in the Hereafter. And as regards a non-believer, he would be made to taste the reward (of virtue in this world) what he has done for himself so much that when it would be the Hereafter, he would find no virtue for which he should be rewarded." [Muslim]

## 1.8 Minor Shirks

In the previous section, we briefly introduced the concept of minor Shirk. At times, acts of Shirk arise from misguided beliefs inherited from forefathers, passed down through generations without question. For example, in some villages, it is common to place a drawing of an eye or similar symbol on a hoarding in pumpkin fields to ward off the evil eye. Similarly, placing a black 'bindiya'—a small dot traditionally worn by Hindu women—on an infant's forehead is often believed to protect the child from harm.

These practices have no foundation in Islamic belief, as all protection and blessings come solely from Allah (SWT). Relying on such objects or rituals, believing they possess protective powers, constitutes minor Shirk—because the person believes that something other than Allah has the power to protect or benefit.

Minor Shirk is forbidden and it results in major sin. This Shirk invalidates one's good deed and render it worthless, and the doer may be punished on the Day of Judgement if not forgiven by the Almighty.

**Hadith**: Mahmud ibn Labid (ra) said: The Messenger of Allah (ﷺ) said: "The thing that I fear most for you is minor Shirk." They said: "O Messenger of Allah (ﷺ), what is minor Shirk?" He (ﷺ) said: Showing off, for Allah will say on the Day when people are recompensed for their actions: 'Go to those for whom you were showing off with your deeds in the world, and see what reward you find with them.' [Musnad Ahmad, Bayhaqi].

The Prophet (ﷺ) was worried much about the minor Shirks of the believers and he (ﷺ) taught us du'a for protection from Shirk. Ma'qil ibn Yasar (ra) reported: I departed with Abu Bakr (ra) to meet the Prophet (ﷺ), and the Prophet (ﷺ) said, "O Abu Bakr, there is Shirk among you more hidden than the crawling of an ant." Abu Bakr (ra) said, "Is there a Shirk other than to believe in a God alongside Allah?" The Prophet (ﷺ) said, "By the One in Whose Hand is my soul, there is Shirk more hidden than the crawling of an ant. Shall I not tell you something to say to rid you of it, both minor and major? Say: *Allahumma inni a'uzu bika an ushrika bika wa ana a'lamu wa astaghfiruka lima la a'lam* (O Allah, I seek refuge in You that I associate partners with You while I know, and I seek Your forgiveness for what I do not know.)" [Bukhari] In Arabic: اللَّهُمَّ إِنِّي أَعُوذُ بِكَ أَنْ أُشْرِكَ بِكَ وَأَنَا أَعْلَمُ وَأَسْتَغْفِرُكَ لِمَا لَا أَعْلَمُ

## 1.9 Riya (show off) is a hidden Shirk

Riya means the intention to show others to gain something, to be praised, to be considered pious or to be treated with respect or to express himself someone in particular in society. Riya invalidates the basic purpose of worshipping Allah SWT because of its wrong intention.

**Hadith**: Narrated 'Umar bin Al-Khattab (ra): I heard Allah's Messenger (ﷺ) saying, "The reward of deeds depends upon the intentions and every person will get the reward according to what he has intended إِنَّمَا الْأَعْمَالُ بِالنِّيَّاتِ، وَإِنَّمَا لِكُلِّ امْرِئٍ مَا نَوَى. So, whoever emigrated for worldly benefits or for a woman to marry, his emigration was for what he emigrated for." [Bukhari]

In Islam, Riya is considered a sin, since it diverts the focus from seeking the pleasure of Allah SWT to seeking admiration of human beings. Allah Almighty says in the Holy Quran (interpretation of meaning):

- *Likewise for those who spend their wealth to show off and do not believe in Allah or the Last Day. And whoever takes Satan as an associate—what an evil associate they have! (An-Nisa Ch 4:38)*

**Hadith**: The Prophet (ﷺ) said: "Shall I not inform you of what I fear for you more than the Masih ad-Dajjal? It is the hidden Shirk. It is when a man stands up for prayer, then beautifies his prayer for another to look at." [Sunan Ibn Majah]

**Hadith:** Abu Huraira (ra) reported: The Messenger of Allah (ﷺ) said: Verily, Allah does not look at your appearance or wealth, but rather He looks at your hearts and actions. [Muslim]

**Consequence of Riya**

Narrated Jundub (ra): The Prophet Muhammad (ﷺ) said, "He who lets the people hear of his good deeds intentionally, to win their praise, Allah will let the people know his real intention (on the Day of resurrection), and he who does good things in public to show off and win the praise of

the people, Allah will disclose his real intention (and humiliate him)."
[Bukhari]

It was narrated on the authority of Abu Hurairah (ra) that the Prophet (ﷺ) said: "The first person to be held accountable on the Day of Resurrection will be a man who had died as a martyr. He will be brought forward, and Allah will remind him of the blessings He had bestowed upon him and he will acknowledge them. Then Allah will ask him: 'What did you do to express gratitude to Me for these blessings?' The man will reply: 'I fought in Your Cause till I was martyred.' Allah will say: 'You have lied. You fought so that people might call you courageous; and they have done so.' He will be then commanded to be dragged on his face and thrown into Hellfire. Next, a man who had acquired and imparted knowledge and read the Quran will be brought forward, Allah will remind him of the blessings He had bestowed upon him, and he will acknowledge them. Then He will ask him: 'What did you do to express gratitude to Me for these blessings?' The man will reply: 'I acquired knowledge and taught it, and I read the Quran for Your sake.' Allah will say to him: 'You have lied. You acquired knowledge so that people might call you a learned (scholar), and you read the Quran so that they might call you a reciter, and they have done so.' Command will then be issued about him, and he will be dragged on his face and thrown into Hellfire. Next, a man, whom Allah had made affluent and blessed with abundant wealth, will be brought forward, and Allah will remind him of the blessings He had bestowed upon him, and the man will acknowledge them. He will ask him: 'What did you do to express gratitude to Me for these blessings?' The man will reply: 'I did not neglect any of the ways You liked wealth to be spent generously for Your sake.' Allah will say to him: 'You have lied. You did it so that people might call you generous, and they have done so.' He will be commanded to be dragged on his face and thrown into Hellfire." [Muslim]

## How to get rid of Riya

Eliminating riya (showing off) is simple in theory but challenging in practice. To overcome it, one must constantly remember that Allah is always watching. Then what other people think will become insignificant. Narrated by Abu Huraira (ra) that the man again asked, "O Allah's Apostle (ﷺ), what is Ihsan (i.e. perfection or Benevolence)?" The Prophet Muhammad (ﷺ) said, "Ihsan is to worship Allah SWT as if you see Him, and if you do not achieve this state of devotion, then (take it for granted that) Allah sees you." [Bukhari]

## 1.10 Superstition, Astrologer and Fortune Teller

Superstitions are beliefs and practices based on the idea that future events can be predicted by unrelated past occurrences. Many people believe these superstitions can influence outcomes by affecting the likelihood of certain events. Interestingly, individuals are more likely to associate negative experiences with superstitious causes than positive ones. In Islam, belief in superstitions is considered a form of minor shirk and a major sin. Visiting a fortune-teller constitutes major shirk. Likewise, astrology becomes major shirk when it involves attributing blessings or control to anyone other than Allah.

There are many superstitious beliefs prevalent in our society. For example:

i.    Tuesday and Saturday are bad luck.

ii.    Owl entering in room is a sign of bad luck.

iii.    If a cat runs in front of a car, immediately one has to stop the car. Otherwise there will be accident.

iv.    Seeing a couple of birds (Common Starling) is a good luck. One has to kiss pointing the birds.

v.    One should not start a journey if a lady with empty water container (pitcher) is met.

vi.    Journey will be bad if a widow is met on the onset of the journey.

vii.    Trimming nails at night invites poverty.

viii.    Brooming rooms during night enhance poverty.

ix.    Looking mirror at night is a cause for poverty.

x.    Itchy palm is a good luck that will bring money.

**Hadith**: Narrated Abdullah ibn Mas'ud (ra): The Prophet (ﷺ) said: Taking tiyarah (omens) is Shirk; taking tiyarah is Shirk. He said it three times. Every one of us has some, but Allah removes it by trust (in Him). [Abu Dawud]

**Hadith**: The Prophet (ﷺ) said: "Whoever goes to a fortune-teller and asks him about something, his prayer will not be accepted for forty nights." [Muslim].

**Hadith**: It was narrated from Abu Mas'ud al-Badri (ra) that the Messenger of Allah (ﷺ) forbade the price of a dog, the fee of a prostitute and the payment of a soothsayer. [Bukhari and Muslim].

**Hadith**: A'isha (ra) said: Some people asked the Messenger of Allah (ﷺ) about soothsayers. The Messenger of Allah (ﷺ) said to them: "They are nothing." They said: O Messenger of Allah (ﷺ), sometimes they tell us something that turns out to be true. The Messenger of Allah (ﷺ) said: "That is a word from the jinn that the jinni snatches, and he cackles it into the ear of his familiar as a hen cackles, but they mix more than a hundred lies with it." [Bukhari, Muslim]

**Hadith**: Narrated Abu Hurairah (ra) that the Prophet (ﷺ) said: "When Allah decrees a matter in heaven, the angels beat their wings in submission to His words, making a sound like a chain striking a rock. When the fear is banished from their hearts, they say: What is it that your Lord has said? They say: The truth, and He is the Most High, the Most Great. Then the one who is listening out hears that, and those who are listening out are standing one above the other" – Sufyaan [one of the narrators] demonstrated with his hand, holding it vertically with the fingers outspread. – "So he hears what is said and passes it on to the one below him, and that one passes it to the one who is below him, and so on until it reaches the lips of the soothsayer or fortune-teller. May be the meteor will hit him before he can pass anything on, or maybe he will pass it on before he is hit. He tells a hundred lies alongside it, but it will be said: Did he not tell us that on such and such a day, such and such would happen? So, they believe him because of the one thing which was heard from heaven." [Bukhari]

**Hadith**: The Prophet (ﷺ) said: "Whoever has intercourse with a menstruating woman or with a woman in her back passage, or goes to a fortune teller and believes what he says, has disbelieved in that which

Allah revealed to Muhammad (ﷺ)." [Abu Dawud, Tirmizi and Sunan Ibn Majah]

**Hadith**: Narrated Abdullah ibn Abbas (ra): The Prophet (ﷺ) said: If anyone acquires any knowledge of astrology, he acquires a branch of magic of which he gets more as long as he continues to do so. [Abu Dawud]

**Hadith**: Zayd ibn Khalid al-Juhani (ra) said: The Messenger of Allah (ﷺ) led the morning prayer for us at al-Hudaybiyah following rainfall during the night. When the Prophet (ﷺ) finished, he turned to face the people and said to them: Do you know what your Lord has said?" They said: "Allah and his Messenger (ﷺ) know the best." He (ﷺ) said: "This morning one of My slaves became a believer in Me and one a disbeliever. As for him who said: 'We have been given rain by the grace of Allah and His mercy,' that one is a believer in Me, a disbeliever in the stars; and as for him who said: 'We have been given rain by such-and-such a star, that one is a disbeliever in Me, a believer in the stars.' [Bukhari, Muslim]

## Incantations (chants), amulets and love spells

**Hadith**: Abdullah ibn Mas'ud (ra) reported: I heard the Messenger of Allah (ﷺ) say: "Incantations (chants), amulets and love spells are Shirk." [Abu Dawud, Sunan Ibn Majah]. According to scholars, what is meant by Shirk here is minor Shirk, not major Shirk.

**Hadith**: Ruwaifi' bin Sabit (ra) said: "The Messenger of Allah [ﷺ] said: 'O Ruwaifi', you may live for a long time after me, so tell the people that whoever ties up his beard, or twists it, or hangs an amulet, or cleans himself (after relieving himself) with animal dung or bones, Muhammad ﷺ has nothing to do with him.'" [Sunan an-Nasai]

**Hadith**: It was narrated from Uqbah Ibn Amir al-Juhani (ra) that a group came to the Messenger of Allah (ﷺ) [to swear their allegiance (bay'ah) to him]. He ﷺ accepted the bay'ah of nine of them but not of one of them. They said, "O Messenger of Allah (ﷺ), you accepted the bay'ah of nine but not of this one." He ﷺ said, "He is wearing an amulet." The man put his hand (in his shirt) and took it off, then he (ﷺ) accepted his bay'ah. He ﷺ said, 'Whoever wears an amulet has committed shirk." [Musnad Ahmad]

Incantations are words that involve polytheism, which the people of jahiliyyah would recite for treatment. Love spells are something that people do, claiming that it will make a woman beloved to her husband and a man beloved to his wife. Amulets are things that are hung on children and calf such as turquoise beads and the like, which they claim will protect them from the evil eye. These actions constitute shirk because they elevate certain objects to the status of causes, even though they are not Shar'i causes backed by proof nor material causes confirmed by experimentation. Shar'i causes, such as the recitation of the Qur'an, and material causes, such as medicines validated by scientific testing, are permissible as long as we understand them to be mere means. Ultimately, all benefit and harm are in the control of Allah SWT.

At times, certain incantations—despite involving **shirk** may appear to be effective. This perceived benefit is often a deception orchestrated by **Shaytan**, who seeks to mislead people and divert them from true faith. Tragically, many Muslims now turn to individuals who claim to offer healing or protection through such forbidden means. What they do not realize is that **Shaytan may cause temporary relief** to validate the incantation, thus strengthening the person's reliance on falsehood. This illusion serves to deepen their deviation and bind them to practices that contradict **Tawhid**. Believers must be cautious and avoid any form of incantation that contains elements of shirk, calling upon jinn, or seeking help from anyone other than **Allah SWT**. The **only type of incantation permitted in Islam** is that which is **free from shirk.**

**Hadith:** It was narrated from Zaynab (ra), the wife of Abdullah Ibn Masood from Abdullah (ra) that he said: "I heard the Messenger of Allah (ﷺ) say, 'Spells (ruqyah), amulets and love-charms are shirks." I said, "Why do you say this? By Allah, my eye was weeping with a discharge and I kept going to so and so, the Jew, who did a spell for me. When he did the spell, it calmed down." Abdullah (ra) said: "That was just the work of the Shaitan who was picking it with his hand, and when (the Jew) uttered the spell, he stopped. All you needed to do was to say as the Messenger of Allah (ﷺ) used to say: *'Adhhib il-ba's Rabb al-naas ishfi anta al-Shaafi laa shifaa'a illa shifaa'uka shifaa'an laa yughaadiru saqaman (Remove the harm, O Lord of mankind, and heal,* You are the Healer. There is no healing but Your healing, a healing which leaves no disease behind.'" [**Sunan Ibn Majah;** Sunan **Abu Dawood**]

**Hadith: Awf ibn Malik (ra) said:** "We used to recite incantations (ruqyah) during the days of ignorance, so we asked the Messenger of Allah ﷺ, 'What is your opinion about that?' He ﷺ said: **'Present your ruqyah to me. There is nothing wrong with ruqyah as long as it does not involve shirk.'"** [**Sahih Muslim**]

Above informations are presented in a **clear and concise tabular form below.**

| Practice | Ruling in Islam | Reason |
| --- | --- | --- |
| Belief in superstitions | Minor Shirk and a major sin. | It contradicts reliance on Allah and gives weight to baseless causes. |
| Visiting a fortune-teller | Major Shirk and a major sin; prayer will not be accepted for forty nights. | It involves claiming knowledge of the unseen, which belongs to Allah alone. |
| Astrology | Major Shirk and a major sin. | Attributing influence to stars or planets is a form of worship to other than Allah. |
| Love spells | Minor Shirk and a major sin. | It is an attempt to create or influence a relationship through the help of Shayṭan |
| Amulets | Minor Shirk and a major sin. | It involves placing reliance on something other than Allah |

## 1.11 Shirk is the biggest sin

Shirk is the act of treating someone in a way that is due only to Allah (SWT). Since the fundamental purpose of creation is to worship Allah alone, directing worship to anyone or anything else is a direct rejection of that divine purpose. Every act of worship must be exclusively for Allah; directing it elsewhere is a grave misplacement and a serious transgression. Allah SWT says:

- *I did not create the Jinns and the human beings except for the purpose that they should worship Me. (Aj-Jariyat Ch 51:56; interpretation of meaning)*

Shirk violates the rights and honor due to Allah alone. It is the gravest form of oppression, as it severs a person from Allah's protection and leads them away from the path of guidance. Its severity is magnified by the fact that the mushrik equates Allah—the Creator—with created beings that lack even the power to produce a single fly. These powerless objects cannot benefit or protect themselves, let alone others. Such a comparison reflects the utmost ingratitude and betrayal toward the One who sustains all. Allah SWT says (interpretation of meaning):

- *humanity! A lesson is set forth, so listen to it carefully: those idols you invoke besides Allah can never create so much as a fly, even if they all were to come together for that. And if a fly were to snatch anything away from them, they cannot even retrieve it from the fly. How powerless are those who invoke and those invoked! (Al-Hajj Ch 22:73)*

- *Ask them, O Prophet, "Have you considered whatever idols you invoke besides Allah? Show me what they have created on earth! Or do they have a share in the creation of the heavens? Bring me a scripture revealed before this Quran or a shred of knowledge, if what you say is true." (Al-Ahqaf Ch 46:4)*

Shirk is the unforgivable sin. On the Day of Judgement, mushrik will find that he/she will be the biggest loser and he will dwel in hellfire forever. Allah SWT says:

- *(Remember) when Luqman said to his son, while he was advising him, "My dear son, do not ascribe partners to Allah. Indeed, ascribing partners to Allah (Shirk) is grave transgression." (Surah Luqman, Ch 31:13; interpretation of meaning)*

**Hadith**: Narrated `Abdullah (ra): I asked Allah's Messenger (ﷺ), "What is the biggest sin in the sight of Allah?" He (ﷺ) said, "To set up rivals unto Allah though He alone created you." I said, "In fact, that is a tremendous sin," and added, "What next?" He (ﷺ) said, "To kill your son being afraid that he may share your food with you." I further asked, "What next?" He (ﷺ) said, "To commit illegal sexual intercourse with the wife of your neighbour." [Bukhari]

## Shirk is one of the destroyers

It was narrated from Abu Hurairah (ra) that the Messenger of Allah (ﷺ) said: "Avoid the seven destroyers." It was said: "What are they, O Messenger of Allah (ﷺ)?" He (ﷺ) said: "Associating others with Allah (Shirk); witchcraft; killing a soul whom Allah has forbidden us to kill, except for a right that is due; consuming orphans' wealth; consuming

Riba (interest/usury); fleeing from the battlefield; and maligning virtuous and innocent women." [Muslim]

## 1.12 Consequence of Shirk

Allah SWT says in the Qur'an: *Indeed, those who disbelieve among the People of the Scripture and the polytheists will be in the Fire of Hell, abiding eternally therein. They are the worst of creatures. (Al-Bayyinah Ch 98:6; interpretation of meaning)*

**Hadith**: Narrated Anas (ra): The Prophet (ﷺ) said: Allah will say to that person of the (Hell) Fire who will receive the least punishment, "If you had everything on the earth, would you give it as a ransom to free yourself (i.e. save yourself from this Fire)?" He will say, 'Yes.' Then Allah will say, "While you were in the backbone of Adam, I asked you much less than this, i.e. not to worship others besides Me, but you insisted on worshipping others besides me." [Bukhari]

### Allah is patient towards disbelievers

Narrated Abu Musa Al-Ash'ari (ra): The Prophet (ﷺ) said, "None is more patient than Allah against the harmful and annoying words He hears (from the people): They ascribe children to Him, yet He bestows upon them health and provision." [Bukhari]

## 1.13 People often commit shirk while mentioning the Creator and creations

We must exercise great care when speaking about Almighty Allah and His creation. All beings, including the Prophets, are creations of Allah. The following hadiths beautifully reflect the teachings of the Prophet (ﷺ), clearly distinguishing between the status of the Creator and that of His creation.

**Hadith 1**: Umar bin Khattab (ra) narrated that the Messenger of Allah (ﷺ) said: "Do not exaggerate in praising me as the Christians praised Messiah (Easa), son of Maryam (as), for I am only his slave. So, call me the slave of Allah and His Messenger (ﷺ)." [Bukhari]

The message conveyed in *hadith1* is crystal clear that the Prophets are creations of Allah and Allah is the Lord. The Prophet (ﷺ) draws a line between **human servitude** and **divine worship**. Love for the Prophet (ﷺ) is a condition of belief — but it must not exceed the bounds set by Allah and His Messenger (ﷺ). This hadith encourages: deep respect and adoration for the Prophet (ﷺ) and a perfect balance of respect without crossing into exaggeration.

Look at hadiths 2 and 3 where the Prophet (ﷺ) disapproved ceratin expressions used by his comapnions due to improper choice of words.

**Hadith 2**: Abdullah Ibn Abbas (ra) narrated: A Companion came to the Prophet (ﷺ) and said: "What Allah Wills **and** you will." He (ﷺ) said: "Are you making me equal to Allah? But say only what Allah alone Wills (مَا شَاءَ اللهُ وَحْدَهُ)." [Musnad Ahmad]

In hadith 2, The 'Will of Allah' refers to the belief that Allah has decreed everything that occurs in the universe, and that nothing happens without His Knowledge. The Qur'anic verses — *'And Allah does what He wills'* (Surah Ibrahim, 14:27) and *'Your Lord creates whatever He wills and chooses'* (Al-Qasas, 28:68) — affirm that this concept is rooted in Allah's Lordship (ar-Rububiyyah). To attribute any share in this divine Lordship to others is an act of shirk. The Prophet (ﷺ) even prohibited the casual use of the word 'and' in certain contexts, as it joins two subjects in equality. Being the best of teachers, he (ﷺ) understood that such phrasing could imply a partnership in Allah's exclusive authority, which contradicts the essence of Tawheed.

**Hadith 3**: Adi bin Hatim Tai (ra) reported that a person (Companion) recited a khutba before the Messenger of Allah (ﷺ) thus: He who obeys Allah and His Apostle (ﷺ), he in fact follows the right path, and he who disobeys **both** of them, he goes astray مَنْ يُطِعِ اللَّهَ وَرَسُولَهُ فَقَدْ رَشِدَ وَمَنْ يَعْصِهِمَا فَقَدْ غَوَى. Upon this, the Messenger of Allah (ﷺ) said, "What a bad speaker you are; say: He who disobeys Allah **and** His Apostle قُلْ وَمَنْ يَعْصِ اللَّهَ وَرَسُولَهُ." Ibn Numair added: He in fact went astray. [Muslim]

In hadith 3, the Prophet (ﷺ) did not object to 'and' in the first phrase. The phrase *'He who obeys Allah and His Apostle (ﷺ), he in fact follows the right path'* aligns with the Quranic verse: (*O you who have believed, obey Allah and obey the Messenger and those in authority among you)"* (An-Nisa Ch 4: 59). This is the essence of Islam: obedience to Allah and His Prophet (ﷺ). Furthermore, the verse "*Whoever obeys the Messenger has indeed obeyed Allah; but those who turn away, We have not sent you as a guardian over them*" (Surah An-Nisa, 4:80) reinforces this connection. Obeying Allah **and** obeying the Messenger — is used to **affirm** the unity of the message and the authority given by Allah to the Prophet (ﷺ). So, while people's obedience is linked (because the Prophet ﷺ only conveys what Allah commands), they are **not parallel in essence or status**.

Narrated Abu Huraira (ra): Allah's Messenger (ﷺ) said, "Whoever obeys me, obeys Allah, and whoever disobeys me, disobeys Allah, and whoever obeys the ruler I appoint, obeys me, and whoever disobeys him, disobeys me." [Bukhari] Therefore, obeying Allah and His Apostle (ﷺ), or simply obeying the Apostle (ﷺ), conveys the same principle of Tawheed. The Prophet (ﷺ) did not object to the phrasing in this hadith, as it expresses the same essential message.

The Prophet (ﷺ) disapproved of the use of the word **"both"** in the phrase *"he who disobeys both of them,"* referring to Allah and His Messenger (ﷺ). The term **"both"** linguistically denotes a pair regarded as equal or similar in rank or kind. When applied to Allah and the Prophet (ﷺ), this phrasing inadvertently implies equality in authority or status—an implication that directly contradicts Tawḥid al-Rububiyyah (the Oneness of Allah's Lordship) and enters into the realm of shirk.

The corrected phrase is: "He who disobeys Allah **and** His Apostle (ﷺ)." This construction conveys disobedience to the divine command without equating the Messenger (ﷺ) with Allah in essence or authority. While disobedience to the Messenger (ﷺ) constitutes a rejection of divine guidance, it is always understood that the Prophet (ﷺ) conveys what Allah has revealed, acting by divine command, not by independent authority.

Importantly, the conjunction **"and"** does not inherently imply equality between the entities it connects. It is a *flexible* grammatical device that can join elements of differing rank or function. In contrast, the term **"both"** is more *rigid* and is typically reserved for two items that are of comparable status. This distinction is critical: using **"both"** for Allah and the Prophet (ﷺ) linguistically places them on the same level, which is theologically unacceptable. Within Islamic doctrine, the Prophet (ﷺ) is the Messenger and servant of Allah, and all of his authority is derived solely through divine revelation.

A question might arise: There are hundreds of hadiths in which the Companions responded with "اللَّهُ وَرَسُولُهُ أَعْلَمُ" (Allah and His Messenger ﷺ know the best) whenever the Prophet (ﷺ) asked them something. Yet, the Prophet (ﷺ) never objected to this response. For reference, Hadiths 4 and 5 are provided below.

**Hadith 4**: Narrated Mu`az bin Jabal (ra): The Prophet (ﷺ) said, "O Mu`az! Do you know what Allah's Right upon His slaves is?" I said, "Allah and His Apostle (ﷺ) know the best." The Prophet (ﷺ) said, "To worship Him (Allah) Alone and to join none in worship with Him (Allah). Do you know what their right upon Him is?" I replied, "Allah **and** His Apostle (ﷺ) know the best." The Prophet (ﷺ) said, "Not to punish them (if they do so)." [Bukhari]

**Hadith 5:** Ubayy bin Ka'b (ra) said: Allah's Messenger (ﷺ) said: "O Abu' al-Munjir (ra), do you know the verse from the Book of Allah which, according to you, is the greatest? I said: Allah **and** His Apostle (ﷺ) know the best. He (ﷺ) again said: Abu'l-Munjir (ra), do you know the verse from the Book of Allah which, according to you, is the greatest? I said: اللَّهُ لاَ إِلَهَ إِلاَّ هُوَ الْحَيُّ الْقَيُّومُ Allah, there is no God but He, the Living, the Eternal.

Thereupon he (ﷺ) struck me on my breast and said: May knowledge be pleasant for you, O Abu'l-Munjir (ra)!" [Bukhari]

In Hadiths 4 and 5, the Prophet (ﷺ) was teaching his companions about the religion. As effective teachers often do, he posed questions not merely to assess knowledge, but to draw attention to specific words, concepts, or broader themes. In Hadiths 4 and 5, the Prophet (ﷺ) already knew the answers, as they were taught to him by Allah. "**Allah and His Messenger (ﷺ) know best**", they were referring to the **source** of divine knowledge — which **flows from Allah**, but is **conveyed** by the Messenger (ﷺ). It recognizes that: Allah is the ultimate knower of all things and the Prophet (ﷺ) knows **only what Allah reveals to him**. So, in this context, the **"and" does not imply equality**, but implies **association by divine authorization**.

**Summary:**

| Phrase | Status | Reason |
|---|---|---|
| "Allah and His Messenger ﷺ know the best" | Approved by the Prophet ﷺ | Acknowledges the Prophet's ﷺ derived knowledge from Allah without equating them. |
| "Obey Allah and His Messenger ﷺ " | Approved by the Prophet ﷺ | Reflects divine command structure; Prophet ﷺ is obeyed **through** Allah SWT. |

| "Disobey both of them" | Disapproved by the Prophet ﷺ | The word **"both"** implies equality/parity, contradicting Tawhid. |
| --- | --- | --- |

## 1.14 Warning by Allah SWT against Shirk

There is severe warning by Allah SWT against Shirk. Allah says:

- *"It has already been revealed to you and to those before you (that): If you associate (partners with Allah), your deeds shall be rendered useless, and you shall be among the losers." (Az-Zumar Ch 39:65; interpretation of meaning)*

This does not mean that there was any chance of the Prophet's (ﷺ) committing Shirk (Allah forbid). Narrated Abu Huraira (ra): Allah's Messenger (ﷺ) said: "I have been sent (as an Apostle) in the best of all the generations of Adam's offspring since their Creation." [Bukhari] The above verse is meant to send strong message by tough words through the Prophet (ﷺ) to the common Muslims that Shirk is the most heinous crime which must be guarded against cautiously.

## 1.15 We have to seek only from Allah, nobody else

The Prophet (ﷺ) never taught us to seek anything from anyone other than Allah (SWT). He (ﷺ) encouraged us to turn to Allah in supplication for all our needs, no matter how small—even for something as trivial as a worn-out shoelace. Anas ibn Malik (ra) reported: The Messenger of Allah (ﷺ) said, **"Let one of you ask his Lord for his needs, all of them, even for**

**a shoe-string when his (shoe-string) breaks**." [Sunan at-Tirmizi]. In the beginning of the Qur'an, Allah SWT taught us in Surah al-Fatihah: إِيَّاكَ نَعْبُدُ وَإِيَّاكَ نَسْتَعِينُ

(*You alone do we worship, and from You alone do we seek help; interpretation of meaning*).

In another place, Allah SWT says in the Qur'an (interpretation of meaning):

- *Do you not know that to Allah alone belongs the kingdom of the heavens and the earth? Other than Allah, you have neither a Guardian, nor a Helper. (Al- Baqarah Ch 2:107)*

**Hadith**: Ibn 'Abbas (ra) narrated: I was behind the Prophet (ﷺ) one day when he said: "O boy! I will teach you a statement: Be mindful of Allah and He will protect you. Be mindful of Allah and you will find Him before you. When you ask, ask Allah, and when you seek aid, seek Allah's aid. Know that if the entire creation were to gather together to do something to benefit you- you would never get any benefit except that Allah had written for you. And if they were to gather to do something to harm you- you would never be harmed except that Allah had written for you. The pens are lifted and the pages are dried." [Tirmizi]

**Hadith**: Mughirah bin Shubah (ra) narrated that whenever the Messenger of Allah (ﷺ) had finished any compulsory prayer, he (ﷺ) used to say these words: "O Allah! Nobody can hold back what You give and nobody can give what You hold back. And the good fortune of any fortunate person is of no avail against You." [Bukhari, Muslim]

**Hadith**: Abdullah bin Mas'ud (ra) narrated that whenever the Messenger of Allah (ﷺ) was distressed, he would say: "O Ever-Living, O Eternal, by Your mercy I seek help." [Al-Mustadrak Hakim, Tirmizi] In Arabic: يَا حَيُّ يَا قَيُّومُ ، بِرَ حْمَتِكَ أَسْتَغِيثُ ،

**Hadith**: Abu Zarr (ra) reported Allah›s Messenger (ﷺ) as saying that Allah, the Exalted and Glorious, said: "My servants, I have made oppression unlawful for Me and unlawful for you, so do not commit oppression against one another. My servants, all of you are liable to err except one whom I guide on the right path, so seek right guidance from Me so that I should direct you to the right path. O My servants, all of you are hungry (needy) except one whom I feed, so beg food from Me, so that I may give that to you. O My servants, all of you are naked (need clothes) except one whom I provide garments, so beg clothes from Me, so that I should clothe you. O My servants, you commit error night and day and I am there to pardon your sins, so beg pardon from Me so that I should grant you pardon. O My servants, you can neither do Me any harm nor can you do Me any good. O My servants, even if the first amongst you and the last amongst you and even the whole of human race of yours, and that of jinns even, become (equal in) God-conscious like the heart of a single person amongst you, nothing would add to My Power. O My servants, even if the first amongst you and the last amongst you and the whole human race of yours and that of the Jinns too in unison become the most wicked (all beating) like the heart of a single person, it would cause no loss to My Power. O My servants, even if the first amongst you and the last amongst you and the whole human race of yours and that of jinns also all stand in one plain ground and you ask Me and I confer upon every person what he asks for, it would not in any way, cause any loss to Me (even less) than that which is caused to the ocean by dipping the needle in it. My servants, these for you I shall reward you for them, so he whose deeds of yours which I am recording finds good should praise Allah and he who does not find that should not blame anyone but his ownself." Sa'id said that when Abu Idris Khaulini narrated this hadith he knelt upon his knees. [Muslim]

Look at the supplications in the Qur'an where the supplications are directly sought to Allah SWT. These supplications are inclusive of worldly affair as well. For example:

- رَبَّنَآ أَتِنَا فِي الدُّنْيَا حَسَنَةً وَّفِي الْأَخِرَةِ حَسَنَةً وَّقِنَا عَذَابَ النَّارِ *(Surah Baqara Ch 2:201; interpretation of meaning)* (Our Lord! Give us in this world that which is good and in the Hereafter that which is good, and save us from the torment of the Fire!)

- رَبَّنَا تَقَبَّلْ مِنَّا ۖ إِنَّكَ أَنتَ السَّمِيعُ الْعَلِيمُ *(Surah Baqarah Ch 2:127; interpretation of meaning)* (Our Lord! Accept (this service) from us: For Thou art the All-Hearing, the All-knowing.)

- رَبَّنَا أَفْرِغْ عَلَيْنَا صَبْراً وَثَبِّتْ أَقْدَامَنَا وَانصُرْنَا عَلَى الْقَوْمِ الْكَافِرِينَ *(Surah Baqarah Ch 2:250; interpretation of meaning)* (Our Lord! Bestow on us endurance, make our foothold sure, and give us help against the disbelieving folk.)

- رَبَّنَا ظَلَمْنَا أَنفُسَنَا وَإِن لَّمْ تَغْفِرْ لَنَا وَتَرْحَمْنَا لَنَكُونَنَّ مِنَ الْخَاسِرِينَ *(Al-A'raf Ch 7:23; interpretation of meaning)* (Our Lord! We have wronged our own souls: If thou forgive us not and bestow not upon us Thy Mercy, we shall certainly be lost.)

Allah SWT says in Surah al-Baqarah (interpretation of the meaning):

- *When My servants ask you about Me, then (tell them that) I am near. I respond to the call of one when he prays to Me; so they should respond to Me, and have faith in Me, so that they may be on the right path. (Al-Baqarah Ch 2:186)*

Allah SWT is very near to us and we have to supplicate to Him only. We have to remember Him in supplications. In another place, Allah SWT says:

- *Indeed We have created man, and We know whatever thoughts his inner self develops, and We are closer to him than (his) jugular vein* (Surah Qaf, Ch 50:16; interpretation of the meaning).*

*The jugular veins are major blood vessels that stretch from our head to our upper chest.

**Hadith**: Narrated from Anas (ra): The prophet (ﷺ) said: Allah the Exalted said, "I am as My servant thinks of Me, and I am with him whenever he invokes Me." [Musnad Ahmad]

**Hadith**: The Prophet (ﷺ) said: "The supplication of the servant will be accepted as long as he does not supplicate for what includes sin, or cutting the relations of the womb, and as long as he does not become hasty." He (ﷺ) was asked, "O Messenger of Allah (ﷺ)! How does one become hasty?" He (ﷺ) said: He (the person) says, 'I supplicated and supplicated, but I do not see that my supplication is being accepted from me.' He thus loses interest and abandons supplicating (to Allah). [Muslim]

Innovators often mislead the public by giving examples such as asking one's living father for money, requesting class notes from a friend, or asking one's mother for a cup of tea. However, these examples pertain to everyday, worldly interactions with people who are alive and present, and they have no connection to Tawheed or Shirk. Such requests are not made with the belief that anyone possesses divine power. The companions of the Prophet (ﷺ) themselves assisted him and one another in various worldly matters, which is a natural part of life. During the battles of Badr and Uhud, around 313 and 700 companions respectively stood by the Prophet (ﷺ) in combat. Numerous hadiths also affirm the permissibility of seeking help from others in worldly affairs.

**Hadith**: Narrated Al-Mughira bin Shu'ba (ra): I helped the Prophet (ﷺ) in performing ablution and he (ﷺ) passed his wet hands over his Khuffs and prayed. [Bukhari]

**Hadith**: Jabir bin Abdullah (ra) reported: I heard Allah's Messenger (ﷺ) exhorting people on the day of the Battle of the Ditch (Khandaq) to fight. Zubair (ra) said: I am ready (to participate). He (ﷺ) then again exhorted and he (Zubair) again said: I am ready to participate. Thereupon Allah's Messenger (ﷺ) said: Behold. For every Prophet there is a helper and my helper is Zubair (ra). [Muslim]

**Hadith**: Narrated Abu Musa (ra): Whenever a beggar or a person in need came to the Prophet (ﷺ), the Prophet (ﷺ) would say, "Help and recommend him and you will receive the reward for it, and Allah will bring about what he will through His Prophet's (ﷺ) tongue." [Bukhari]

**Hadith**: It was narrated that Abu Hurairah (ra) said: We were with the Messenger of Allah (ﷺ) in the year of Khaibar, and we did not get any spoils of war except for wealth, goods and clothes. Then a man from Banu Ad-Dubaib, who was called Rifa'ah bin Zaid, gave the Messenger of Allah a black slave who was called Mid'am (ra). The Messenger of Allah (ﷺ) set out for Wadi Al-Qura. When we were in Wadi Al-Qura, while Mid'am (ra) was unloading the luggage of the Messenger of Allah (ﷺ), an arrow came and killed him. The people said: 'Congratulations! You will go to Paradise,' but the Messenger of Allah (ﷺ) said: 'No, by the One in Whose hand is my soul! The cloak that he took from the spoils of war on the Day of Khaibar is burning him with fire.' When the people heard that, a man brought one or two shoelaces to the Messenger of Allah (ﷺ) and the Messenger of Allah (ﷺ) said: 'One or two shoelaces of fire.' [Sunan an-Nasai]

**Hadith**: It was narrated that Abu Salamah bin Abdul-Rahman said: Usman (ra) looked out from the house when he was under siege and said: I adjure by Allah anyone who was present with the Messenger of Allah (ﷺ), on the day of Hira, when the mountain shook beneath his feet; he kicked it with his foot and said: "Be still, Hira, there is no one on you but a Prophet (ﷺ), a Siddiq or a martyr, and I was with him. And some men testified to what he said. Then he said: I adjure by Allah anyone who was present with the Messenger of Allah (ﷺ) on the day of Bai'atul-Ridwan, when he had sent me to the mushrikeen, the people of Makkah; he (ﷺ) said: This is my hand and this is the hand of Usman, and he swore allegiance on my behalf. And some men testified to what he said. Then he said: I adjure by Allah anyone who was present when the Messenger of Allah (ﷺ) said: 'Who will expand the mosque by incorporating this house into it, in return for a house in Paradise?' and I bought it with my wealth and expanded the mosque by incorporating it into it. And some men testified to what he said. Then he said: 'I adjure by Allah anyone who saw the Messenger of Allah (ﷺ) on the day of the army of hardship (i.e., Tabuk), when he said: Who will spend today a spending that will be accepted by Allah? and I equipped half of the army with my wealth. And some men testified to what he said: Then he said: I adjure by Allah anyone who saw the water of Rumah (a well) being sold to wayfarers, then I bought it with my own wealth and gave it to wayfarers for free. And some men testified to what he said. [Musnad Ahmad]

**Hadith**: Narrated Ya'la ibn Umayyah (ra): The Messenger of Allah (ﷺ) said to me: When my messengers come to you, give them thirty coats of mail, and thirty camels. I asked: Messenger of Allah (ﷺ), is it a loan with a guarantee of its return, or a loan to be paid back? He replied: It is a loan to be paid back. [Abu Dawud]

**Hadith:** It was narrated that 'Imran bin Hudaifah said: Maimunah (ra) used to take out loans frequently, and some of her family criticized her and denounced her for that. She said: I will not stop taking loans, for I heard my close friend and my beloved [i.e. the Prophet (ﷺ)] say: "There is no one who takes out a loan, and Allah knows that he intends to pay it back, but Allah will pay it back for him in this world." [Sunan an-Nasai]

**Hadith**: Jaibir (ra) reported that a woman from the tribe of Makhzum committed theft. She was brought to Allah's Apostle (ﷺ) and she sought refuge (intercession) from Umm Salama (ra), the wife of Allah's Apostle (ﷺ). Thereupon Allah's Apostle (ﷺ) said: By Allah, even if she were Fatima (ra), I would have her hand cut off. And thus, her hand was cut off. [Muslim] Ibn Hajar Asqalani said in Fath al-Baari about this hadith of Muslim: "So she sought refuge in Umm Salamah (ra)", meaning she sought protection [assistance/help] from her." The Islamic scholars are of the opinion that "As for seeking help of a creature in that which he is able to do during his life, then this is permissible, whether this is called seeking refuge, or seeking help, or otherwise."

In the Qur'an, Allah SWT is commanding the Companions to help the Prophet (ﷺ). Allah says (interpretation of meaning):

- *If you do not help him, then Allah has already helped him when the disbelievers expelled him, he being the second of the two, when the two of them were in the cave, he said to his companion 'Do not grieve; Allah is indeed with us.' Then Allah sent down His tranquility upon him and strengthened him with hosts you did not see, and He made lowest the word of the unbelievers; and the Word of Allah is the highest; and Allah is all-Mighty, all-Wise. (At-Tawbah, Ch 9:40)*

The verse above was revealed as a warning to those Muslims who showed reluctance to join the Battle of Tabuk. Allah reminds them that if they do not support the Prophet (ﷺ) in his mission, He will still aid him—just as He had in the past. One such instance was during the Hijrah, when the Prophet (ﷺ) and Abu Bakr (ra) took refuge in the Cave of Sawr while migrating from Makkah to Madinah, and Allah protected them from their enemies. Allah SWT says (interpretation of meaning)

- *Or ask them, "Who responds to the distressed when they cry to Him, relieving their affliction, and Who makes you successors in the earth? Is it another god besides Allah? Yet you are hardly mindful!" (An-Naml Ch 27:62)*

## Ghausul Azam

The title *Ghausul Azam* translates as *"The Greatest Helper"*. It is a title traditionally associated with virtuous dead persons (people believe *awliya*) who are believed to be the chief helpers— someone who relieves the hardships of others. So, instead of calling Allah SWT during trouble, people call Ghausul Azam for help directly. Calling for worldly affair who is alive is already discussed in detail in preceeding paragraphs. The topic of *Ghausul Azam* can be critically examined under the two fundamental theological categories of *Rububiyyah* (Lordship) and *Uluhiyyah* (Worship).

The Qur'an affirms repeatedly that Allah is the only true Helper, Protector, and Ally. These roles are conveyed through divine names and attributes such as نَصِير (Nasir – Helper), وَلِيّ (Wali – Ally), and مَوْلَى (Mawla – Protector). Below are several verses that emphasize this truth (interpretation of meaning):

- بَلِ ٱللَّهُ مَوْلَىٰكُمْ وَهُوَ خَيْرُ ٱلنَّاصِرِينَ

  *"But Allah is your protector, and He is the best of helpers."* *(Surah Al-Imran Ch 3:150)*

- وَٱعْتَصِمُوا بِٱللَّهِ هُوَ مَوْلَىٰكُمْ فَنِعْمَ ٱلْمَوْلَىٰ وَنِعْمَ ٱلنَّصِيرُ

  *"And hold fast to Allah. He is your protector—the best protector and the best helper."* *(Surah Al-Hajj Ch 22:78)*

- وَإِن تَوَلَّوْا فَٱعْلَمُوا أَنَّ ٱللَّهَ مَوْلَىٰكُمْ نِعْمَ ٱلْمَوْلَىٰ وَنِعْمَ ٱلنَّصِيرُ

  *"And if they turn away, then know that Allah is your protector. What an excellent protector, and what an excellent helper!"* *(Surah Al-Anfal Ch 8:40)*

In light of these verses, it is clear that **only Allah** is the Helper and the Protector. These are the attributes of action of Allah and are frequently mentioned in the Qur'an, and they affirm that none but Allah has the ultimate power to assist, safeguard, and govern the affairs of His creation. These are practical manifestations of Allah's Lordship—His sole authority and control over creation, sustenance, guidance, and protection. While we may honour and love the righteous people, we must not believe they have any independent power. Attributing divine qualities of Lordship to anyone besides Allah in an ultimate or independent sense, constitutes major shirk, the gravest sin in Islam.

However, if a person directs their prayer or plea for help to anyone other than Allah, this constitutes an act of this person directed toward one who does not inherently possess the divine attributes of absolute help and protection. Such an act infringes upon the exclusive right of Allah to be worshipped (Uluhiyyah) and amounts to associating partners with Him (shirk), as it attributes divine qualities to the creation which belong to Allah alone.

The Prophet Muhammad (ﷺ) used these phrases in times of trials. Narrated Ibn `Abbas (ra): 'Allah is sufficient for us and He is the best Disposer of affairs," was said by Ibrahim (as) when he was thrown into the fire; and it was said by Muhammad (ﷺ) when they (i.e. hypocrites) said, "A great army is gathering against you, therefore, fear them," but it only increased their faith and they said: " حَسْبُنَا ٱللَّهُ وَنِعْمَ ٱلْوَكِيلُ Allah is Sufficient for us, and He is the Best Disposer (of affairs, for us)." (3.173) [Bukhari] This incident referred to aftermath of the **Battle of Uhud.**

**Allah SWT says:**

قُلْ إِنِّى لَآ أَمْلِكُ لَكُمْ ضَرًّا وَلَا رَشَدًا

*Say (O Prophet), "It is not in my power to harm or benefit you." (Surah Al-Jinn Ch 72:21; interpretation of meaning)*

Surah Al-Jinn (Ch 72:21) powerfully teaches that even the Prophet Muhammad ﷺ does **not own** the ability to bring **harm or benefit**, nor to **guide** people by his own will. It is a declaration of **pure monotheism**, affirming that **only Allah** has complete control over all matters. Related Verses in the Qur'an are (interpretation of meaning):

- قُل لَّآ أَمْلِكُ لِنَفْسِي نَفْعًا وَلَا ضَرًّا إِلَّا مَا شَآءَ ٱللَّهُ

  *"Say, 'I hold not for myself [the power of] benefit or harm, except what Allah has willed...'"* Surah Al-A'raf (Ch 7:188)

- قُل لَّآ أَمْلِكُ لِنَفْسِي ضَرًّا وَلَا نَفْعًا إِلَّا مَا شَآءَ ٱللَّهُ

  *"Say, 'I possess not for myself any harm or benefit except what Allah should will...'"* Surah Yunus (Ch 10:49)

## 1.16 Intermediation

To understand the concept of intermediation in Islam in a simplified way, it can be discussed in two parts based on the purpose it serves:

1. Seeking intermediation to attain closeness to Allah.

2. Seeking intermediation in the hope of having one's supplications (du'a) accepted by Allah.

Discussing the nature and legitimacy of intermediation according to these two purposes makes the matter clearer and easier to comprehend.

## 1. Seeking intermediation to attain closeness to Allah SWT

People of the Indian subcontinent often believe that in order to reach Allah SWT and elevate the rank and dignity of the soul, one must seek intermediation through another virtous person (spiritual guide). They frequently interpret the Qur'anic term *wasila* as "intercession" or "intermediation," commonly citing the verse from Surah Al-Ma'idah (Ch 5:35) in support of this view.

Based on this interpretation, they hold the belief that a person cannot approach Allah directly; rather, they must reach Him through a righteous or saintly individual who acts as an intermediary. Through such a person, the servant embarks on a journey of spiritual purification and may attain a position among those close to Allah (*awliya* of Allah). A commonly used analogy in this context is that just as one needs a ladder to reach the roof of a building from the ground, one also needs an intermediary to approach Allah SWT. However, this analogy does not accurately apply to the matter of supplication (*du'a*) to Allah. Allah directly hears and responds to our *du'as*; therefore, the concept of needing a "ladder" or intermediary is irrelevant in this case. What truly hinders our supplications from reaching Allah is not the absence of an intermediary but rather the ingratitude or insincerity within our own hearts.  Allah SWT says:

يَـٰٓأَيُّهَا ٱلَّذِينَ ءَامَنُوا۟ ٱتَّقُوا۟ ٱللَّهَ وَٱبْتَغُوٓا۟ إِلَيْهِ ٱلْوَسِيلَةَ وَجَـٰهِدُوا۟ فِى سَبِيلِهِۦ لَعَلَّكُمْ تُفْلِحُونَ

*O believers! Be mindful of Allah and seek **wasila** and struggle in His Way, so you may be successful. (Al-Mai'dah Ch 5:35; interpretation of meaning)*

Ibn Kasir writes in his Tafseer: Wasilah means 'the means of approach.' Mujahid, Abu Wa'il, Al-Hasan, Qatadah, `Abdullah bin Kasir, As-Suddi, Ibn Zayd and others gave the same meaning for Wasilah. Qatadah said that the Ayah means, "Seek the means of approach to Him by obeying Him and performing the acts that please Him."

أُولَـئِكَ الَّذِينَ يَدْعُونَ يَبْتَغُونَ إِلَى رَبِّهِمُ الْوَسِيلَةَ

*Those whom they call upon seek a means of access to their Lord Allah. (Ch 17:57)*

Wasilah is a means of approach to achieve something, and it is also used to refer to the highest grade in Paradise, and it is the grade of the Messenger of Allah (ﷺ), his residence and the nearest grade in Paradise to Allah's Throne. Al-Bukhari recorded that Jabir bin `Abdullah (ra) said that the Messenger of Allah ﷺ said, "Whoever, after hearing to the Azan says, "O Allah! Lord of this perfect call and of the regular prayer which is going to be established! Grant Muhammad ﷺ the **Wasilah** and superiority and send him on the Day of Judgment to the praiseworthy station which You have promised him," then intercession from me will be permitted for him on the Day of Resurrection.) Muslim recorded that `Abdullah bin `Amr bin Al-`As (ra) said that he heard the Prophet ﷺ saying, "When you hear the Mu'azzin, repeat what he says, and then ask for Salah (blessing, mercy from Allah) for me. Verily, whoever asks for Salah for me, then Allah will grant ten Salah to him. Then, ask for the **Wasilah** for me, for it is a grade in Paradise that only one servant of Allah deserves, and I hope that I am that servant. Verily, whoever asks (Allah) for **Wasilah** for me, he will earn the right of my intercession. These hadiths tell us that 'Wasila' is a particular rank of Paradise designated mainly for our Prophet (ﷺ).

**Hadith**: Al-Nu'man ibn Bashir (ra) reported: The Prophet (ﷺ) said, **"Supplication is worship itself."** Then, the Prophet (ﷺ) recited the verse, *"Your Lord said: Call upon Me and I will answer you. Verily, those who disdain My worship will enter Hell in humiliation."* (Ch 40:60) [Tirmizi]

As long as the relationship with the intermediary remains a sincere and healthy teacher-student relationship aimed at gaining knowledge of the Qur'an and Sunnah, there is no cause for objection. In fact, such a relationship is praiseworthy and has historically been regarded as an essential means of spreading Islamic teachings across generations. However, the problem arises when a particular belief infiltrates this relationship—namely, that without the intermediary, attaining closeness to Allah SWT is impossible, and that one *must* use the intermediary in order for their supplications (*du'a*) to be accepted. This kind of belief contradicts the fundamental tenets of Islamic creed and undermines the beauty and simplicity of *tawhid*. In Islam, **Allah is the only true guide**, and any human mentor is just a helper, not a divine intermediary. Allah SWT says (interpretation of meaning):

- *You cannot give guidance to whomsoever you wish (O Prophet), but Allah gives guidance to whomsoever He wills, and He best knows the ones who are on the right path. (Al Qasas Ch 28:56)*

- *Similarly, We made enemies for every prophet from among the wicked, but sufficient is your Lord as a Guide and Helper. (Al Furqan Ch 25:31)*

The situation becomes particularly dangerous when a person begins to assume that the intermediary will *definitely* intercede for them on the Day of Judgment. Considering this as a guaranteed assurance or divine guarantee can be spiritually harmful, as it places reliance on a creation rather than on the decision and Will of Allah. Such a mindset goes against the core principle of *tawhid*. True safety and salvation lie in seeking the pleasure of Allah, in self-purification, and in following the Sunnah of the Messenger of Allah (ﷺ). Allah says (interpretation of the meaning):

- *"Who is it that can intercede with Him except by His permission?" (Surah Al-Baqarah, 2:255)*

This verse clearly states that the right to intercede is entirely dependent on Allah's permission. Only those to whom Allah grants permission will be able to intercede. Allah further says (interpretation of the meaning):

- *"Guard yourselves against the Day on which no soul will be of help to another. No intercession will be accepted, no ransom taken, and no help will be given." (Surah Al-Baqarah, 2:48)*

This verse explicitly conveys that no soul will be of benefit to another unless Allah permits it. Abu Hurairah (ra) narrated that the Messenger of Allah (ﷺ) said: "Every Prophet has a (special) supplication which is answered. Verily, I have reserved mine as intercession for my nation, and it shall reach, if Allah wills, those of them who die, not associating anything with Allah." [Tirmizi] The highest form of intercession belongs to the Prophet Muhammad (ﷺ) himself, and even he (ﷺ) will intercede only by the permission of Allah.

## 2. Seeking intermediation in the hope of having du'a accepted by Allah

There are several valid methods of seeking intermediation in the hope that one's *du'a* will be accepted by Allah. These methods are supported by the Qur'an and authentic hadith. For example:

**Intermediation through Righteous Deeds:** It is permissible to seek intermediation through all kinds of righteous deeds. One significant and well-known example is found in an authentic hadith commonly referred to as *"The Story of the Three Men Who Took Shelter in a Cave."*

**Hadith**: Narrated Abdullah Ibn `Umar (ra): The Prophet (ﷺ) said: While three persons were walking, rain began to fall and they had to enter a cave in a mountain. A big rock rolled over and blocked the mouth of the cave. They said to each other, "Invoke Allah with the best deed you have performed (so Allah might remove the rock)". One of them said, "O Allah! My parents were old and I used to go out for grazing (my animals). On my return I would milk (the animals) and take the milk in a vessel to my parents to drink. After they had drunk from it, I would give it to my children, family and wife. One day I was delayed and, on my return, I found my parents sleeping, and I disliked to wake them up. The children were crying at my feet (because of hunger). That state of affairs continued till it was dawn. O Allah! If You regard that I did it for Your sake, then please remove this rock so that we may see the sky." So, the rock was moved a bit. The second said, "O Allah! You know that I was in love with a cousin of mine, like the deepest love a man may have for a woman, and she told me that I would not get my desire fulfilled unless I paid her one-hundred Dinars (gold pieces). So, I struggled for it till I gathered the desired amount, and when I sat in between her legs, she told me to be afraid of Allah, and asked me not to deflower her except rightfully (by marriage). So, I got up and left her. O Allah! If You regard that I did if for Your sake, kindly remove this rock." So, two-thirds of the rock was removed. Then the third man said, "O Allah! No doubt You know that once I employed a worker for one Faraq (three Sa's) of millet, and when I wanted to pay him, he refused to take it, so I sowed it and from its yield I bought cows and a shepherd. After a time that man came and demanded his money. I said to him: Go to those cows and the shepherd and take them for they are for you. He asked me whether I was joking with him. I told him that I was not joking with him, and all that belonged to him. O Allah! If You regard that I did it sincerely for Your sake, then please remove the rock." So, the rock was removed completely from the mouth of the cave. [Bukhari]

**Intermediation through Allah's Names and Attributes**: Seeking to draw close to Allah by means of His names and attributes, faith and Tawheed are also recommended. Allah SWT says (interpretation of the meaning):

- *"And (all) the Most Beautiful Names belong to Allah, so call on Him by them, and leave the company of those who belie or deny (or utter impious speech against) His names. They will be requited for what they used to do." [al-A'raf Ch 7:180]*

**Hadith**: Narrated Abdullah ibn Mas'ud (ra): The Messenger of Allah ﷺ said, "No servant says when he is afflicted with sorrow or grief: 'O Allah, I am Your servant, the son of Your servant, the son of Your maidservant. My forelock is in Your hand, Your command over me is forever executed and Your decree over me is just. **I ask You by every name belonging to You which You have named Yourself with**, or revealed in Your Book, or You taught to any of Your creation, or You have preserved in the knowledge of the unseen with You, that You make the Quran the life of my heart and the light of my breast, and a departure for my sorrow and a release for my anxiety,' except that Allah will take away his distress and replace it with joy." They said, "O Messenger of Allah ﷺ, should we not learn these words?" He ﷺ said, "Certainly, whoever hears them should learn them." [Musnad Ahmad]

**Intermediation through the Status of the Prophet ﷺ:** The status and intercession of the Prophet (ﷺ) are recognized by Allah SWT. The Prophet (ﷺ) is a noble and honored figure for us, and many imams and scholars have regarded it as permissible to ask Allah through the honor and rank of the Messenger (ﷺ), although there exists some scholarly disagreement regarding the interpretation of the following hadith.

**Hadith**: It is narrated by 'Usman ibn Ḥunayf (ra) that a blind man once came to the Prophet ﷺ and said, "O Messenger of Allah □, pray to Allah to cure me." The Prophet ﷺ replied: "If you wish, I will make du'a for you right now. And if you wish, be patient, for that is better for you." The man said, "No, please make du'a for me." So, the Prophet ﷺ said: "Then perform ablution (wuḍu), and do it well. Then pray two rak'ahs of prayer, and say this du'a: "O Allah, I ask You and turn to You through Your Prophet Muḥammad ﷺ, the Prophet of mercy. O Muḥammad ﷺ, I turn to my Lord through you for this need of mine, so that it may be fulfilled. O Allah, accept his intercession for me and accept my intercession for myself." [Sunan at-Tirmizi]

**Requesting du'a from a righteous, living person:** Usair b. Jabir reported that when people from Yemen came to help (the Muslim army at the time of jihad) he (Umar ra) asked them: Is there amongst you Uwais b. 'Amir? (He continued finding him out) until he met Uwais. He said: Are you Uwais b., Amir? He said: Yes. He said: Are you from the tribe of Qaran? He said: Yes. He (Hadrat) 'Umar (again) said: Did you suffer from leprosy and then you were cured from it but for the space of a dirham? He said: Yes. He ('Umar) said: Is your mother (living)? He said: Yes. He ('Umar) said: I heard Allah's Messenger (ﷺ) say: There would come to you Uwais b. Amir with the reinforcement from the people of Yemen. (He would be) from Qaran, (the branch) of Murid. He had been suffering from leprosy from which he was cured but for a spot of a dirham. His treatment with his mother would have been excellent. If he were to take an oath in the name of Allah, He would honour that. And if it is possible for you, then do ask him to beg forgiveness for you (from your Lord). So he (Uwais) begged forgiveness for him. Umar said: Where do you intend to go? He said: To Kufa. He ('Umar) said: Let me write a letter for you to its governor, whereupon he (Uwais) said: I love to live amongst the poor people. When it was the next year, a person from among the elite (of Kufa) performed Hajj and he met Umar. He asked him about Uwais. He said: I left him in a state with meagre means of sustenance. (Thereupon) Umar said: I heard Allah's Messenger (ﷺ) as saying: There would come to you Uwais b. 'Amir, of Qaran, a branch (of the tribe) of Murid, along with the reinforcement of the people of Yemen. He had been suffering from leprosy which would have been cured but for the space of a dirham. His treatment with his mother would have been very kind. If he would take an oath in the name of Allah (for something) He would honour it. Ask him to beg forgiveness for you (from Allah) in case it is possible for you. So he came to Uwais and said.: Beg forgiveness (from Allah) for me. He (Uwais) said: You have just come from a sacred journey (Hajj); you, therefore, ask forgiveness for me. He (the person who had performed Hajj) said: Ask forgiveness for me (from Allah). He (Uwais again) said: You have just come from the sacred journey, so you ask forgiveness for me. (Uwais further) said: Did you meet Umar? He said: Yes. He (Uwais) then begged forgiveness for him (from Allah). So the people came to know about (the status of religious piety) of Uwais. He went away (from that place). Usair said: His clothing consisted of a mantle, and whosoever saw him said: From where did Uwais get this mantle? [Muslim]

**Beginning du'a with Praise and *durud* upon the Prophet (ﷺ):** Faḍalah ibn 'Ubayd (ra) reported that the Prophet ﷺ said: "When one of you prays, let him begin by praising Allah, then sending blessings upon the Prophet ﷺ, then let him supplicate for whatever he wishes." [Tirmizi]

Abdullah ibn Mas'ud (ra) said: "When any of you wishes to ask from Allah, let him begin by praising Allah in the way He deserves to be praised, then send blessings upon the Prophet ﷺ, and then make his supplication. For this increases the likelihood of it being accepted." [al-Mu'jam al-Kabir, Ṭabarani]

## 1.17 Swearing by something other than Allah is a Shirk

Swearing by anything or anyone other than Allah is a grave issue in Islam and is regarded as minor shirk and a major sin, even if the person swears truthfully. This act signifies giving ultimate respect or reverence, which stems from qualities such as dignity, wisdom, or dedication—honor that belongs solely to Allah SWT.

**Hadith**: Ibn 'Umar (ra) reported that the Prophet (ﷺ) said: "Allah has prohibited that you should swear by your fathers. If anyone swears, let him swear by Allah, or else remain silent." [Bukhari]

**Hadith**: Ibn 'Umar (ra) reported that the Prophet (ﷺ) said: "Whoever swears by something other than Allah is guilty of Shirk." [Musnad Ahmad]

**Hadith**: It was narrated on the authority of Sa'd ibn 'Ubaydah that Ibn 'Umar (ra) heard a man swearing, "No, by the Ka'bah!" Ibn 'Umar (ra) said to him: I heard the Prophet (ﷺ) say: 'Whoever swears by other than Allah has fallen into Shirk.' [Abu Dawud]

In conclusion of this Chapter 1, it may be said that **Tawheed** is the foundation of Islam, and the defines line between faith and disbelief. It affirms that Allah alone is the authority in worship, guidance, and judgment. Any act that assigns divine qualities to others besides Him constitutes **shirk**, the gravest sin in Islam. Upholding Tawheed secures eternal success, while shirk corrupts faith and endangers the soul. Therefore, understanding and safeguarding Tawheed is a lifelong commitment to sincere devotion and unwavering loyalty to Allah alone.

# Chapter 2

# Innovation (Bid'ah)

Bid'at or Bid'ah (بدعة) is a newly invented, changed or introduced worship which is neither revealed in the Qur'an and nor is available in the Sunnah of the Prophet (ﷺ). The word 'Bid'ah' here is only relevant to the religion. There is no place of Bid'ah in Islam and are forbidden. Every Bid'ah is misguidance due to the saying of the Prophet (ﷺ): "Every newly introduced matter is a Bid'at, and every Bid'at is misguidance."

Islamic scholars have put forward several classification or types of Bid'at. For example: al-bid'ah al-haqeeqah (real innovation) and **al-bid'ah al-idaafiyyah** (innovation by addition); bid'ah sayyiah (that opposes the Qur'an and Sunnah) and bid'ah hasanah (good bid'ah); bid'ah which constitutes kufr and bid'at which does not constitute kufr and so on. On the other hand, some scholars are of the opinion that Bid'ah in religion is a Bid'ah and it has no place in Islam.

## 2.1 Characterization of Bid'at

Rather than focusing on classification, this discussion presents a characterization of Bid'at. Characterization seeks to offer detailed insights into the nature or attributes of the subject, emphasizing what makes it distinct. This approach will facilitate easier identification and exclusion of Bid'at. It is important to note that systematic attempt to characterize Bid'ats in a comprehensive manner is limited in literature.

Characterization of bid'ah may be discussed under two major heads viz. action based bid'ah and 'Aqeedah based bid'ah.

## i. 'Aqeedah based bid'ah

After the death of the Prophet Muhammad ﷺ, several **innovations in 'Aqeedah** (the core set of beliefs/creed) arose, particularly as Islam expanded into new regions, encountered foreign philosophies, and as some individuals attempted to re-interpret Islamic teachings using speculative reasoning. These innovations often deviated from the **pure teachings of the Qur'an and Sunnah** and the understanding of the **Sahabah. This type of innovations may be termed as 'fallacious bid'ah' which are not action based, but based on corrupted belief. Some scholars are of the view that** *"The innovations in belief are more harmful to the Ummah than innovations in actions."* Innovations in 'aqeedah **corrupt the foundation of Islam**—the core beliefs and eventually lead to action based bid'ah in some cases. Historically, many sects formed due to 'aqeedah-innovation and these sects caused bloodshed, and confusion in the Ummah, especially in early Islamic history. The subject 'Aqeedah is very vast topic in Islam and beyond the scope of the book. Some examples of fallacious bid'ah are: denial of Allah's many attributes, believing that Qur'an was created, labeling sinful Muslims as disbelievers, claiming that **faith alone** is sufficient for salvation, even without actions, etc.

## ii. Action based bid'ah

Bid'at can be described in the language of Algebra like this: Suppose Islam is the set $I$ and Bid'at is the set $B$ comprising some activities as its elements, then intersection of sets $I$ and $B$ is a null set i.e. the sets $I$ and $B$ do not have anything in common.

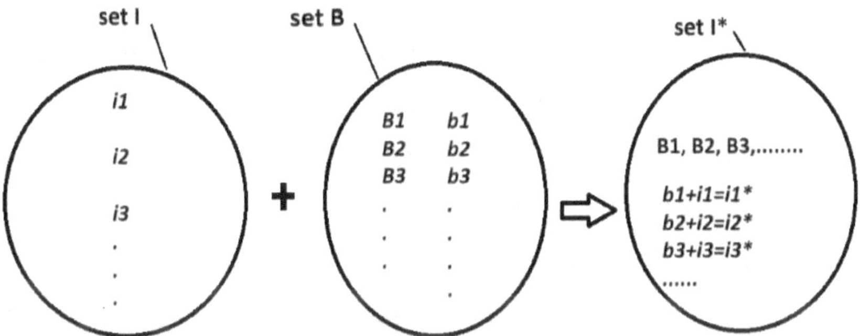


**Fig 3**: Bid'ah explained. (Note: set $I^*$ is not a 'union')

Bid'at can be characterized by studying the mode of action or mechanism of Bid'at activities by which these activites established themselves within the boundary of Islam. Elements within boundary of $I$ are already predefined plus agreed upon. With passage of time, elements of $B$ penetrated into the set $I$ altering its composition, and the reasons for penetration is discussed in subsequent sections. As a result, set $I$ transformed into a new set $I^*$. Set $B$ contains two types of activities or elements. The first type, {B1, B2, B3, …}, penetrated into $I$ and became static, coexisting alongside the original elements of $I$ without further interaction. This type of element may be termed as a **coexistent Bid'at**. Each coexistant Bid'at exists as a complete package of az-Zikr and does not interfere with other elements of the set $I$. The manner in which each coexistent Bid'at is to be performed is specified by their innovator(s). The size of coexistent Bid'ats are large or very large on time scale and while some of these involve Shirk, others do not. Detail analysis and examples this type of bid'ah is appended in **Section 2.24.**

Reactivity of the second type of elements $\{b_1, b_2, b_3, ....\}$ continued further after penetration and they merged with some elements of $I$ thereby forming doped or amalgamated or unified elements. Thus, some of the original elements of $I$ are modified to $\{i_1^*, i_2^*, i_3^*, ...\}$. These types of elements of $B$ may be termed as **integrating Bid'ats**. Bid'ats are always additive, meaning they introduce something new to the original practices. This is because people often perform these Bid'ats in the name of religious practices to seek additional virtue and draw closer to Allah SWT. Unlike coexistent Bid'ats, integrating Bid'ats do not exist as a complete package of az-Zikr, and their time scale is typically small or very small. The specifications of integrating Bid'at is also established by the innovator(s). Mechanism of Bid'at is depicted in Figure 3.

Integrating Bid'at can be illustrated taking *wudu* for example. Review of authentic sources reveals that one has to say '*Bismillah*' before starting, although considered not obligatory by some scholars [Tirmizi] and '*Ashhadu an la ilaha ill-Allah wahdahu la sharika lah, wa ashhadu anna Muhammadan 'abduhu wa rasuluhu*' after wudu. [Muslim] There is no proof that the Prophet (ﷺ) recited any du'a during wudu while washing or wiping his parts of body.

But in the sub-continent, there are many du'as before, during and after wudu. One such du'a while washing the nose during wudu is as follows:

اَللّٰهُمَّ لَا تُحَرِّمْ عَلَىَّ رِيْحَ الْجَنَّةِ وَاجْعَلْنِىْ مِمَّنْ يَشَمُّ رِيْحَهَا وَرَوْحَهَا وَطِيْبَهَا

*O Lord! Do not deprive me of the fragrance of Paradise, and make me of those who smell its fragrance and perfume.*

Meaning of the above du'a is heart touching. We all aspire of fragrance of Paradise. Definitely there is nothing wrong in its meaning and there is no involvement of Shirk in it. The Prophet (ﷺ) did not teach us this du'a during washing of nose and it unified later on with wudu. Thus, it is an integrating Bid'at. Question may arise: What is wrong reciting those meaningful du'as that do not contradict Tawheed? The answer is, this is not the right place to recite this du'a and this is not as per the teaching of the Prophet (ﷺ). Following hadith is an excellent riposte.

**Hadith**: A man sneezed next to Abdullah ibn 'Umar (ra) and said '*Alhamdu lillah was-salamu 'ala Rasulillah*' (praise be to Allah and peace be upon the Messenger of Allah). Ibn 'Umar (ra) said: "I too say (at other times) *Alhamdu lillah was salamu 'ala Rasulillah*, but this is not how Rasulullah (ﷺ) taught us, rather he taught us to say, '*Alhamdulillahi 'ala kulli hal*' (Praise be to Allah in all circumstances)." [Sunan at-Tirmizi, Al-Mustadrak Hakim].

**Hadith**: Narrated Al-Bara 'bin `Azib (ra): The Prophet (ﷺ) said to me, "Whenever you go to bed perform ablution like that for the prayer, lie or your right side and say:

اللَّهُمَّ أَسْلَمْتُ وَجْهِي إِلَيْكَ، وَفَوَّضْتُ أَمْرِي إِلَيْكَ، وَأَلْجَأْتُ ظَهْرِي إِلَيْكَ، رَغْبَةً وَرَهْبَةً إِلَيْكَ، لاَ مَلْجَأَ وَلاَ مَنْجَا مِنْكَ إِلاَّ إِلَيْكَ، اللَّهُمَّ آمَنْتُ بِكِتَابِكَ الَّذِي أَنْزَلْتَ، وَبِنَبِيِّكَ الَّذِي أَرْسَلْتَ

*(O Allah! I surrender to You and entrust all my affairs to You and depend upon You for Your Blessings both with hope and fear of You. There is no fleeing from You, and there is no place of protection and safety except with You. O Allah! I believe in Your Book (the Qur'an) which You have revealed and, in Your **Nabi**, whom You have sent).*

Then if you die on that very night, you will die with faith (i.e. or the religion of Islam). Let the aforesaid words be your last utterance (before sleep)." I repeated it before the Prophet (ﷺ) and when I reached "Allahumma amantu bikitabika-l-laji anzalta (O Allah I believe in Your Book which You have revealed)." I said, "Wa-**rasulika** (وَرَسُولِكَ)." The Prophet (ﷺ) said, "No, (but say): 'Wa **nabiyika**-l-laji arsalta (وَنَبِيِّكَ الَّذِي أَرْسَلْتَ), instead." [Bukhari]

Indeed, every **Rasul** (Messenger) is also a **Nabi** (Prophet), but not every Nabi is a Rasul. The status of a Rasul is higher than that of a Nabi. Outwardly, referring to the Prophet Muḥammad ﷺ as a *Rasul* in place of *Nabi* in a supplication may seem technically correct here, as it denotes a higher rank. It is possible that the Companion intended to express greater reverence and honor by using the title *Rasul*. However, the Prophet ﷺ did not approve of this substitution and instructed the Companion to say, **"wa nabiyyika** al-laji arsalta" (and in Your Prophet whom You have sent), rather than **"wa rasulika"** (and Your Messenger). This highlights the importance of adhering precisely to the wordings taught by the Prophet ﷺ, especially in matters of du'a and worship, even if alternative expressions may appear more respectful or appropriate from a personal perspective. We have to practise the way Allah's Apostle (ﷺ) taught or practised. Allah SWT says:

*Indeed in the Messenger of Allah (Muhammad) you have a good example to follow for him who hopes for Allah and the Last Day and remembers Allah much. (Al-Ahzab Ch 33:21; interpretation of meaning)*

The Prophet (ﷺ) said: "Whoever does something that is not part of our way will have it rejected." [Sahih Muslim] This reminds us that in matters of worship, what truly matters is not how emotionally uplifting or meaningful an act may appear, but whether it aligns with the Sunnah of the Prophet ﷺ. No matter how noble an action may seem, if it was not practiced or approved by the Messenger of Allah ﷺ, we must refrain from it. Indeed, only Allah and His Messenger ﷺ have the authority to prescribe the correct forms of worship. True devotion lies in obedience, not in innovation.

Between coexistent Bid'at and integrating Bid'at, the latter is more frequently practised. A person may not perform coexistent Bid'at during his whole lifetime whereas he is performing wudu (for instance) daily in the fabricated manner. Fortunately, the expression $I+B{\rightarrow}I^*$ is reversible. There is a continuous scope of identification of $B$, separation of $I$ and $B$ by acquiring proper knowledge.

## 2.2 Negligence and Bid'ah

As explained earlier, Bid'ah is always additive in nature i.e $I+B{\rightarrow}I^*$. If there is any subtraction of obligatory act in the set $I$, it cannot be called a Bid'ah, it is a negligence of a believer. Thus, negligence is '$I$ *minus*' whereas Bid'ah is '$I$ *plus*'. Negligence is a state of distraction where one is not mindful of Allah SWT. He is not afraid of punishments and has taken Allah's Orders lightly. Prevalent examples of negligence among Muslims are: missing Fajr prayer daily, offering only Friday and Eid prayers, offering prayers only during Ramadan, and so on. Negligence on part of a believer is a major sin and severe punishment is associated with it.

**Hadith**: Samurah ibn Jundub (ra) reported: The Prophet (ﷺ) saw in a dream, **"As for the one whose head was crushed by a stone, he had taken the Quran but refused to act upon it, and he slept through the prescribed prayers."** [Bukhari]

**Hadith**: Abu Zuhayr 'Umara ibn Ruwayba (ra) said: I heard the Messenger of Allah (ﷺ) say, "No one who used to pray before the rising of the sun and before its setting will enter the Fire, meaning Fajr and 'Asr. [Muslim]

Allah SWT says (interpretation of meaning): *But there came after them successors who neglected prayer and pursued desires; so they are going to meet evil.* (Surah Maryam Ch 19: 59)

Most interpreters of the Quran believe that this verse is about those who delay the prayer from its prescribed fixed time. Allah warned them of being thrown in a valley in Hell.

Merely not performing optional deeds is not automatically negligence. Following hadith may be referred in this regard.

**Hadith**: It was narrated from Abu Suhail, from his father, that he heard Talhah bin 'Ubaidullah (ra) say: A man from the people of Najd came to the Messenger of Allah (ﷺ) with unkempt hair. We could hear him talking loudly but we could not understand what he was saying until he came closer. He was asking about Islam. The Messenger of Allah (ﷺ) said to him: 'Five prayers each day and night.' He said: 'Do I have to do anything else' He (ﷺ) said: 'No, unless you do it voluntarily.' He (ﷺ) said: 'And fasting the month of Ramadan.' He said: 'Do I have to do anything else?' He (ﷺ) said: 'No, unless you do it voluntarily.' And the Messenger of Allah (ﷺ) mentioned Zakat to him, and he said: 'Do I have to do anything else?' He (ﷺ) said: 'No, unless you do it voluntarily.' The man left saying: 'By Allah, I will not do any **more** than this or any **less**.' The Messenger of Allah (ﷺ) said: 'He will achieve salvation, if he is speaking the truth.' [Sunan an-Nasa'i]

This does not mean that we should neglect our optional righteous deeds. These voluntary acts are means of attaining Allah's love and mercy. When a servant earns Allah's love, Allah guides their actions and choices, leading them toward what pleases Him and what He loves.

**Hadith**: On the authority of Abu Hurayrah (ra) who said: The Messenger of Allah (ﷺ) said, "Verily Allah Ta'ala has said: 'Whosoever shows enmity to a wali (friend) of Mine, then I have declared war against him. And My servant does not draw near to Me with anything more loved to Me than the religious duties I have obligated upon him. *And My servant continues to draw near to me with nawafil (supererogatory) deeds until I Love him.* When I Love him, I am his hearing with which he hears, and his sight with which he sees, and his hand with which he strikes, and his foot with which he walks. Were he to ask [something] of Me, I would surely give it to him; and were he to seek refuge with Me, I would surely grant him refuge.'" [Bukhari]

**Hadith**: Hurais bin Qabisah narrated: "I arrived in Al-Madinah and said: 'O Allah! Facilitate me to be in a righteous gathering.'" He said: "I sat with Abu Hurairah (ra) and said: 'Indeed I asked Allah to provide me with a righteous gathering. So narrate a hadith to me which you heard from Allah's Messenger (ﷺ) so that perhaps Allah would cause me to benefit from it.' He (Abu Huraira) said: 'I heard Allah's Messenger (ﷺ) say: "Indeed the first deed by which a servant will be called to account on the Day of Resurrection is his Salat. If it is complete, he is successful and saved, but if it is defective, he has failed and lost. So if something is deficient in his obligatory (prayers) then the Lord, Mighty and Sublime says: 'Look! *Are there any voluntary (prayers) for my worshipper?*' So with them, what was deficient in his obligatory (prayers) will be completed. Then the rest of his deeds will be treated like that." [Tirmizi]

**Hadith**: Narrated Abu Huraira (ra): At the time of the Fajr prayer, the Prophet (ﷺ) asked Bilal (ra), "Tell me of the best deed you did after embracing Islam, for I heard your footsteps in front of me in Paradise." Bilal (ra) replied, "I did not do anything worth mentioning except that whenever I performed ablution during the day or night, I *prayed after that ablution* as much as was written for me." [Bukhari and Muslim]

Negligence on part of a believer is caused by the whisper of Satan. Abu Sa'id al-Khudri (ra) reported: The Messenger of Allah (ﷺ) said, "**Satan** said: By Your might, O Lord, I will continue to mislead the children of Adam, as long as their souls are in their bodies. The Lord said: By My might and majesty, I will continue to forgive them, as long as they seek My forgiveness." [Musnad Ahmad]

Sa'id ibn Jubair reported: Abdullah Ibn Abbas (ra) said, "Satan is perched over the heart of the son of Adam. If he is unmindful and he forgets, Satan whispers. If he remembers Allah, Satan withdraws." [Musannaf Ibn Abi Shaybah]

The cure for negligence is the rememberance of Allah SWT (zikr). Zikr restrains and hurts Satan. Narrated Al-Haris Al-Ash'ari (ra): The Messenger of Allah (ﷺ) said: "Indeed Allah commanded Yahya bin

Zakariyya with five commandments to abide by, and to command the Children of Isra'il to abide by them……….. Then he (Yahya alayhis-salam) said: "I can ransom myself from you with a little or a lot" so he ransoms himself from them. And He commands you to remember Allah. For indeed the parable of that, is a man whose enemy quickly tracks him until he reaches an impermeable fortress in which he protects himself from them. This is how the worshiper is; he does not protect himself from Ash-Shaytan except by the remembrance of Allah.' [Tirmizi]

Negligence discussed above is not the same as disbelief or kufr and a negligent is still within Islam. A disbeliever completely rejects Tawheed and it is a **complete negligence**. In case of complete negligence, and **set *I*** will be a null set. Following verse and verses of similar meanings in the Qur'an are applicable to complete negligence. Allah SWT says (interpretation of the meaning):

*Await they just for the final fullfilment of the event? On the Day the event is finally fulfilled (i.e. the Day of Resurrection), those who **neglected** it before will say: "Verily, the Messengers of our Lord did come with the truth, now are there any intercessors for us that they might intercede on our behalf? Or could we be sent back (to the first life of the world) so that we might do (good) deeds other than those (evil) deeds which we used to do?" Verily, they have lost their ownselves (i.e. destroyed themselves) and that which they used to fabricate (invoking and worshipping others besides Allah) has gone away from them. (Al-A'raaf, Ch 7: 53)*

## 2.3 Why should not there be any innovation?

Allah SWT says (interpretation of meaning):

*Then We sent Our messengers in succession: whenever a messenger came to his people, they denied him. So, We destroyed them, one after the other, reducing them to cautionary tales. So away with the people who refuse to believe! (Al-Mu'minun Ch 23:44)*

Allah SWT sent large number of prophets on the earth from time to time. The prophets whose names have been mentioned in the Qur'an are: Adam, Idris, Nuh, Hud, Salih, Ibrahim, Lut, Isma'il, Ishaq, Ya'qub, Yusuf, Ayyub, Shu'ayb, Musa, Harun, Yunus, Dawud, Sulaiman, Ilyas, al-Yasa', Zakariyya, Yahya, 'Issa and Muhammad (blessings and peace of Allah be upon them).

The religion during a particular Prophet was complete during the respective era of that Prophet. Other Prophets knew that another Prophet would again come after his death and there was no question of last Prophethood. But absolute perfection reached during the Holy Prophet Muhammad (ﷺ) and will continue till the Last Day. Since no Prophet will come after him, last prophethood is a concern in Islam. Allah SWT says in the Book:

*Muḥammad is not the father of any of your men, but is the Messenger of Allah and the seal of the prophets. And Allah has perfect Knowledge of all things. (Al-Ahzab Ch 33:40; interpretation of the meaning)*

Islam is complete and that the Prophet (ﷺ) disclosed everything to Ummah. On the occasion of the Last Hajj of the Prophet (ﷺ), he (ﷺ)

asked his companions: 'You people will be asked about me, so what is it that you will say?' So, the companions responded by saying, 'We bear witness that indeed you conveyed the message.' [Part of a Hadith from Sunan Abu Dawud and Sunan Ibn Majah]. Allah SWT mentions in the Qur'an:

*'This day I have perfected your religion for you, completed My favours upon you, and have chosen for you, Islam as your religion.' (Al- Ma'idah, Ch 5:3; interpretation of the meaning).*

Ibn Kasir writes about this verse as: "This, indeed, is the biggest favour from Allah to this Ummah, for He has completed their religion for them, and they, thus, do not need any other religion or any other Prophet except Muhammad (ﷺ). This is why Allah made Muhammad (ﷺ) the final Prophet and sent him to all humans and Jinns. Therefore, the permissible is what he allows, the impermissible is what he prohibits, the Law is what he legislates and everything that he conveys is true and authentic and does not contain lies or contradictions." Umar (ra) said about this verse: I know definitely on what day this Verse was revealed; it was revealed on the day of Arafat (during Last Hajj), on Friday. [Bukhari]"

Imams of the misguidance say that the Prophet (ﷺ) conveyed some confidential knowledge to some of his companions [Ali (ra) in particular] and this knowledge is transferred from person to person (chest to chest) till today (we seek refuge in Allah!). These knowledges are not available in recorded form. One can acquire this confidential knowledge only by taking an intermediary. Narrated Aisha (ra): Whoever tells you that the Prophet (ﷺ) concealed something of the Divine Inspiration, do not believe him, for Allah said (that means): *'O Apostle Muhammad! Proclaim (the*

*Message) which has been sent down to you from your Lord, and if you do it not, then you have not conveyed His Message.'* (Al-Ma'idah, Ch 5:67) [Bukhari].

The Prophet (ﷺ) undoubtedly performed his duties and the performance certificate has been recognized in the Qur'an. Allah SWT says (interpretation of meaning):

وَٱلنَّجْمِ إِذَا هَوَىٰ

مَا ضَلَّ صَاحِبُكُمْ وَمَا غَوَىٰ

وَمَا يَنطِقُ عَنِ ٱلْهَوَىٰ

إِنْ هُوَ إِلَّا وَحْيٌ يُوحَىٰ

عَلَّمَهُ شَدِيدُ ٱلْقُوَىٰ

By the star when it sets: Your companion [i.e., Muḥammad] has not strayed, nor has he erred, nor does he speak from [his own] inclination. This is nothing but a revelation that is conveyed to him, taught to him by one intense in strength [i.e., Jibriel] (Surah An-Najm Ch 53:1-5)

Allah SWT says in another place:

*Had he (the prophet) forged some statements in Our name, We would have certainly seized him by the right hand, and then severed his life-artery, and none of you could have saved him from it. (Al-Haqqah Ch 69:44-47; interpretation of meaning)*

"The foregoing verses were revealed to rebut the outrageous thoughts of the disbelievers. They used to accuse the Prophet (ﷺ) of being a poet and a soothsayer. The invincible argument is put forward in a strong language - assuming the impossible. This verse refers to a theoretical situation." (Ibn Kasir)

Ali ibn Abi Talib (ra) faced the same question of secret knowledge repeatedly. It was narrated that Amir bin Wasilah said: A man asked Ali (ra): "Did the Messenger of Allah (ﷺ) used to tell you anything in secret that he (ﷺ) did not tell the people?" Ali (ra) got so angry that his face turned red, and he said: "He (ﷺ) used not to tell me anything in secret that he (ﷺ) did not tell the people except that he (ﷺ) told me four things when he (ﷺ) and I were alone in the house. He (ﷺ) said:

- Allah curses the one who curses his father,

- Allah curses the one who offers a sacrifice to anyone other than Allah,

- Allah curses the one who gives refuge to an offender and

- Allah curses the one who changes boundary markers (of the land).

[Sunan an-Nasai]

**Hadith**: Abu Tufail Amir b. Wisila reported: I was in the company of Ali bin Abi Talib (ra), when a person came to him, and said: What was it that Allah's Apostle (ﷺ) told you in secret? Thereupon he (Ali) was enraged and said: Allah's Apostle (ﷺ) did not tell me anything in secret that he hid from people, except that he told me four things. He said: Commander of Faithful, what are these? He (ﷺ) said:

- Allah cursed him who cursed his father;

- Allah cursed him who sacrificed for anyone besides Allah;

- Allah cursed him who accommodates an innovator (in religion); and

- Allah cursed him who changed the minarets (the boundary lines) of the land. [Muslim]

**Hadith**: Narrated Ash-Shu`bi: Abu Juhaifa said, "I asked `Ali (ra): 'Have you got any book (which has been revealed to the Prophet (ﷺ) apart from the Qur'an)?' `Ali (ra) replied, 'No, except Allah's Book or the power of understanding which has been bestowed (by Allah) upon a Muslim or what is (written) in this sheet of paper (with me). Abu Juhaifa said: I asked, "What is (written) in this sheet of paper?" Ali (ra) replied, "It deals with the Diyya (compensation, blood money paid by the killer to the relatives of the victim), the ransom for the releasing of the captives from the hands of the enemies, and the law that no Muslim should be killed in Qisas (equality in punishment) for the killing of (a disbeliever)." [Bukhari]

**Hadith**: It was narrated that Abdullah bin Abbas (ra) said: "The Messenger of Allah (ﷺ) drew back the curtain, and his head was bandaged during the sickness of which he (ﷺ) died. He (ﷺ) said: 'O Allah, have I conveyed (the message)?' (And he ﷺ repeated this) Three times, "There is nothing left of the glad tidings of Prophethood except a good dream that a Muslim sees or that is seen for him." [A part of the Hadith from Muslim]

From the preceeding discussion, it may be inferred that anything religious innovated or invented or appended means:

- The Prophet (ﷺ) missed something to preach during his holy life time (Na'uzubillahi-min-zalik); or

- The innovator understands better than the Prophet (ﷺ) or his companions (Na'uzubillahi-min-zalik).

In that case, the innovator is:

- contempting Almighty's verse in the Qur'an الْيَوْمَ أَكْمَلْتُ لَكُمْ دِينَكُمْ وَأَتْمَمْتُ عَلَيْكُمْ نِعْمَتِي

- telling a lie on the Prophet (ﷺ); and

- insulting the Sunnah of the Prophet (ﷺ).

- The innovator has, in fact put a question mark (?) on the prophecy of the Prophet (ﷺ).

And the end result is very severe. The Prophet (ﷺ) said: "Whoever knowingly lies upon me, then let him occupy his seat in the Fire (of Hell)" [Bukhari, Muslim]. People may twist or fabricate Hadiths or references from the Quran to justify their actions that can take one out of Islam. The Prophet (ﷺ) said in the Khutbah, on day of Arafat in the Farewell Hajj, where he (ﷺ) said: "You people will be asked about me, so what is it that you will say?" So, the Companions responded by saying, "We bear witness that indeed you conveyed the message." [Part of a Hadith collected from Abu Dawud].

**Hadith**: Ibn Abbas (ra) said: "Indeed the most detestable of things to Allah are the innovations." [al-Bayhaqi in as-Sunan al-Kubra]

**Hadith**: The Prophet (ﷺ) said, "………..Don't go astray after me by striking the necks of one another. Lo! It is incumbent upon those who are present to inform it to those who are absent for perhaps the informed one might comprehend it (understand it) better than some of the present audience." Whenever the sub-narrator Muhammad mentioned that statement, he would say, "The Prophet (ﷺ) said the truth." And then the Prophet (ﷺ) added, "No doubt! Haven't I conveyed Allah's Message to you! No doubt! Haven't I conveyed Allah's Message to you?" [a part of the Hadith from al-Bukhari]

When two of the Prophet's ﷺ closest companions, Abu Bakr and 'Umar (ra), raised their voices in disagreement in his blessed presence, Allah SWT did not permit even that. It is important to note that they were neither raising their voices at the Prophet ﷺ nor arguing with him directly—yet Allah revealed a verse in the Qur'an to correct this subtle breach of etiquette. If such a gentle misstep by the best of this Ummah warranted divine correction, then what about one who introduces an innovation that contradicts the command of Allah and the Sunnah of His Messenger ﷺ? Such a person (innovator), whether knowingly or unknowingly, displays disapproval of the Prophet ﷺ and the guidance he ﷺ brought. One can only imagine the gravity of the consequences for such an individual in the sight of Allah. Allah SWT says:

*O you who believe, do not raise your voices above the voice of the Prophet, and be not loud when speaking to him, as you are loud when speaking to one another, lest your good deeds should become void while you are not aware. (Al-Hujurat Ch 49:2; interpretation of meaning)*

**Hadith**: Narrated Ibn Abi Mulaika: Once the two righteous men, i.e., Abu Bakr (ra) and `Umar (ra) were on the verge of destruction (and that was because): When the delegate of Bani Tamim came to the Prophet (ﷺ), one of them (either Abu Bakr or `Umar) recommended Al-Aqra' bin H`abis at-Tamimi Al-Hanzali, the brother of Bani Majashi (to be appointed as their chief), while the other recommended somebody else. Abu Bakr (ra) said to `Umar (ra), "You intended only to oppose me." Umar (ra) said, "I did not intend to oppose you!" Then their voices grew louder in front of the Prophet (ﷺ) whereupon there was revealed: *'O you who believe! Do not raise your voices above the voice of the Prophet.....a great reward.'* (Ch *49:2-3*) Ibn Az-Zubair said, "Thence forward when `Umar (ra) talked to the Prophet (ﷺ), he would talk like one who whispered a secret and would even fail to make the Prophet (ﷺ) hear him, in which case the Prophet (ﷺ) would ask him (to repeat his words)." [Bukhari]

## 2.4 Why is the last prophethood important?

Belief in the last prophethood is a part of Faith. Finality of prophethood is important because otherwise one is advancing the concept that Islam is incomplete and one is attempting to open the door for possible changes, corruption, fabrication, innovation or rejection of the messages of the Prophet (ﷺ). Allah SWT says (interpretation of meaning): *"Today, I have perfected your religion for you, and have completed My blessing upon you, and chosen Islam as Deen (religion and a way of life) for you."* (Al-Ma'idah Ch 5:3)

Abu Huraira (ra) reported Allah's Messenger (ﷺ) as saying: The similitude of mine and that of the Apostles (before me) is that of a person who constructed a building and he built it fine and well and the people went around it saying: Never have we seen a building more imposing than this, but for **one brick**, and I am that brick (with which you give the finishing touch to the building). [Muslim] The Prophet of Allah (ﷺ) mentioned about 'one brick' which is the declaration of finality of prophethood by the Messenger of Allah (ﷺ) himself.

Narrated Sad (ra): Allah's Messenger (ﷺ) set out for Tabuk appointing Ali (ra) as his deputy (in Madinah). Ali (ra) said, "Do you want to leave me with the children and women?" The Prophet (ﷺ) said, "Will you not be pleased that you will be to me like Harun to Musa? But there will be **no prophet after me**." [Bukhari]

The finality of prophethood highlights the completeness and universal acceptance of his message for all mankind. Ibn Kasir writes in his commentary, "Hence this verse (i.e Ch 5:3) is a clear proof of the fact that no prophet will come after Muhammad (ﷺ) and when it is said that no prophet will come after him it is a foregone conclusion that no messenger will succeed him either, for the office of a messenger holds prominence over the office of a prophet. Every messenger is a prophet, but all prophets are not messengers. Anyone who lays a claim to prophethood after Muhammad (ﷺ), is a liar, a disrupter, an imposter, depraved and a seducer despite his wonderous jugglery and magical feats. Anyone who would make this claim in future till the end of the world belongs to this class."

The Holy Quran states that Prophet Muhammad (ﷺ) was sent as a guide for all of humanity. Since the Quran and the Sunnah of the Prophet (ﷺ) have been preserved in their original, complete forms, and the Divine mission has been fulfilled by him, the need for additional Divine revelations has been fully met. Now, only scholars/Imams/Mujaddids are needed to address human flaws and guide people, but there is no longer a need for new prophets.

## 2.5 Treatment with innovators

The Messenger (ﷺ) warned against the people of innovation from befriending and supporting. The Messenger (ﷺ) said: "Whoever innovates or accommodates an innovator then upon him is the curse of Allah, His Angels and the whole of mankind." [Bukhari, Muslim]

**Hadith**: Al-Hasan al-Basree said: "Do not sit with the people of innovation and desires, nor argue with them, nor listen to them." [Sunan ad-Darimee]

**Hadith**: Narrated Ali (ra): "We have no Book to recite except the Book of Allah (Qur'an) and this paper. Then Ali (ra) took out the paper, and behold! There was written in it, legal verdicts about the retaliation for wounds, the ages of the camels (to be paid as Zakat or as blood money). In it was also written: 'Madinah is a sanctuary from Air (mountain) to Saur (mountain). So, whoever innovates in it a heresy (something new in religion) or commits a crime in it or gives shelter to such an innovator, will incur the curse of Allah, the angels and all the people, and none of his compulsory or optional good deeds will be accepted on the Day of Resurrection…." [Part of Hadith from Bukhari]

Islamic scholars are of the opinion that question of whether to boycott individuals involved in bid'ah must be approached with wisdom, sincerity, and a consideration of the broader objectives of Islam. While it is part of faith to love for the sake of Allah and hate for the sake of Allah, this principle must be applied with a keen awareness of context and consequences. If boycotting an innovator is likely to bring about reform, protect the community, and deter others from misguidance, then it may be the correct course of action. However, if advice, and da'wah are more likely to lead to repentance and guidance, then maintaining communication and outreach is more beneficial.

## 2.6 Examples often quoted by innovators for misguidance

Innovations in religion are strictly forbidden. However, advancements and inventions in science and technology—such as cars, air conditioners, airplanes, or the internet—are not considered *bid'ah* because they are unrelated to matters of worship or belief. These developments are intended for the comfort and progress of human civilization. Similarly, using microphones in masajid, performing Hajj by airplane instead of camel, or benefiting from air conditioning, electric fans, and lighting are not *bid'ah*. These are technological tools that support religious practices and do not contradict Islamic teachings. Before air conditioning was installed in the masajid (for example), the Maghrib prayer was three rak'ahs. After the installation, it is still three rak'ahs. This shows that air conditioning has no effect on the core practices of worship. Therefore, it is not a bid'ah.

Among the common arguments presented by the imams of misguidance and innovators is the claim: *"Where is it written that this (innovative practice) is prohibited?"* This rhetorical question aims to create confusion, suggesting that unless something is explicitly and directly *forbidden*, it can be considered acceptable in Islam. However, this argument is fundamentally flawed and dangerous, as it misrepresents the principles of *Shari'ah* and the methodology of the Prophet Muhammad ﷺ. The Correct Principle is: Islam is a complete and perfect religion. Everything that is part of the religion must be proven by authentic evidence; otherwise it is rejected. Therefore, it is not required to prove that a practice is *prohibited* in order to consider it a *bid'ah*. Instead, the burden of proof lies on the one who introduces any act of worship—he must show that it was practiced or permitted by the Prophet ﷺ or his Companions (ra). If people were allowed to insert acts into the religion just because "there is no verse or hadith that prohibits it," the structure and purity of Islam would collapse under endless additions. Religion would then become a playground for personal preference, firqa, culture, or emotion. For instance:

- **Where is it written that Azan before Salatul Janazah is prohibited?** There is no specific hadith that says, *"Do not call Azan before Janazah."* But there is also no evidence that the Sahabah ever gave Azan before Janazah. Therefore, adding it becomes a condemnable innovation (bid'ah).

- **Where is it written that the Khutbah of Eid cannot be before the Eid prayer?** Again, there is no hadith that directly says, *"Do not deliver the Eid Khutbah before the prayer."* But what is established beyond doubt is the practice of the Prophet ﷺ—he ﷺ always prayed the Eid Salah first, followed by the Khutbah. Reversing this order is a clear departure from the Sunnah and is an innovation.

Thus, absence of prohibition does not imply permissibility. What matters is presence of precedent from the Qur'an and the Sunnah. Just as no one is allowed to offer four rak'ah Maghrib Salat on the excuse that "it's not prohibited," similarly, no innovative religious act—no matter how logical, emotional, or well-intended—can be justified without clear evidence from the Qur'an, Sunnah, and the understanding of the Sahabah. The religion of Islam is based on divine guidance, not human innovation.

Adhering to what the Prophet ﷺ did is the essence of obedience, and introducing new ways of worship—even without explicit prohibition—is the door to misguidance. A hadith may be reproduced in this regard (of worldly affair) from the Prophet (ﷺ) that teaches us that in worldly matters, we are permitted to use our own skills and judgment.

**Hadith**: Musa b. Talha (ra) reported: I and Allah's Messenger (ﷺ) happened to pass by people near the date-palm trees. He (the Holy Prophet ﷺ) said: What are these people doing? They said: They are grafting, i. e. they combine the male with the female (tree) and thus they yield more fruit. Thereupon Allah's Messenger (ﷺ) said: I do not find it to be of any use. The people were informed about it and they abandoned this practice. Allah's Messenger (ﷺ) (was later) on informed (that the yield had dwindled), whereupon he ﷺ said: If there is any use of it, then they should do it, for it was just a personal opinion of mine, and do not go after my personal opinion; but when I say to you anything on behalf of Allah, then do accept it, for I do not attribute lie to Allah, the Exalted and Glorious. [Muslim]

## 2.7 Warning against Bid'at in the Qur'an

- *"... Whatever the Messenger gives you, take it. And whatever he forbids you from, leave it. And fear Allah. Surely Allah is severe in punishment." (Al-Hashr Ch 59:7)*

- *"... Do not treat the Messenger's summons to you ˈas lightlyˈ as your summons to one another. Allah certainly knows those of you who slip away, hiding behind others. So let those who disobey his orders beware, for an affliction may befall them, or a painful torment may overtake them." (An-Noor Ch 24:63).*

- *O believers! Obey Allah and obey the Messenger and those in authority among you. Should you disagree on anything, then refer it to Allah and His Messenger, if you ˈtrulyˈ believe in Allah and the Last Day. This is the best and fairest resolution." (An-Nisa Ch 4:59).*

- *"That is because Allah has revealed the Book in truth. And surely those who differ regarding it are totally engrossed in opposition." (Al- Baqarah Ch 2:176); (interpretation of meanings)*

## 2.8 Warning against Bid'at by the Prophet (ﷺ)

Narrated Abu Huraira (ra): The Prophet (ﷺ) said, "Name yourselves with my name (use my name) but do not name yourselves with my Kunya name (i.e. Abul Qasim). And whoever sees me in a dream then surely, he has seen me for Satan cannot impersonate me. And whoever tells a lie against me (intentionally), then (surely) let him occupy his seat in Hell-fire." [Bukhari]

Narrated ˈAbdullah bin ˈAmr (ra): The Prophet (ﷺ) said, "Convey (my teachings) to the people even if it were a single sentence, and tell others the stories of Bani Israel (which have been taught to you), for it is not sinful to do so. And whoever tells a lie on me intentionally, will surely take his place in the (Hell) Fire." [Bukhari]

Abu Hurairah (ra) narrated that the Messenger of Allah (ﷺ) said: "At the end of time there will be imposters and liars who will bring hadiths that neither you nor your forefathers ever heard. Beware of them and stay away from them, and do not let them mislead you or confuse you." [Muslim]

Aishah (ra) narrated that the Messenger of Allah (ﷺ) said: "Whoever innovates something in this matter of ours (i.e. Islam) that is not part of it, will have it rejected." [Sunan Ibn Majah]

Narrated Abu Huraira (ra): The Prophet (ﷺ) said, "The Hour (Doomsday) will not be established till my followers copy the deeds of the previous nations and follow them very closely, span by span, and cubit by cubit (i.e., inch by inch)." It was said, "O Allah's Messenger (ﷺ)! Do you mean by those (nations) the Persians and the Byzantines?" The Prophet (ﷺ) said, "Who can it be other than they?" [Bukhari]

Narrated Abu Sa`id (ra): The Prophet (ﷺ) said, "You will follow the wrong ways, of your predecessors so completely and literally that if they should go into the hole of a mastigure, you too will go there." We said, "O Allah's Messenger (ﷺ)! Do you mean the Jews and the Christians?" He replied, "Whom else?" (Meaning, of course, the Jews and the Christians.) [Bukhari]

## 2.9 Who is responsible for introducing Bid'at?

Scholars and religious leaders are responsible to guide the community. This responsibility is particularly grave if they knowingly promote practices that go against the Qur'an and Sunnah. The followers are also equally responsible of Bid'ah if they blindly follow innovations as well as for not seeking knowledge and understanding the truth of their faith. Allah SWT created human being and provided them with the tools for acquiring knowledge, namely hearing, sight and wisdom. Allah SWT says (interpretation of the meaning):

- *And Allah has brought you out from the wombs of your mothers while you know nothing. And He gave you hearing, sight, and hearts that you might give thanks (to Allah). (al-Nahl Ch 16:78)*

- *And do not follow a thing about which you have no knowledge. Surely, the ear, the eye and the heart - each one of them shall be interrogated about. (Al- Isra Ch 17:36)*

**Hadith:** Abu Zarr (ra) reported: I said, "O Messenger of Allah (ﷺ), what do you fear for your nation more than the False Messiah (Dajjal)?" The Prophet (ﷺ) said, "**The Imams of misguidance.**" [Musnad Ahmad]

**Hadith:** Shaddad ibn Aws (ra) reported: The Prophet (ﷺ) said, "Verily, I do not fear for my nation anything but the Imams of misguidance. For when the sword is raised among my nation, it will not be removed from them until the Day of Resurrection." [Sahih Ibn Hibban]

**Hadith:** Narrated `Abdullah bin `Amr (ra): I heard the Prophet (ﷺ) saying, "Allah will not deprive you of knowledge after he has given it to you, but it will be taken away through the death of the religious learned men with their knowledge. Then there will remain ignorant people who, when consulted, will give verdicts according to their opinions whereby they will mislead others and go astray." [Bukhari]

**Hadith:** It was narrated that Jabir bin 'Abdullah (ra) said: "When the Messenger of Allah (ﷺ) delivered a sermon, his eyes would turn red, he would raise his voice and he would speak with intensity, as if he were warning of an (enemy) army, saying, 'They will surely attack you in the morning, or they will surely attack you in the evening!' He would say: 'I and the Hour have been sent like these two,' and he would hold his index and middle finger. Then he would say: 'The best of guidance is the guidance of Muhammad (ﷺ). The most evil matters are those that are newly-invented, and every innovation (Bid'ah) is a going astray.' And he (ﷺ) used to say: 'Whoever dies and leaves behind some wealth, it is for his family, and whoever leaves behind a debt or dependent children, then they are both my responsibility.' [Sunan Ibn Majah]

**Hadith:** Abu Burda reported on the authority of his father: We offered the sunset prayer along with Allah's Apostle (ﷺ). We then said: If we sit (along with Allah's Messenger ﷺ) and observe night prayer with him it would be very good, so we sat down and he (ﷺ) came to us and said: "You are still sitting here." I said: "Allah's Messenger (ﷺ), we observed evening prayer with you, then we said: Let us sit down and observe night prayer along with you", whereupon he (ﷺ) said: "You have done well or you have done right." He (ﷺ) then lifted his head towards the sky and it often happened that as he lifted his head towards the sky, he said: "The stars are a source of security for the sky and when the stars disappear there comes to the sky, i. e. (it meets the same fate) as it has been promised (it would plunge into darkness). And I am a source of safety and security to my Companions and when I would go away there would fall to the lot (of my Companions) as they have been promised with and my Companions are a source of security for the Ummah and as they would go there would fall to the lot of my Ummah as (its people) have been promised (i.e. disasters which is destined)." [Muslim]

**Hadith:** Abu Darda' (ra) said: The Messenger of Allah (ﷺ) came out to us when we were speaking of poverty and how we feared it. He said: "Is it poverty that you fear? By the One in Whose Hand is my soul, (the delights and luxuries of) this world will come to you in plenty, and nothing will cause the heart of anyone of you to deviate except that. By Allah, I am leaving you upon something like Bayda (white, bright, clear path) the night and day of which are the same." [Sunan Ibn Majah]

**Hadith:** Miqdam bin Ma'dikarib Al-Kindi (ra) narrated that: The Messenger of Allah (ﷺ) said: "Soon there will come a time that a man will be reclining on his pillow, and when one of my hadiths is narrated he will say: 'The Book of Allah is (sufficient) between us and you. Whatever it states is permissible, we will take as permissible, and whatever it states is forbidden, we will take as forbidden.' Verily, whatever the Messenger of Allah (ﷺ) has forbidden is like that which Allah has forbidden." [Sunan Ibn Majah]

## 2.10 Whom to follow in case of Bid'ah

Allah SWT guided us to act in cases of Bid'at. Allah says in the Qur'an (interpretation of meaning):

- *'Say: 'Obey Allah and obey the Messenger'* (An-Nur, Ch ٢٤:٥٤)

- *'It is not for a believer, man or woman, when Allah and His Messenger have decreed a matter that they should have any option in their decision'* (Al-Ahzab, Ch 33:36)

In the beginning of the Qur'an in Surah al-Fatiha, Allah SWT instructed us to follow the *'Sirat al-Mustaqim: straight path'*. Allah SWT says (interpretation of meaning):

اهْدِنَا ٱلصِّرَٰطَ ٱلْمُسْتَقِيمَ

صِرَٰطَ ٱلَّذِينَ أَنْعَمْتَ عَلَيْهِمْ

(Guide us along the Straight Path, the path of those on whom You have bestowed Your grace)

**'Straight path'** is mentioned in the Qur'an several times. Allah SWT says (interpretation of meaning):

- *but to worship Me ʿaloneʾ? This is the Straight Path. (Surah Yasin, Ch 36: 61)*

- *Indeed, that is My Path—perfectly straight. So follow it and do not follow other ways, for they will lead you away from His Way. This is what He has commanded you, so perhaps you will be conscious ʿof Allahʾ (Surah Al-An'am Ch 6:153)*

The term "Straight Path" is mentioned in the Qur'an approximately 33 times. Yet, what's striking is that the Qur'an does not describe its precise location, landmarks, or geographical direction. We are not given a visual map, nor a checklist of physical signs to follow. Instead, the Qur'an defines this path in just one profound way:

*The path of those upon whom You have bestowed Your favour. (Al-Fatihah Ch 1:7; interpretation of meaning)*

Rather than directing us to abstract ideas or philosophical ideals to individually explore, Allah SWT pointed us to *people*. The guidance comes not merely through concepts, but through lives lived—individuals who embody the truth of this path. In doing so, we are subtly taught that the Straight Path is found by looking towards those who have already been guided. But who are these people? Who are the recipients of Allah's favour?

Imam Ibn Kasir (رحمه الله) explains in his *Tafsir* that this verse is clarified by another portion of the Qur'an (interpretation of meaning):

*And whoever obeys Allah and the Messenger (ﷺ), then they will be in the company of those on whom Allah has bestowed His grace, the **Prophets, the Siddiqin (the truly faithful), the martyrs, and the righteous**. And how excellent these companions are! Such is the bounty from Allah, and Allah is sufficient to know. (Al-Nisa Ch 4:69-70).*

These are the ones Allah honored with His grace. They form the living example of the Straight Path. To follow it, therefore, is to emulate their faith, their conduct, and their unwavering commitment to the truth. They are the human compass that points us toward divine guidance. Each of these groups reflects a unique dimension of the Straight Path. Allah SWT says in another place (interpretation of meaning):

*And those who believed in Allah and His messengers, - those are the **Siddiqun (the most righteous after prophets) and the Shuhada'** (martyrs) in the sight of your Lord. For them shall be their reward and their light. As for those who disbelieved and rejected Our verses, they are the inmates of Hell. (Al-Hadid, Ch 57:19)*

The companions of the Prophet ﷺ embodied all these noble qualities— namely, the Ṣiddiqun, the Shuhada, and the Ṣaliḥun. Therefore, the path shown by the Prophet ﷺ and practiced by the Companions (ra) is the Straight Path, as affirmed in the following aḥadith among others. It is worth mentioning that the '*path shown by the Prophet* (ﷺ) *as instructed by Allah SWT and practiced by the Companions'* is none other than the Sunnah and thus Sunnah is the straight path.

**Hadith:** Allah's Messenger (ﷺ) said: "…my Ummah will be fragmented into seventy-three groups. All of them will be in Hell-Fire except one. They (the Companions) said: Allah's Messenger (ﷺ), which is that? Where upon he (ﷺ) said: It is one to which I and my companions belong." [Tirmizi]

**Hadith:** Narrated Abdullah ibn Mas'ud (ra): One day Prophet Muhammad (ﷺ) drew a line on the sand for them and said, "This is Allah's path." He (ﷺ) then drew several lines to the right and to the left and said, "These are the paths [of misguidance] on each of which is a devil inviting people to follow it." He (ﷺ) then recited the verse: *Verily, this is my path, leading straight, so follow it. And do not follow the [other] paths for they will scatter you about from Allah's path. That is His command to you in order that you may be conscious of Allah (Ch 6:153).* [Musnad Ahmad]

A key point to note here is that in Surah Al-Fatiha and Al-An'am (6:153), the term used is '**path**' in the singular, not 'paths'. Similarly, in the hadiths mentioned above (and in others not included here), the singular 'path' is emphasized. Ibn Kasir writes: "Allah's statement, فَاتَّبِعُوهُ وَلاَ تَتَّبِعُواْ السُّبُلَ (so follow it, and follow not (other) paths...) describes Allah's path in the singular sense, because truth is one. Allah describes the other paths in the plural, because they are many and are divided." Multiple paths would imply deviation from the practices of the Prophet (ﷺ) and his Companions (ra).

## 2.11 Sunnah of Righty guided Khalifas

On the authority of Abu Najeeh al- 'Irbaad ibn Saariyah (ra) who said: The Messenger of Allah (ﷺ) gave us a sermon by which our hearts were filled with fear and tears came to our eyes. So, we said, "O Messenger of Allah (ﷺ)! It is as though this is a farewell sermon, so counsel us." He (ﷺ) said, "I counsel you to have taqwa (fear) of Allah, and to listen and obey [your leader], even if a slave were to become your ameer (leader). Verily he among you who lives long will see great controversy, so you must keep to my Sunnah and to the Sunnah of the Khulafa ar-Rashideen (the rightly guided caliphs), those who guide to the right way. Cling to it stubbornly (literally: with your molar teeth). Beware of newly invented matters [in the religion], for verily every bidah (innovation) is misguidance." [Abu Dawud, Tirmizi]

Abu Hurairah (ra) narrated that the Prophet (ﷺ) said: "Whatever I have commanded you do it, and whatever I have forbidden you, refrain from it." [Sunan Ibn Majah]

Narrated Anas bin Malik (ra) that he heard 'Umar (ra) speaking while standing on the pulpit of the Prophet (ﷺ) in the morning (following the death of the Prophet ﷺ), when the people had sworn allegiance to Abu Bakr (ra). He said the Tashah-hud before Abu Bakr (ra), and said, "Amma Ba'du (then after) Allah has chosen for his Apostle (ﷺ) what is with Him (Paradise) rather than what is with you (the world). This is that Book (Qur'an) with which Allah guided your Apostle (ﷺ), so stick to it, for then you will be guided on the right path as Allah guided His Apostle (ﷺ) with it." [Bukhari]

Narrated Abu Wail: I sat with Shaiba in this Mosque (Al-Masjid-Al-Haram) and he said: `Umar (ra) once sat beside me here as you are now sitting, and said, 'I feel like distributing all the gold and silver that are in it (i.e., the Ka`ba) among the Muslims'. I said, 'You cannot do that.' `Umar (ra) said, 'Why?' I said, 'Your two (previous) companions [the Prophet (ﷺ) and Abu Bakr (ra)] did not do it'. `Umar (ra) said, 'They are the two persons whom one must follow.' [Bukhari]

Narrated Huzaifa (ra): Allah's Messenger (ﷺ) said to us, "Honesty descended from the Heavens and settled in the roots of the hearts of men (faithful believers), and then the Qur'an was revealed and the people read the Qur'an, (and learnt it from it) and also learnt it from the Sunnah." Both Qur'an and Sunnah strengthened their (the faithful believers') honesty. [Bukhari]

Narrated `Abdullah (ra): The best talk (speech) is Allah's Book 'Qur'an), and the best way is the way of Muhammad (ﷺ), and the worst matters are the heresies (those new things which are introduced into the religion); and whatever you have been promised will surely come to pass, and you cannot escape (it). [Bukhari]

Narrated Abu Musa (ra): The Prophet (ﷺ) said: "My example and the example of what I have been sent with is that of a man who came to some people and said, 'O people! I have seen the enemy's army with my own eyes, and I am the naked warner; so protect yourselves!' Then a group of his people obeyed him and fled at night proceeding stealthily till they were safe, while another group of them disbelieved him and stayed at their places till morning when the army came upon them, and killed and ruined them completely. So, this is the example of that person who obeys me and follows what I have brought (the Qur'an and the Sunnah), and the example of the one who disobeys me and disbelieves the truth I have brought." [Bukhari]

## 2.12 Who are Khulafa ar-Rashideen?

The Rashidun caliphs or *al-Khulafa al-Rashidun*, meaning 'rightly guided caliphs', often simply called the Rashidun, are the Caliphs (meaning successor) who led the Ummah following the death of the prophet (ﷺ). They are Abu Bakr (ra), Umar (ra), Usman (ra) and Ali ibn Abi Talib (ra). The reign of these caliphs, called the Rashidun Caliphate (632–661CE), is considered to have been 'rightly guided', meaning that it constitutes a model to be followed.

The first four caliphs were among the earliest and closest Companions of the Prophet Muhammad (ﷺ). They lived simple and righteous lives and sacrificed for the religion of Allah SWT. Their justice was impartial, their treatment towards others was kind and merciful, and they were one with the people – the first among equals. As a successor to the Prophet (ﷺ), the Caliph was the head of the Muslim community and his primary responsibility was to continue in the path of the Prophet (ﷺ).

Since religion was complete and the door of Divine revelation was closed after the demise of the Prophet (ﷺ), the Caliph was to make all laws in accordance with the Qur'an and the Sunnah. Caliph was responsible for maintaining conditions under which it would be easy for Muslims to live according to Islamic principles, and to see that justice was done to all. Following Hadiths are reproduced here to indicate the Khilafat of Islamic history after the death of the Prophet (ﷺ).

**Hadith**: Narrated by Safeenah (ra), that the Prophet (ﷺ) said: "The Prophetic Khalifa will last for 30 years. Then Allah will give the dominion to whomever He wills." [Abu Dawud, Al-Mustadrak Hakim]

In the Sunan of Abu Dawud, there occurs after this Hadith, said by Sa'eed bin Jamhaan, who narrated from Safeenah (ra): Safeenah said (to me): "Hold on (meaning listen), the Khilafah of Abu Bakr (ra) was 2 years, and Umar (ra) was 10 years, Usman (ra) 12 years, and Ali (ra) 6 years (Total 30 years)." [Abu Dawud].

Also reported by Safeenah (ra), the saying of the Prophet (ﷺ): "The Khilafah after me in my Ummah will last for 30 years. Then there will be kingship after that." [Musnad Ahmad, Tirmizi, Musnad Abi Ya'laa, Ibn Hibbaan, Saheeh al-Jaami' as-Sagheer]

**Hadith**: Narrated Huzayfah (ra) that the Prophet (ﷺ) said: "The Prophethood will remain amongst you for as long as Allah wills it to be. Then Allah will raise it when He wills to raise it. Then there will be the Khilafah upon the Prophetic methodology. And it will last for as long as Allah wills it to last. Then Allah will raise it when He wills to raise it. Then there will be biting kingship, and it will remain for as long as Allah wills it to remain. Then Allah will raise it when He wills to raise it. Then there will be tyrannical (forceful) kingship and it will remain for as long as Allah wills it to remain. Then He will raise it when He wills to raise it. Then there will be a Khilafah upon the Prophetic methodology. Then he (the Prophet ﷺ) was silent. [Musnad Ahmad and Abu Dawud]

## 2.13 Whoever obeys the Prophet (ﷺ) will enter Paradise

Allah SWT says:

وَمَن يُطِعِ ٱللَّهَ وَٱلرَّسُولَ فَأُو۟لَٰٓئِكَ مَعَ ٱلَّذِينَ أَنْعَمَ ٱللَّهُ عَلَيْهِم مِّنَ ٱلنَّبِيِّـۧنَ وَٱلصِّدِّيقِينَ وَٱلشُّهَدَآءِ وَٱلصَّٰلِحِينَ ۚ وَحَسُنَ أُو۟لَٰٓئِكَ رَفِيقًا

*And whoever obeys Allah and the Messenger will be in the company of those blessed by Allah: the prophets, the people of truth, the martyrs, and the righteous—what honourable company! (An-Nisa Ch 4:69; interpretation of meaning)*

**Hadith**: Narrated Abu Huraira (ra): Allah's Messenger (ﷺ) said, "All my followers will enter Paradise except those who refuse." They said, "O Allah's Messenger (ﷺ)! Who will refuse?" He (ﷺ) said, "Whoever obeys me will enter Paradise, and whoever disobeys me is the one who refuses (to enter it)." [Bukhari]

**Hadith:** Narrated Jabir bin ʿAbdullah (ra): Some angels came to the Prophet (ﷺ) while he was sleeping. Some of them said, "He is sleeping." Others said, "His eyes are sleeping but his heart is awake." Then they said, "There is an example for this companion of yours." One of them said, "Then set forth an example for him." Some of them said, "He is sleeping." The others said, "His eyes are sleeping but his heart is awake." Then they said, "His example is that of a man who has built a house and then offered therein a banquet and sent an inviter (messenger) to invite the people. So, whoever accepted the invitation of the inviter, entered the house and ate of the banquet, and whoever did not accept the invitation of the inviter, did not enter the house, nor did he eat of the banquet." Then the angels said, "Interpret this example to him so that he may understand it." Some of them said, "He is sleeping." The others said, "His eyes are sleeping but his heart is awake." And then they said, "The houses stand for Paradise and the call maker is Muhammad; and whoever obeys Muhammad, obeys Allah; and whoever disobeys Muhammad, disobeys Allah. Muhammad separated the people (i.e., through his message, the good is distinguished from the bad, and the believers from the disbelievers). [Bukhari]

## 2.14 Whom to follow if there is no righteous group of Muslims

Narrated Huzaifa bin Al-Yaman (ra): The people used to ask Allah's Messenger (ﷺ) about the good but I used to ask him about the evil lest I should be overtaken by them. So, I said, "O Allah's Messenger (ﷺ)! We were living in ignorance and in an (extremely) worst atmosphere, then Allah brought to us this good (i.e., Islam); will there be any evil after this good?" He (ﷺ) said, "Yes." I said, 'Will there be any good after that evil?" He (ﷺ) replied, "Yes, but it will be tainted (not pure.)" I asked, "What will be its taint?" He (ﷺ) replied, "(There will be) some people who will guide others not according to my tradition? You will approve of some of their deeds and disapprove of some others." I asked, "Will there be any evil after that good?" He (ﷺ) replied, "Yes, (there will be) some people calling at the gates of the (Hell) Fire, and whoever will respond to their call, will be thrown by them into the (Hell) Fire." I said, "O Allah s Apostle (ﷺ)! Will you describe them to us?" He (ﷺ) said, "They will be from our own people and will speak our language." I said, "What do you order me to do if such a state should take place in my life?" He (ﷺ) said, "Stick to the group of Muslims and their Imam (ruler)." I said, "If there is neither a group of Muslims nor an Imam (ruler)?" He (ﷺ) said, "Then turn away from all those sects even if you were to bite (eat) the roots of a tree till death overtakes you while you are in that state." [Bukhari]

## 2.15 Consequence of Bid'ats

**Every misguidance is in the Hellfire:** Jabir ibn Abdullah (ra) reported: The Messenger of Allah (ﷺ) would praise Allah in his Khutbah, as He deserves to be praised, and then he (ﷺ) would say:

مَنْ يَهْدِهِ اللَّهُ فَلاَ مُضِلَّ لَهُ وَمَنْ يُضْلِلْهُ فَلاَ هَادِيَ لَهُ إِنَّ أَصْدَقَ الْحَدِيثِ كِتَابُ اللَّهِ وَأَحْسَنَ الْهَدْيِ هَدْئُ مُحَمَّدٍ وَشَرَّ الأُمُورِ مُحْدَثَاتُهَا وَكُلَّ مُحْدَثَةٍ بِدْعَةٌ وَكُلَّ بِدْعَةٍ ضَلاَلَةٌ وَكُلَّ ضَلاَلَةٍ فِي النَّارِ

"Whomever Allah guides, no one can lead him astray. Whomever Allah sends astray, no one can guide him. The truest word is the Book of Allah, and the best guidance is the guidance of Muhammad (ﷺ). The evilest matters in religion are those that are newly invented, **for every newly invented matter is an innovation (Bid'at), every innovation is misguidance, and every misguidance is in the Hellfire.**" [Sunan an-Nasai]

**Innovators will be driven away from the Cistern:** It was narrated that Abu Hurairah (ra) said: The Messenger of Allah (ﷺ) said: 'My Ummah will come to me at the Cistern *(Hawd),* and I will be driving the people away from it as a man drives another man's camels away from his own camels." They said: "O Prophet of Allah (ﷺ), will you recognize us?" He (ﷺ) said: "Yes. You will have a feature that no one else will have. You will come to me with glimmering faces and limbs because of the traces of *wudu.* But a group of you will be prevented from reaching me. I will say: 'O Lord, these are from among my followers.' An angel will reply and say to me: 'Do you know what they innovated after you were gone?' [Muslim]

It was narrated from Abu Hurairah (ra) that the Messenger of Allah (ﷺ) came to the graveyard and said: "Peace be upon the abode of believing people, and if Allah Wills we will join you soon. Would that we could see our brothers." They said: "Are we not your brothers, O Messenger of Allah (ﷺ)?" He (ﷺ) said: "You are my Companions. Our brothers are those who have not come yet." They said: "How will you recognize those of your Ummah who have not come yet, O Messenger of Allah (ﷺ)?" He said: "Do you not see that if a man has a horse that has a white blaze and white feet among horses that are all black, will he not recognize his horse?" They said: "Of course, O Messenger of Allah (ﷺ)!" He (ﷺ) said: "You will come to me with glimmering faces and limbs (like the white markings of a horse) because of the traces of w*udu. I* will reach the Cistern *(Hawd)* before them. And Lo! Men will be driven away from my Cistern as stray camels are driven away. I will call out to them: 'Come here!' but it will be said: 'They changed after you were gone.' And I will say: 'Away with you, away with you!" [Muslim]

Note: It is said that these were the people who became murtad (apostate) during the Khilafat of Abu Bakr (ra).

**Sunnah is dead when Bid'at is alive:** Ibn Abbas (ra) said, "When bid'ah is created then the Sunnah dies and this continues until that bid'ah is living and the Sunnah is dead." And also, the Prophet (ﷺ) said: "Islam began as something strange, and it shall return as something strange as it began. So, give glad tidings to the strangers." It was asked, "Who are the strangers?" He (ﷺ) replied, "Those that purify and correct what the people have corrupted of my Sunnah" [at -Tabarani].

**The prohibition of plastering graves or erecting structures over them:** Jabir (ra) said: Allah's Messenger (ﷺ) forbade that the graves should be plastered or they be used as sitting places (for the people), or a building should be built over them. [Muslim]

**Not to pray facing towards graves:** It was narrated that 'Abdullah ibn Abi Awfa said: when Mu'az ibn Jabal (ra) came from Syria, he prostrated to the Prophet (ﷺ), who said, "What is this, O Mu'az?" He said: I went to Syria and saw them prostrating to their archbishops and patriarchs, and I wanted to do that for you. The Messenger of Allah (ﷺ) said, "Do not do that. If I were to command anyone to prostrate to anyone other than Allah, I would have commanded women to prostrate to their husbands. By the One in Whose hand is the soul of Muhammad (ﷺ), no woman can fulfil her duty towards Allah until she fulfils her duty towards her husband." [Sunan Ibn Majah]

Abu Marsad al-Ghanawi (ra) reported Allah's Messenger (ﷺ) as saying: Do not sit on the graves and do not pray facing towards them. [Muslim]

## 2.16 The grant is from Allah SWT only

Allah SWT says (interpretation of meaning):

When My servants ask you 'O Prophet' about Me: I am truly near. I respond to one's prayer when they call upon Me. So let them respond 'with obedience' to Me and believe in Me, perhaps they will be guided 'to the Right Way'. (Al- Baqarah Ch 2:186)

Some people seek health, wealth, children, relief from acute diseases and so on from the dead virtuous person in the grave. The grant is from Allah and we have to supplicate and beg before the Almighty. A dead person does not possess anything for himself. Instead, we pray for the dead to the Almighty for His forgiveness. The Prophet (ﷺ) used to invoke for the dead. Once a person dies, all his deeds are stopped except Sadaqa Jariya (ongoing charity), beneficial knowledge and virtuous child supplicating for him. Abu Qatadah (ra) reported: The Messenger of Allah (ﷺ) said, **"The best of what a man leaves behind are three: a righteous child who supplicates for him, ongoing charity the reward of which reaches him, and knowledge that is acted upon after him."** [Sunan Ibn Majah]

**Hadith**: The Prophet (ﷺ) also invoked for the dead. Umm Salama (ra) reported: The Messenger of Allah (ﷺ) came to Abu Salama (as he died). His eyes were fixedly open. He (ﷺ) closed them, and then said: When the soul is taken away the sight follows it. Some of the people of his family wept and wailed. So, he (ﷺ) said: Do not supplicate for yourselves anything but good, for angels say 'Ameen' to what you say. He (ﷺ) then said: **"O Allah, forgive Abu Salama, raise his degree among those who are rightly guided, grant him a successor in his descendants who remain. Forgive us and him, O Lord of the Universe, and make his grave spacious, and grant him light in it."** [Muslim]

**Hadith**: Jubair bin Nufair says: I heard it from 'Auf bin Malik (ra) that the Prophet (ﷺ) said prayer on the dead body, and I remembered his prayer: **"O Allah! forgive him, have mercy upon him, give him peace and forgive him. Receive him with honour and make his grave spacious; wash him with water, snow and hail. Cleanse him from faults as Thou wouldst cleanse a white garment from impurity. Requite him with an abode more excellent than his abode, with a family better than his family, and with a mate better than his mate.**

**Admit him to the Garden, and protect him from the torment of the grave and the torment of the Fire." [Muslim]**

**Hadith**: Narrated Muawiya (ra): I heard Allah's Messenger (ﷺ) saying, "If Allah wants to do good to a person, He makes him comprehend the religion. I am just a distributor, but the grant is from Allah. (And remember) that this nation (true Muslims) will keep on following Allah's teachings strictly and they will not be harmed by any one going on a different path till Allah's order (Day of Judgment) is established." [Bukhari]

## 2.17 Graves

One of the most widespread forms of shirk in the contemporary Muslim world is the veneration of graves. This includes constructing shrines over them, organizing festivals at these sites, prostrating before them, adorning them with flowers and decorative cloths, lighting candles and incense, tying threads to them, and engaging in similar acts. True honor for the righteous lies in following their example, not in worshiping them. One of the most visible examples of shrine-building over the graves of righteous people can be seen in the history of Jannat al-Baqi' in Madina. Over time, domes and structures were erected over the graves of the Prophet's Companions and family members, and others. During last century, these shrines were demolished in an effort to restore the graveyard to its original Sunnah-based simplicity.

**Hadith**: Sumama bin Shafayy reported: When we were with Fadala bin 'Ubaid in the country of the Romans at a place (known as) Rudis, a friend of ours died. Fadala bin 'Ubaid ordered to prepare a grave for him and then it was levelled; and then he said: I heard the Messenger of Allah (ﷺ) commanding (us) to level the grave. [Muslim]

**Hadith**: Narrated `Aisha (ra): Um Salama (ra) told Allah's Messenger (ﷺ) about a church which she had seen in Ethiopia and which was called Mariya. She told him about the pictures which she had seen in it. Allah's Messenger (ﷺ) said, "If any righteous pious man dies amongst them, they would build a place of worship at his grave and make these pictures in it; they are the worst creatures in the sight of Allah." [Bukhari, Muslim]

**Hadith**: Narrated `Aisha (ra) and `Abdullah bin `Abbas (ra): When the last moment of the life of Allah's Messenger (ﷺ) came, he (ﷺ) started putting his 'Khamisa' on his face and when he felt hot and short of breath he took it off his face and said, "May Allah curse the Jews and Christians for they built the places of worship at the graves of their Prophets." The Prophet (ﷺ) was warning (Muslims) of what those had done. [Bukhari, Muslim]

**Hadith**: Jundub ibn 'Abd-Allah al-Bajali (ra) said: I heard the Messenger of Allah (ﷺ) say, "Allah has taken me as a close friend (khaleel) as He took Ibraahim (as) as a close friend. If I were to take anyone among my ummah as a close friend, I would have taken Abu Bakr (ra) as a close friend. Those who came before you took the graves of their Prophets and righteous people as places of worship. Do not take graves as places of worship, for I forbid you to do that." [Muslim].

**Hadith**: Narrated `Urwa: Aisha (ra) said: The Prophet (ﷺ) in his fatal illness said, "Allah cursed the Jews and the Christians because they took the graves of their Prophets as places for praying." Aisha (ra) added, "Had it not been for that, the grave of the Prophet (ﷺ) would have been made prominent but I am afraid it might be taken (as a) place for praying." [Bukhari]

Note: Prophet's (ﷺ) grave was in the room of Aisha (ra) until Umar (ra) was buried. Also note the utmost care of Mother of the believers, Aisha (ra). She could anticipate the Shirk activities at graves by later generations.

## 2.18 Part of the Head is Shaved and Other Parts are Left Long

Shaving a part of the head of a man while leaving another part long is known as Qaza' and is done to imitate the singers, musicians, actors, sports personalities, fashion models, and celebrities. Qaza is forbidden in Islam. Ibn 'Umar (ﷺ) said: "The Messenger (ﷺ) prohibited shaving a part of the head and leaving another part long." [Sunan an-Nasa'i]

**Hadith**: It is narrated Ubaidullah bin Hafs: that `Umar bin Nafi` told him that Nafi, Maula `Abdullah had heard `Umar (ra) saying, "I heard Allah's Apostle (ﷺ) forbidding Al-Qaza." 'Ubaidullah added: I said, "What is Al-Qaza?" 'Ubaidullah pointed (towards his head) to show us and added, "Nafi` said, 'It is when a boy has his head shaved leaving a tuft of hair here and a tuft of hair there." Ubaidullah pointed towards his forehead and the sides of his head. 'Ubaidullah was asked, "Does this apply to both girls and boys?" He said, "I don't know, but Nafi` said, 'The boy.' 'Ubaidullah added: I asked Nafi` again, and he said, 'As for leaving hair on the temples and the back part of the boy's head, there is no harm, but Al-Qaza is to leave a tuft of hair on his forehead unshaved while there is no hair on the rest of his head, and also to leave hair on either side of his head.' [Bukhari]

## 2.19 Not to narrate from tampered Torah and Bible

Many fabricated stories are being narrated from tampered Torah and Bible to bring emotions among the listeners; e.g: dramatic narration regarding Prophet Yusuf (as) and a lady beyond the narrations in the Qur'an and Hadiths. Another example is the fake story of wedding by the Prophet Dawud (as) with the wife of his army general. In these tampered Books, we do not know which are the verses revealed from Allah SWT and which are fabricated.

**Hadith**: Narrated Abu Huraira (ra): The people of the Book used to read the Torah in Hebrew and then explain it in Arabic to the Muslims. Allah's Messenger (ﷺ) said (to the Muslims): Do not believe the people of the Book, nor disbelieve them, but say, 'We believe in Allah and whatever is revealed to us, and whatever is revealed to you.' [Bukhari]

**Hadith**: Ibn ʿAbbas (ra) said, "Why do you ask the people of the scripture about anything while your Book (Qur'an) which has been revealed to Allah's Messenger (ﷺ) is newer and the latest? You read it pure, undistorted and unchanged, and Allah has told you that the people of the scripture (Jews and Christians) changed their scripture and distorted it, and wrote the scripture with their own hands and said, 'It is from Allah,' to sell it for a little gain. Does not the knowledge which has come to you prevent you from asking them about anything? No, by Allah, we have never seen any man from them asking you regarding what has been revealed to you!" [Bukhari]

**Hadith:** It was narrated from Jaabir ibn 'Abdullah (ra) that 'Umar ibn al-Khattaab (ra) came to the Prophet (ﷺ) with some written material he had got from one of the people of the Book. He read it to the Prophet (ﷺ), and he got angry and said: "Are you confused (about your religion), O son of al-Khattaab? By the One in Whose hand is my soul, I have brought it (the message of Islam) to you clear and pure. Do not ask them about anything, lest they tell you something true and you disbelieve it, or they tell you something false and you believe it. By the One in Whose hand is my soul, if Musa (sa) were alive, he would have no option but to follow me." [Musnad Ahmad]

## 2.20 Why does Bid'ah exist?

**Ignorance and following blindly:** One of the key reasons for the spread of *bid'ah* is the widespread ignorance among common people. Many either lack knowledge altogether or hold incorrect understandings. A significant number of Muslims today remain unaware because they do not study the Qur'an and Sunnah. Instead, they blindly follow the practices of their fathers and forefathers without reflecting on whether these align with true Islamic teachings. This uncritical following has led many to wrongly believe that such inherited practices define Islam. They are often influenced—or even misled—by individuals with vested interests, sometimes referred to as the 'Imams of misguidance.' When *bid'ah* is pointed out, people often respond with arrogance or become defensive, questioning whether their ancestors could have been wrong. While it's true that our forefathers were not always mistaken, the term **'forefathers'** becomes problematic in this context. The Qur'an repeatedly mentions how past nations rejected prophets, including the final Prophet (ﷺ), by clinging to the practices of their forefathers, using them as a reason to reject the truth. In this regard, Allah SWT mentions (interpretation of meaning):

- *"When it is said to them, "Follow what Allah has revealed," they reply, "No! We 'only' follow what we found our **forefathers** practicing." ˈWould they still do so, even if their forefathers had absolutely no understanding or guidance." (Surah Baqarah Ch 2:170)*

- *In fact, they say, "We found our **forefathers** following a ˈparticularˈ way, and we are following in their footsteps." Similarly, whenever We sent a warner to a society before you ˈO Prophetˈ, its ˈspoiledˈ elite would say, "We found our **forefathers** following a ˈparticularˈ way, and we are walking in their footsteps." (Az-Zukhruf Ch 43:22-23)*

Prophet Ibrahim (as) was also rejected on the ground of the religion of forefathers. Allah SWT says:

*And indeed, We had granted Ibrahim sound judgment early on, for We knew him well ˈto be worthy of itˈ. ˈRememberˈ when he questioned his father and his people, "What are these statues to which you are so devoted?" They replied, "We found our **forefathers** worshipping them." He responded, "Indeed, you and your forefathers have been clearly astray." (Al-Anbiya Ch 21: 51-54; interpretation of meaning)*

Leaders of misguidance with vested interest knowingly brainwash people and present narrow interpretations to preserve their own agenda. In some cases, common people are even discouraged from questioning, or seeking knowledge from the Qur'an and Sunnah directly. It is told that if one studies the Qur'an and Sunnah directly, he will go astray. This is dangerous because it suffocates intellectual growth. Community has to be vigilant in this regard. On the day of Judgement, we will be liable for our own deeds whether guided or misguided. Anas ibn Malik (ra) reported: The Messenger of Allah (ﷺ) said, "I saw some men on the night of my ascension (Mi'raj), whose lips were being sheared by scissors of fire. I said: O Jibriel, who are these people? Jibriel (as) said: Preachers from your nation who commanded people to be righteous but they forgot it themselves, yet they recited the Book. Will they not reason?" [Musnad Aḥmad] Allah SWT warns people against intentional misguidance. Allah says (interpretation of meaning):

- *Who can be more unjust than the one who conceals the testimony he has from Allah? (Al-Baqarah Ch 2:140)*

- *Those who hide the clear proofs and guidance that We have revealed—after We made it clear for humanity in the Book—will be condemned by Allah and all those who condemn. (Al-Baqarah Ch 2:159)*

Above verses were revealed about the People of the Scripture (Jews and Christians) who intentionally hid the description of the Prophet (ﷺ) although they testified to these facts.

**Imitating the disbelievers:** Abu Waqid Al-Laisi narrated that when the Messenger of Allah (ﷺ) went out to Hunain, he passed a tree that the idolaters called Jat Anwat upon which they hung their weapons. They (the Companions) said: "O Messenger of Allah (ﷺ)! Make a Jat Anwat for us as they have a Jat Anwat.' The Prophet (ﷺ) said: "Subhan Allah!

This is like what Musa's people said: Make for us a God like their Gods. By the One in Whose is my soul! You shall follow the way of those who were before you." [Tirmizi]

In the abobe hadith, the Prophet (ﷺ) was pointing towards some Israelites, who under the guidance of Prophet Musa (as), could not cleanse themselves from Shirk activities that had been stamped in their hearts during their slavery under the Pharaohs. This incident is stated in the Qur'an.

*We took the Children of Israel across the sea, but when they came upon a people who worshipped idols, they said, 'Moses, make a god for us like theirs.' He said, 'You really are foolish people: What these people are engaged in is sure to be destroyed; and false is what they are doing." (Al A'raf Ch 7:138-139; interpretation of meaning)*

**Thinking one is becoming more virtuous:** Most common people who engage in *bid'ah* do so without bad intentions. In fact, many believe they are earning greater reward and drawing closer to Allah (SWT). However, Allah only accepts deeds that are in accordance with the Qur'an and Sunnah. Our acts of worship must be performed exactly as the Prophet (ﷺ) did, and as practiced by his Companions. Any additional religious acts not prescribed by Islam have no place in the faith. Just as a student's self-made questions and answers outside the syllabus hold no value in an examination, such innovations will not be accepted on the Day of Judgment. In Islam, there is no room for a **'Sunnah plus'**—we are to follow, not add. Allah SWT says (interpretation of meaning):

*For those people who are differing from the commands of Prophet, there will come to them either a Fitnah (test or trial from Allah) or a severe punishment. (An-Nur Ch 24:63)*

## 2.21 Good Practices and Bid'at

Practices in support of religion are not Bid'ats. Practices recommended or prohibited by the Prophet (ﷺ) are his Sunnah and part of religion. Good practices should not be confused with Bid'at. Example of good practice can be to donate (charity) using digital transfer such as net-banking, UPI, QR code etc instead of physical transactions. Following Hadith is an example of good practice recommended by the Prophet (ﷺ).

**Hadith**: Jarir bin Abdullah (ra) reported that some desert Arabs clad in woollen clothes came to Allah's Messenger (ﷺ). He (ﷺ) saw them in sad plight as they had been hard pressed by need. He (ﷺ) exhorted people to give charity, but they showed some reluctance until (signs) of anger could be seen on his face. Then a person from the Ansar came with a purse containing silver. Then came another person and then other persons followed them in succession until signs of happiness could be seen on his (sacred) face. Thereupon Allah's Messenger (ﷺ) said: He who introduced some good practice (سُنَّةً حَسَنَةً) in Islam which was followed after him (by people) he would be assured of reward like one who followed it, without their rewards being diminished in any respect. And he who introduced some evil practice (سُنَّةً سَيِّئَةً) in Islam which had been followed subsequently (by others), he would be required to bear the burden like that of one who followed this (evil practice) without their being diminished in any respect. [Muslim, a part from Tirmizi]

Further explanation may be found in a report recorded in Sunan an-Nasa'i, also from Jarir ibn 'Abdullah (ra) who said: "We were with the Messenger of Allah (ﷺ) early one day, when some people who were almost naked (not dressed properly) and barefoot, with their swords by their sides, came to him. Most, if not all of them, were of (the tribe of) Mudar. The Messenger's (ﷺ) face changed when he (ﷺ) saw how poor they were [i.e., he (ﷺ) became upset]. He (ﷺ) went into (his house), then he (ﷺ) came out and ordered Bilal to give the call to prayer. He (ﷺ) led the people in prayer, then he (ﷺ) addressed them, saying: O people, be dutiful to your Lord, Who created you from a single person, and from him He created his wife, and from them both he created many men and women, and fear Allah through Whom you demand your mutual (rights), and (do not cut the relations of) the wombs (kinship). "Fear Allah, and keep your duty to Him. And let every person look to what he has sent forth for the morrow" [al-Hashr, Ch 59:18]. Let a man give charity from his dinars, his dirhams, his clothing, his wheat or his dates - even if it is only half a date. A man from the Ansar brought a package which he could hardly carry in his hand, then another and another came, until there were two piles, of food and clothing, and I saw the face of the Messenger of Allah (ﷺ) beaming with joy. The Messenger of Allah (ﷺ) said: 'Whoever starts a good thing in Islam will have his own reward and a reward equal to that of those who follow him, without it detracting in the least from their reward, and whoever starts a bad thing in Islam will have to bear the burden of his own sin and a burden equal to that of those who followed him, without it detracting in the least from their burden. [Sunan an-Nasa'i].

From the context of the hadith, it is clear that what is meant by the words "whoever starts a good thing (sunnah hasanah) in Islam" means: Whoever revives a part of the Sunnah of the Prophet (ﷺ), or teaches it to others, or commands others to follow it, or acts according to it so that others see him or hear about it and follow his example. This is also indicated by the hadith narrated by Abu Hurairah (ra) who said: A man came to the Prophet (ﷺ), and he urged the people to give him charity. A man said: 'I have such-and-such,' and there was no person left in the gathering who did not give something in charity to him, whether it was a large amount or a little. The Messenger of Allah (ﷺ) said: 'Whoever starts something good, and others follow his lead, will have a complete reward and a reward like that of those who followed him, without it detracting in the least from their reward. Whoever starts something bad, and others follow his lead, will bear a complete burden of sin, and a burden like that of those who followed him, without it detracting in the least from their burden.' [Sunan Ibn Majah]

## 2.22 Night Prayer during Ramadan in congregation

Narrated 'Urwa that he was informed by Aisha (ra): Allah's Messenger (ﷺ) went out in the middle of the night and prayed in the mosque and some men prayed behind him. In the morning, the people spoke about it and then a large number of them gathered and prayed behind him (on the second night). In the next morning the people again talked about it and on the third night the mosque was full with a large number of people. Allah's Messenger (ﷺ) came out and the people prayed behind him. On the fourth night the Mosque was overwhelmed with people and could not accommodate them, but the Prophet (ﷺ) came out (only) for the morning prayer. When the morning prayer was finished he (ﷺ) recited Tashah-hud and (addressing the people) said, "Amma ba'du, your presence was not hidden from me but I was afraid lest the night prayer (Qiyamul lail) should be enjoined on you and you might not be able to carry it on." So, Allah's Apostle (ﷺ) died and the situation remained like that (i.e. people prayed individually). [Bukhari]

It was narrated that Abdur Rahman bin Abdul Qari said: I went out in the company of 'Umar bin Al-Khattab (ra) one night in Ramadan to the mosque and found the people praying in different groups. A man praying alone or a man praying with a little group behind him. So, 'Umar (ra) said, "In my opinion, I would better collect these (people) under the leadership of one Qari (Reciter) (i.e. let them pray in congregation!)." So, he made up his mind to congregate them behind Ubai bin Ka'b (ra). Then on another night I went again in his company and the people were praying behind their reciter. On that, 'Umar (ra) remarked, "What an **excellent Bid'at** this is, but the prayer which they do not perform, but sleep at its time is better than the one they are offering." He meant the prayer in the last part of the night. (In those days) people used to pray in the early part of the night." [Bukhari]

The Prophet (ﷺ) explained the reason why he (ﷺ) did not come out for congregation which was the fear that it might be made 'obligatory'. But at the time of 'Umar's (ra) caliphate, he re-started the Qiyamul-lail in congregation that was something new in the sense that people had not practised it during the caliphate of Abu Bakr (ra) and the first half of 'Umar's (ra) caliphate. Islamic scholars are of the opinion that the term 'Bid'at' used by Umar (ra) here should be treated as a linguistic term and should not be misused. It was in accordance with what the Prophet (ﷺ) did, it is revival of Sunnah and is not an innovation in real sense.

## 2.23 Congregational coexistent Bid'ah in Masjid

These are among the most commonly practiced innovations in the mosque; therefore, a detailed analysis is presented below.

**Hadith**: Narrated 'Amr bin Salamah: We were sitting by the door of Abdullah ibn Mas'ud (ra) before lunch, so that if he came out, we could walk with him to the Masjid. Abu Musa al-Ash'aree (ra) came and said: Has Abu Abdur-Rahman come out yet? We said: No. So, he sat down with us, waiting for him to come out, and when he came out, we all gathered towards him, and Abu Musa (ra) said: O Abu Abdur-Rahman! Previously I saw something in the Masjid, which I disliked. But, Alhamdulillah, what I saw, was nothing but good.' He said: What was it? Abu Musa (ra) said, 'If you live, you will see it.' Then Abu Musa (ra) said, 'I saw a group of people, sitting in circles waiting for the prayer. In every circle there was a man and in their hands were small stones and he would say: 'Say ١٠٠ الله أكبر times' and they would say '100 الله أكبر' times. Then, he would say, 'Say 100 لا إله إلا الله times' and they would say '100 لا إله إلا الله' times and he would say, 'Say 100 سُبْحَانَ ٱللَّهِ' times and they would say '100 سُبْحَانَ ٱللَّهِ' times.'

Abdullah ibn Mas'ud (ra) said, 'So what did you say to them?' He said: 'I did not say anything to them, rather I waited for your opinion [or 'I waited for your command'].' He said: 'Why did you not command them to count their bad deeds [i.e. seek forgiveness from your deeds] and guarantee them that their good deeds would not be lost?!' Then he walked and we walked with him until he reached one of those circles and he stood there and said, 'What is this that I see you doing?' They said: 'O Abu Abdur-

Rahman! These are nothing but small stones with which we are counting, saying 'Allaahu Akbar, laa ilaaha illallaah and Subhan Allah.'

He said, 'Count your sins; I guarantee that you will not lose anything of your good deeds! Beware, O Ummah of Muhammad (ﷺ)! How quick you are to your destruction! Here we are, the Companions of your Prophet (ﷺ) – abundant, everywhere and here is his clothing which has not been [wasted away] and his utensils have not been broken [Means, the Prophet (ﷺ) departed not many days/months ago]. I swear by Him in Whose Hand is my soul, either you are an Ummah more rightly-guided than the Ummah of Muhammad (ﷺ) or you are opening the door of misguidance.' They said; 'We swear by Allah, O Abu Abdur-Rahman, we did not intend anything but good.' He said: 'How many people intend good but never achieve it. Verily the Messenger of Allah (ﷺ) narrated to us, 'Indeed there will be a people who read the Qur'an but it does not pass beyond their throats.' I swear by Allah, I do not know. Perhaps most of them are from amongst you.' Then he went away. 'Amr bin Salamah said, 'We saw some of those sitting in those circles fighting on the Day of Nahrawan, along with the Khawarij.' [Musnad ad-Darimi]

The incident mentioned above occurred during the period when Abdullah ibn Mas'ud (ra) served as the governor under the caliphate of Umar ibn al-Khattab (ra). Abu Musa al-Ash'aree (ra) wanted that the verdict be given by Abdullah ibn Mas'ud (ra) as a governor. The above hadith is very crucial in the sense that it condemns the coexistent Bid'ats performed in congregation daily, weekly, monthly, annually as a routine. Let us analyse critically the components of this hadith and examine the probable reason for objection by Abdullah ibn Mas'ud (ra), a companion of the Prophet (ﷺ).

**Rememberance of Allah SWT (i.e. az- Zikr):** The Messenger of Allah (ﷺ) said: "The Mufarridun have outdone everyone." They (companions) asked: "Who are the Mufarridun?" He (ﷺ) replied: "The men and women who frequently remember Allah." [Muslim]

Besides, the Prophet (ﷺ) said: Allah SWT says, "I am as My Servant thinks of Me (expects of me); I am with him when he mentions Me. If he mentions Me to himself, I mention him to Myself; and if he mentions Me in a gathering, I mention him in a gathering that is much better than his (i.e. with the angels)." [Muslim]

Allah SWT says (interpretation of meaning): *O you who believe, remember Allah abundantly, and glorify Him morning and evening. (Al-Ahzab Ch33:41-42)* Zikr is a means of blessings and reward from Allah. It is a protection against Satan and is required for our salvation that we remember Allah in private and public.

**Sitting in Masjid before prayer:** Abu Hurairah (ra) narrated that: Allah's Messenger (ﷺ) said: "One of you does not cease to be in Salat as long as he is waiting for it. And the angels do not cease praying for one of you as long as he remains in the Masjid (saying): 'Allah! Forgive him. O Allah! Have mercy upon him' - as long as he does not commit hadath." A man from Hadramawt said: "And just what is hadath Abu Hurairah?" He said: "Breaking wind, or passing gas." [Tirmizi] There is no mention of zikr in congregation and recititation of the same verse/du'a in unison.

**Sitting in Masjid after prayer:** Simak b. Harb reported: I said to Jabir bin Sámura (ra): Did you sit in the company of the Messenger of Allah (ﷺ)? He said: Yes, very often. He (ﷺ) used to sit at the place where he observed the morning or dawn prayer till the sun rose or when it had risen; he would stand, and they (his Companions) would talk about matters (pertaining to the days) of ignorance, and they would laugh (on these matters) while (the Holy Prophet ﷺ) only smiled. [Muslim]

There is no mention of zikr in congregation and recitation of the same verse/du'a in unison.

**To gather for rememberance:** Mu'awiyah ibn Abi Sufyaan (ra) narrated: The Messenger of Allah (ﷺ) came out to a circle of his companions and said: "Why are you sitting here?" They said: We are sitting to remember Allah and praise Him for having guided us to Islam and blessed us with it. He (ﷺ) said: "By Allah, are you only sitting for that purpose? They said: By Allah, we are only sitting for that purpose. He (ﷺ) said: "I did not ask you to swear because I am accusing you, but Jibril came to me and told me that Allah was boasting of you to the angels." [Muslim]

There was a gathering but there is no mention that they were remembering Allah in unison either loudly or in low voice. It is also not mentioned that they were remembering by saying the same word or phrase or sentence all at a time by specified number of times.

**Counting by pebbles:** Counting by pebbles cannot be an innovation because the counter in whatever form (digital counter, mechanical counter etc) is a device supportive of religion. The detail discussion on these has already been presented in preceeding section.

**Specifying numbers:** Abu Huraira (ra) reported Allah's Messenger (ﷺ) as saying: If anyone extols Allah after every prayer 33 times (*Subhan Allah*), and praises Allah 33 times (*al hamdulillah*), and declares His

Greatness 33 times (*Allahu akbar*), ninety-nine times in all, and says to complete a 100: *There is no god but Allah, having no partner with Him, to Him belongs sovereignty and to Him is praise due, and He is Potent over everything,* لاَ إِلَهَ إِلاَّ اللَّهُ وَحْدَهُ لاَ شَرِيكَ لَهُ لَهُ الْمُلْكُ وَلَهُ الْحَمْدُ وَهُوَ عَلَى كُلِّ شَىْءٍ قَدِيرٌ his sins will be forgiven even If these are as abundant as the foam of the sea. [Muslim]

It was narrated from Juwayriyah (ra), Ummul Muminin, that the Prophet (ﷺ) left her house one morning when he prayed Fajr, and she was in her prayer-place, then he (ﷺ) came back after the forenoon had come, and she was still sitting there. He (ﷺ) said: "Are you still as you were when I left you?" She said: Yes. The Prophet (ﷺ) said: "After I left you I said four words 3 times, which if they were weighed against what you have said today, they would outweigh it: *Subhaan Allah wa bi hamdihi, 'adada khalqihi, wa ridaa nafsihi, wazinata 'arshihi, wa midaada kalimaatihi* (Glory and praise be to Allah, as much as the number of His creation, as much as pleases Him, as much as the weight of His Throne and as much as the ink of His words)." [Muslim] Narrated Abu Huraira (ra): Allah's Messenger (ﷺ) said, "Whoever says, '*Subhan Allahi wa bihamdihi,*' 100 times a day, will be forgiven all his sins even if they were as much as the foam of the sea." [Bukhari]

Narrated Abu Huraira (ra): Allah's Messenger (ﷺ) said, "If one says 100 times in one day: Laa ilaaha ill-Allah wahdahu laa shareeka lah, lahu'l-mulk wa lahu'l-hamd wa huwa 'ala kulli shay'in qadeer (*None has the right to be worshipped but Allah, the Alone Who has no partners, to Him belongs Dominion and to Him belong all the Praises, and He has power over all things)*", one will get the reward of manumitting ten slaves, and one-hundred good deeds will be written in his account, and one-hundred bad deeds will be wiped off or erased from his account, and on that day he will be protected from the morning till evening from Satan, and nobody will be superior to him except one who has done more than that which he has done." [Bukhari]

Thus, numbers like 3, 33, 100 (and other numbers) are reported in the hadiths. Virtue of reciting "Subhan Allah" 100 times, "Alhamdulillah" 100 times in the morning and evening is reported in the Sunan Tirmizi.

**The persons were Tabi'un:** Imran bin Husain (ra) reported the Messenger of Allah (ﷺ) as saying: The best of my people is the generation in which I have been sent (i.e Companions), then their immediate followers (Tabi'in), then their immediate followers (Tabiu at-Tabi'in). Allah knows the best whether he mentioned the third or not. After them will be people who will give testimony without being asked, who will make vows which they do not fulfil, who will be treacherous and not to be trusted, among whom fatness will appear. [Sunan Abu Dawud]

Last part of the hadith under consideration shows that although they were companion of the companions of the Prophet (ﷺ), later on they became Khawarij. The virtue attributed by the Prophet (ﷺ) is not applicable to them.

From the above discussion, it becomes evident—through the method of elimination—that the practice of performing zikr in a congregation, with all participants reciting the same phrases in unison for a specified number of times, is not in accordance with the Sunnah of the Prophet (ﷺ). Moreover, presenting this form of zikr as a complete and packaged mode of worship as wazifa—detached from the way it was practiced during the blessed life of the Prophet (ﷺ)—constitutes an innovative practice. While it does not involve Shirk, it remains a coexistent form of Bid'ah.

Creating one's own ways of zikr unless there is evidence of it in the Quran and the Sunnah, is to be avoided as it may fall into the category of Bida'h. Allah SWT sent Messengers to show us the right path and the Messengers explained what Allah loves. The Prophet (ﷺ) was very kind towards his Ummah with utmost caring and he (ﷺ) explained everything to the Ummah.  Following the path of the Prophet (ﷺ) strictly is an obligation. Allah SWT says (interpretation of the meaning):

*"Whatever the Messenger gives you, take it. And whatever he forbids you from, leave it. And fear Allah. Surely Allah is severe in punishment."* (al-Hashr Ch 59:7)

There are numerous verses in the Qur'an that emphasize the importance of performing **zikr (remembrance of Allah)** with **heartfelt humility, fear of Allah (khawf)**, and **humble submission (khushu)**, and that it should be done **in a low and modest voice**, not for show or public display. Allah says (interpretation of meaning):

- *Remember your Lord in your heart with humility and awe, and without speaking loudly, in mornings and evenings, and do not be among the heedless. (Al-A'raf Ch 7:205)*

- *Has the time not come for those who have believed that their hearts should become humbly submissive at the remembrance of Allah and what has come down of the truth?" (Al-Ḥadid Ch 57:16)*

Similarly, there are authentic **ḥadiths** in which the Prophet ﷺ encouraged **private and sincere zikr**, especially in **isolation**, where the heart is truly present. Such remembrance often leads to **tears flowing from the eyes—** whether out of **fear, love**, or **longing for Allah**.

**Hadith**: Abu Hurayrah (ra) reported that the Messenger of Allah ﷺ said: "Seven types of people will be shaded by Allah in His Shade on the Day when there is no shade but His: … and a man who remembers Allah in solitude, and his eyes overflow with tears." [Muslim, Bukhari]

**Hadith**: Narrated by **Abdullah ibn ʿAbbas (ra):** The Messenger of Allah ﷺ said: "Two eyes will never be touched by the Fire: an eye that wept out of fear of Allah, and an eye that stayed awake guarding in the path of Allah." [al-Bukhari]

## 2.24 Mid Sha'ban/Lailatul Barat Prayer

The importance of the month of Sha'ban has been strongly emphasized in the Sunnah as a warm-up to Ramadan. There are many authentic hadiths and some are as follows.

**Hadith**: Aisha (ra) reported: The Messenger of Allah (ﷺ) would fast until we said he (ﷺ) will never break his fast, and he (ﷺ) would not fast until we said he (ﷺ) would never fast. I did not see the Prophet (ﷺ) complete an entire month of fasting except for Ramadan, and I did not see him complete more voluntary fasts than in the month of Sha'ban. [Bukhari and Muslim]

**Hadith**: Usamah ibn Zayd (ra) reported: I said, "O Messenger of Allah (ﷺ), I do not see you fasting any month as much as you fast during

Sha'ban." The Prophet (ﷺ) said, **"It is a month people neglect between Rajab and Ramadan. It is a month in which the deeds are raised to the Lord of the worlds, and I like for my deeds to be raised while I am fasting."** [Sunan an-Nasai]

**Hadith**: Aisha (ra) reported: The most beloved month to the Messenger of Allah (ﷺ) for fasting was Sha'ban, then he (ﷺ) would connect it with Ramadan. [Sunan Abu Dawud]

**Hadith**: Umm Salamah (ra) reported: I did not see the Prophet (ﷺ) fast for two consecutive months in a row except for Sha'ban and Ramadan. [Sunan at-Tirmizi]

Nisfu Sha'ban is a mid Sha'ban (Sha'ban is the $8^{th}$ month of Islamic calender) related religious Salat celebrated in many places on the $15^{th}$ night of the month. It is believed to reward them with fortune for the whole year. Following authentic hadiths may be referred.

**Hadith**: Mu'az ibn Jabal (ra) reported: The Prophet (ﷺ) said, **"Allah looks down at His creation on the middle night of Sha'ban and He forgives all of His creatures, except for an idolater or one filled with malice."** [Sahih Ibn Hibban; similar narration from Abu Musa (ra) in Sunan Ibn Majah]

**Hadith**: Abu Sa'labah (ra) reported: The Prophet (ﷺ) said, **"On the middle night of Sha'ban, Allah looks down upon His creation and He forgives the believers, gives respite to the unbelievers, and He abandons the people of malice to their malice until they give it up."** [Shu'ab al-Iman lil-Bayhaqi]

Thus, the vitue of the mid Sha'ban is proved in many narrations. However, there is no authentic source that explicitly mentions the importance of Prayer and fasting especially in the mid Sha'ban. As mentioned above, the Prophet (ﷺ) used to fast frequently during this month. So mid Sha'ban cannot be singled out for Prayer and fasting. There is no report from the Messenger of Allah (ﷺ) or from his companions (ra) concerning the prayer in the night of the middle of Shaban (i.e. lailatul barat).

Again, a group of scholars are of strong opinion that the blessed night in Ch 44 refers to mid-Sha'ban when every matter is decreed and when the Qur'an was revealed. Allah SWT says:

حمّ

وَٱلْكِتَٰبِ ٱلْمُبِينِ

إِنَّآ أَنزَلْنَٰهُ فِى لَيْلَةٍ مُّبَٰرَكَةٍ ۚ إِنَّا كُنَّا مُنذِرِينَ

فِيهَا يُفْرَقُ كُلُّ أَمْرٍ حَكِيمٍ

أَمْرًا مِّنْ عِندِنَآ ۚ إِنَّا كُنَّا مُرْسِلِينَ

رَحْمَةً مِّن رَّبِّكَ ۚ إِنَّهُۥ هُوَ ٱلسَّمِيعُ ٱلْعَلِيمُ

Hā Mīm

By the clear Book!

*Indeed, We sent it down on a blessed night, for We always warn ˹against evil˺.*

*On that night every matter of wisdom is ordained*

*by a command from Us, for We have always sent 'messengers' (Surah Ad-Dukhan Ch 44:1-4; interpretation of meaning)*

Ibn Kasir writes in his Tafseer about these verses: "Allah tells us that He revealed the Magnificent Qur'an on a blessed night, Laylatul-Qadr (the Night of Decree), as He says elsewhere: إِنَّا أَنزَلْنَـهُ فِى لَيْلَةِ الْقَدْرِ

(Verily, We have sent it down in the Night of Al-Qadr) (Ch 97:1). This was in the month of Ramadan, as Allah tells us: شَهْرُ رَمَضَانَ الَّذِى أُنزِلَ فِيهِ الْقُرْآنُ

(The month of Ramadan in which was revealed the Qur'an) (Ch 2:185)." Thus, the blessed night referred here is in Ramadan, not in Shaban.

## 2.25 Bid'at has made Islam bulky

The introduction of Bid'ah into Islam has greatly increased the physical size of the religion due to its additive nature. The current generation, already struggling with the demands of survival, finds it difficult to explore the vast resources of Islam. We have made the religion heavy, complicated, and hard to follow. However, Allah designed Islam to be accessible to everyone—whether someone has the simplest understanding or the intellect of a Nobel Laureate. Islam was meant to be both easy to comprehend and practice for all levels of intellect. The Prophet (ﷺ) said, "Religion is very easy and whoever overburdens himself in his religion will not be able to continue in that way. So, you should not be extremists, but try to be near to perfection and receive the good tidings that you will be rewarded; and gain strength by worshipping in the mornings, the afternoons, and during the last hours of the nights." [Bukhari]

Secondly, stories of Muslim saints about their extremely difficult level of worships and adorations are terrifying. People are afraid of such frightening acts and they are going far away from the religion with the frustration that getting closer to Allah SWT is simply unachieveable.

**Hadith**: The Prophet (ﷺ) said, "Make things easy for the people, and do not make it difficult for them, and make them calm (with glad tidings) and do not repulse (them)." [Bukhari]

**Hadith**: Anas (ra) reported that the Messenger of Allah (ﷺ) entered the mosque (and he found) a rope tied between the two pillars; so he (ﷺ) said: What is this? They said: It is for Zainab (ra). She prays and when she slackens or feels tired she holds it. Upon this he (the Holy Prophet ﷺ) said: Untie it. Let one pray as long as one feels fresh but when one slackens or becomes tired one must stop it. (And in the hadith transmitted by Zuhair it is:" He should sit down.") [Muslim]

**Hadith**: Mihjan ibn al-Adra' (ra) reported: The Messenger of Allah (ﷺ) said, "Verily, Allah Almighty is pleased for this Ummah to be at ease, and He is displeased for it to be in difficulty," and the Prophet (ﷺ) said it three times. [al-Mu'jam al-Kabir lil-Ṭabarani]

**Hadith**: Narrated Aishah (ra): "I do not know that the Messenger of Allah (ﷺ) recited the whole Quran in one night, or prayed Qiyam (Salat) until morning, or ever fasted an entire month, except Ramadan." [Sunan an-Nasai]

The role of common people here in preserving the purity of Islam is vital, as they form the foundation of the Muslim community. Their responsibilities include learning Islam from the Quran and Sunnah, as well as from reliable scholars. Remember, we all have to face the Lord on the Day of Judgement and for some unfortunate people, our kind Prophet (ﷺ) will be a witness against them instead of intercession. Allah SWT says:

*So how will it be when We bring a witness from every faith-community and bring you ˹O Prophet˺ as a witness against yours? (An-Nisa Ch 4:41; interpretation of the meaning)*

Abdullah bin Mas`ud (ra) said: The Messenger of Allah (ﷺ) said to me, "Recite to me." I said, "O Messenger of Allah (ﷺ)! Should I recite (the Qur'an) to you, while it was revealed to you?" He (ﷺ) said, "Yes, for I like to hear it from other people." I recited Surat An-Nisa' until I reached this Ayah, فَكَيْفَ إِذَا جِئْنَا مِن كُلِّ أُمَّةٍ بِشَهِيدٍ وَجِئْنَا بِكَ عَلَى هَؤُلَاءِ شَهِيداً

He (ﷺ) then said, "Stop now." I found that his eyes were tearful." [Bukhari]

## 2.26 Sects (Firqa) in Islam

A sect is a subgroup within a larger religion that holds distinct beliefs based on their interpretation of key religious principles and core rules of Shari'ah. Over time, some groups have diverged from the mainstream Muslim community, creating their own unique practices and approaches. A defining characteristic of a sect is its departure from the Quran, Sunnah, and scholarly consensus (ijma). Differences of opinion on minor matters, however, do not necessarily constitute a sect. The Prophet (ﷺ) said: "Whoever among you lives after I am gone will see a great deal of dissent." [Abu Dawud]

Following verses of the Qur'an prove that Allah dislikes sects (interpretation of meaning):

- *And hold firmly together to the **rope of Allah*** and do not be divided. (Ali Imran Ch ٣:١٠٣)

- *Indeed, you ˹O Prophet˺ are not responsible whatsoever for those who have divided their faith and split into sects. Their judgment rests only with Allah. And He will inform them of what they used to do. (Al-An'am Ch 6:159)*

- *And do not be like those who split ˹into sects˺ and differed after clear proofs had come to them. It is they who will suffer a tremendous punishment. (Ali Imran Ch 3:105)*

**Rope of Allah* means the Qur'an. Holding fast to His rope will protect one from going astray and will lead him on the path of guidance and help him to follow the guide. 'Rope' establishes a bond between man and the Almighty and joins all believers together. Abu Shurayh al-Khuza'i (ra) reported: The Messenger of Allah (ﷺ) came out to them one day and he (ﷺ) said, "Rejoice! Do you not witness that there is no God but Allah and I am the messenger of Allah?" They said, "Yes". The Prophet (ﷺ) said, "Verily, this Quran is a rope. One end is in the hand of Allah and the other end is in your hands. Hold fast to it, for you will never be led astray or ruined ever again." [Sahih Ibn Hibban]

**Hadith**: Narrated Zaid bin Arqam (ra) that the Messenger of Allah (ﷺ) said: "Indeed, I am leaving among you, that which if you hold fast to them, you shall not be misguided after me. One of them is greater than the other: The Book of Allah is a rope extended from the sky to the earth, and my family - the people of my house - and they shall not split until they meet at the Hawd (cistern), so look at how you deal with them after me." [Tirmizi]

Consequence of division of sect is horrible and the destination is Hell-fire. The Prophet (ﷺ) warned against the sects. Following Hadiths may be referred to in this regard.

**Hadith**: Abu Huraira (ra) reported: The Messenger of Allah (ﷺ) said, "Verily, Allah Almighty is pleased with you by three things and displeased by three things. He is pleased for you to worship Him without associating anything with Him, to hold fast to the rope of Allah altogether, and to not become divided. He is displeased for you to gossip among yourselves, to ask many unnecessary questions, and to waste your wealth. [Muslim]

**Hadith**: Allah's Messenger (ﷺ) said: "…my Ummah will be fragmented into seventy-three groups. All of them will be in Hell-Fire except one. They (the Companions) said: Allah's Messenger (ﷺ), which is that? Where upon he (ﷺ) said: It is one to which I and my companions belong." [Tirmizi]

**Hadith**: The Prophet (ﷺ) said: The Jews were split up into seventy-one or seventy-two sects, and the Christians were split up into seventy-one or seventy-two sects, and my community will be split up into seventy-three groups. [Abu Dawud]

**Hadith**: It was narrated from 'Awf bin Malik (ra) that the Messenger of Allah (ﷺ) said: "The Jews split into seventy-one sects, one of which will be in Paradise and seventy in Hell. The Christians split into seventy-two sects, seventy-one of which will be in Hell and one in Paradise. I swear by the One Whose Hand is the soul of Muhammad, my nation will split into seventy-three, one of which will be in Paradise and seventy-two in Hell." It was said: "O Messenger of Allah (ﷺ), who are they?" He (ﷺ) said: "الْجَمَاعَةُ (The main body)." [Sunan Ibn Majah]

What is meant by الْجَمَاعَة is the 'aqeedah and actions of the Prophet (ﷺ) and his Companions, as reported in the hadith of Tirmizi above. It is to be mentioned that Prophet (ﷺ) said that his Ummah **will be divided.** He (ﷺ) never told us to divide and he (ﷺ) never supported division amongst Muslims; it was his prediction (and his predictions are always true).

Division into sects (firqa) is a grave matter in Islam and is strongly condemned. Identifying ourselves with labels such as *Deobandi, Barelvi, Ahl-e-Hadees,* or any other sectarian affiliation goes against the spirit of Islamic unity. These divisions often lead to disunity, prejudice, and deviation from the pure teachings of Islam. We must strive to rise above such labels and sincerely return to the identity that Allah SWT has given us—*Muslim.* This is the name that unites the followers of Prophets under one creed, and it is the name mentioned in the Qur'an. Allah SWT says (interpretation of meaning):

*And strive for Allah with the striving due to Him. He has chosen you and has not placed upon you in the religion any difficulty. [It is] the religion of your father, Abraham. Allah named you "Muslims" before [in former scriptures] and in this [revelation] that the Messenger may be a witness over you and you may be witnesses over the people. So establish prayer and give zakah and hold fast to Allah. He is your protector; and excellent is the protector, and excellent is the helper. (Al-Hajj Ch 22:78; interpretation of meaning)*

## 2.27 Islamic Brotherhood

One of the greatest harms caused by division within Islam is the breakdown of unity and brotherhood among the Ummah. While political factors have played a role, a major source of division among Sunnis began with the formation of different *mazhabs* (schools of thought). A historical example of this is the presence of designated *maqamat* (prayer stations) for the four Imams within Masjid al-Haram, where separate Imams led the daily prayers according to their respective *mazhabs*—a practice that continued until 1925 CE.

Today, one of the key challenges faced by new Muslims (reverts) is the confusion surrounding which path to follow after embracing Islam. Upon entering the faith, they are often met with multiple groups, each claiming, 'This is the right way.' In the Indian subcontinent, the majority of Muslims follow the Fiqh of Imam Abu Hanifa (rahimahullah). However, even among Hanafi followers, divisions have arisen due to differing opinions on various matters, including those listed below.

- The Prophet (ﷺ) is alive in the grave as he (ﷺ) was alive on the earth or not;

- The Prophet (ﷺ) in the grave can hear us or not;

- The Prophet (ﷺ) is made of 'Noor' of Allah or not;

- All the Prophets and awliya can come out their graves and go anywhere or not;

- It is possible to see dead awliya and Prophets when awake or not;

- Awliya are also alive and you get their blessings if you visit their graves or not;

- If you do not practise Mawlid, you are a true lover of the Prophet (ﷺ) or not;

- Spiritual leaders (awliya) have ilmul gaib or not;

- We should do raful yadain or not in salah;

- We should say 'Ameen' loudly or silently after Surah Fatiha;

- We should place our hand below the naval or above during prayer;

- We should do congregational du'a after each salat or not;

- Whether we have to offer 8 rak'ah taraweeh or 20 rak'ah;

- Lailatul Barat is to be celebrated or not;

- 'Urs' observed at a shrine is allowed or not;

- Construction of a permanent structures over graves of awliya is allowed or not and so on.

The divisions among Sunni Muslims are starkly evident in the signboards displayed on mosques. In the subcontinent, mosques are often labeled as "Salafi Masjid," "Deobandi Masjid," or "Barelvi Masjid." In some places, only specific groups are permitted to perform Salat, while others are restricted. While mosques are meant to be the houses of Allah* (SWT), such group-specific claims are deeply regrettable and contradict the spirit of Islamic unity and brotherhood. The Prophet (ﷺ) said, "Houses of Allah in the world are masajid. Allah bestows blessing to those who come there." [Tabarani, Mu'jam al-Kabir]

*Note: The Masjid is called the "House of Allah" as a title of honor, not to suggest a physical dwelling, for Allah SWT is the Creator of time and space, exalted above both. Allah SWT says (interpretation of meaning):

*Who does more wrong than those who prevent Allah's Name from being mentioned in His places of worship and strive to destroy them? Such people have no right to enter these places except with fear. For them is disgrace in this world, and they will suffer a tremendous punishment in the Hereafter. (Al-Baqarah Ch 2: 114)*

Despite our differences, all Muslims are united in their belief in the five pillars of Islam. It is essential that we respect one another and strive to spread authentic knowledge to help bridge the gaps between us. These divisions will begin to dissolve when the concepts of *Tawheed*, *Shirk*, and *Bid'ah* are properly understood. True unity will come when we all acknowledge that the path to righteousness lies in following the Book of Allah and the Sunnah of the Prophet (ﷺ). As Muslims, we must cultivate tolerance and mutual respect—now more than ever. The following hadiths shed light on the importance of brotherhood in Islam.

**Hadith**: Al-Nu'man ibn Bashir (ra) reported: The Messenger of Allah (ﷺ) said, "The parable of the believers in their affection, mercy, and compassion for each other is that of a body. When any limb aches, the whole body reacts with sleeplessness and fever." [Bukhari, Muslim]

**Hadith**: Abu Musa (ra) reported: The Messenger of Allah (ﷺ) said, "Verily, the believers are like bricks of a building, each part strengthening the other," and the Prophet (ﷺ) clasped his fingers together. [Bukhari, Muslim]

**Hadith**: Anas ibn Malik (ra) reported: The Messenger of Allah (ﷺ) said, "Do not hate each other, do not envy each other, do not turn away from each other, but rather be servants of Allah as brothers. It is not lawful for a Muslim to boycott his brother for more than three days." [Bukhari, Muslim]

**Hadith**: Suwayd ibn Hanzalah (ra) reported: We went out intending to meet the Messenger of Allah (ﷺ) and with us was Wa'il ibn Hujr (ra). Then, one of his enemies seized him, and the people resisted swearing an oath, but I swore an oath, saying, "He is my brother!" They let him go on his way, and we came to the Messenger of Allah (ﷺ). I told him that the people resisted swearing an oath, but I swore an oath that he was my brother. The Prophet (ﷺ) said, "You spoke the truth. The Muslim is the brother of another Muslim." [Abu Dawud]

**Hadith**: Narrated `Abdullah (ra): I heard a man reciting a verse (of the Holy Qur'an) but I had heard the Prophet (ﷺ) reciting it differently. So, I caught hold of the man by the hand and took him to Allah's Messenger (ﷺ) who said, "Both of you are right." Shu`ba, the sub-narrator said, "I think he said to them, "Don't differ, for the nations before you differed and perished (because of their differences)." [Bukhari]

**Hadith**: Narrated Anas (ra): Allah's Messenger (ﷺ) said, "Help your brother, whether he is an oppressor or he is an oppressed one. People asked, "O Allah's Messenger (ﷺ)! It is all right to help him if he is oppressed, but how should we help him if he is an oppressor?" The Prophet (ﷺ) said, "By preventing him from oppressing others." [Bukhari]

**Hadith**: Abu Malik Al-Ash'ari (ra) narrated from Allah's Messenger (ﷺ) that he said: "There are people from the worshippers of Allah who are neither prophets nor martyrs, yet they will be the envy of the prophets and martyrs on the Day of Resurrection due to their rank in the sight of Allah." The Companions asked, "O Messenger of Allah (ﷺ), inform us as to who they are." He (ﷺ) replied, "They are a people who love one another for the sake of Allah, without having any blood relationship between them, nor any exchange of wealth between them. By Allah, their faces will be light, and they will be seated upon pulpits of light. They shall not fear when the people are afraid, and they shall not grieve when the people grieve." Then he (ﷺ) recited this verse, "Behold, indeed for the allies of Allah there is no fear, nor shall they grieve." [Abu Dawud]

**Hadith**: Abu Huraira (ra) reported Allah's Messenger (ﷺ) as saying: Avoid suspicion, for suspicion is the gravest lie in talk and do not be inquisitive about one another and do not spy upon one another and do not feel envy with the other, and nurse no malice, and nurse no aversion and hostility against one another. And be fellow-brothers and servants of Allah. [Muslim]

**Hadith**: Abu Huraira (ra) reported Allah's Messenger (ﷺ) as saying: Don't nurse grudge and don't bid him out for raising the price and don't nurse aversion or enmity and don't enter into a transaction when the others have entered into that transaction and be as fellow-brothers and servants of Allah. A Muslim is the brother of a Muslim. He neither oppresses him nor humiliates him nor looks down upon him. The piety is here, (and while saying so) he pointed towards his chest thrice. It is a serious evil for a Muslim that he should look down upon his brother Muslim. All things of a Muslim are inviolable for his brother in faith: his blood, his wealth and his honour. [Muslim]

**Hadith**: Salim reported on the authority of his father that Allah's Messenger (ﷺ) said: A Muslim is the brother of a fellow-Muslim. He should neither commit oppression upon him nor ruin him, and he who meets the need of a brother, Allah would meet big needs, and he who relieved a Muslim from hardship Allah would relieve him from the hardships to which he would be put on the Day of Resurrection, and he who did not expose (the follies of a Muslim) Allah would conceal his follies on the Day of Resurrection. [Muslim]

## 2.28 Mujaddid (Revivalist)

A *Mujaddid* is someone who appears at the beginning of every Islamic century to revive the faith, remove innovations, and restore Islam to its original purity. This individual may be a caliph, a renowned teacher, a scholar, or another influential figure—or even a group of people. The concept of Mujaddid is based on the hadith: Abu Hurairah (ra) narrated that the Prophet (ﷺ) said, "Allah shall raise for this Ummah at the head of every century a man who shall renew (or revive) for it its religion." [Sunan Abu Dawud, Bayhaqi]

Narrated Abu Hurairah (ra): Allah's Apostle (ﷺ) said, "There will always be in my nation a group who will safeguard the truth until the day of resurrection comes." [Mustadrak al-Hakim]

Notable figures often regarded as Mujaddids include ʿUmar ibn ʿAbd al-ʿAziz (d. 720 CE), known for his just rule; Imam ash-Shafiʿi (d. 820 CE), and Imam al-Ḥakim al-Nishapuri (d. 1014 CE). The concept of the *Mujaddid*—a reviver of Islam at the turn of every century—is based on Prophetic tradition but remains interpretive, not doctrinal. Scholars and sects may differ in identifying Mujaddids, often influenced by theological or political contexts. While many individuals have been claimed or have claimed to be Mujaddids, such assertions are not always credible and have, at times, been misused for personal or political gain.

Many scholars also consider **Imam al-Mahdi** a future *mujaddid* in the most complete sense. His role, however, is exceptional. He will restore justice, eliminate corruption, and prepare the world for the return of ʿIsa (as). Though not a prophet, his emergence marks the culmination of Islamic history and transcends the regular pattern of century-based revival. His mission is eschatological (end-times), not part of the ongoing sequence of scholarly Mujaddids.

The Prophet Muhammad (ﷺ) said: "If there were only one day left of this world, Allah would extend it until He sends a man from me or from my family—his name will be like mine and his father's name like my father's—he will fill the earth with fairness and justice as it was filled with oppression and injustice." [Musnad Ahmad]

In conclusion, it can be said that introducing innovations into the religion is a major sin, as the Qur'an and Hadith contain stern warnings of severe punishment regarding this matter. Although some people take this issue lightly due to their personal inclinations or sectarian identity, many Islamic scholars have regarded Bid'ah as far more serious than major sins. This is because a person who engages in Bid'ah indirectly questions the completeness and perfection of the Prophethood of the Messenger of Allah (ﷺ)—which clearly contradicts the core principles of Islam and indicates a form of disbelief in Prophethood. Therefore, being aware of Bid'ah and completely avoiding it is essential for every Muslim. Recognizing and rejecting Bid'ah is not about rigidity, but about loyalty to the divine guidance that ensures the unity and integrity of the ummah and safeguards the path to salvation.

# Chapter 3

# Knowledge of Unseen

Knowledge is commonly defined as the information and understanding that an individual or society holds about a particular subject. In the Islamic worldview, all knowledge originates from Allah SWT, the All-Knowing. Human beings acquire knowledge through two primary means:

1. Divine Revelation (*Wahi*), which was granted to the Prophets to guide humanity in matters of faith, morality, and ultimate purpose.

2. Human Endeavour, which includes the observation of the natural world, logical reasoning, and experimentation.

Thus, whether through revealed guidance or intellectual inquiry, all true knowledge leads to the recognition of the Creator and the fulfillment of human purpose. Allah SWT says (interpretation of meaning):

*"and you 'O humanity' have been given but little knowledge." (Al-Isra Ch 17:85)*

In Islam, *al-Ghaib* refers to matters that lie beyond human perception or understanding. *Ilm al-Ghaib*—knowledge of the unseen—encompasses things that are entirely unknown and inaccessible to us, but fully known to Allah, the All-Knowing. The Qur'an contains over 50 verses that emphasize Allah's exclusive knowledge of the unseen, reinforcing that only He has complete awareness of what is hidden. Allah SWT says (interpretation of the meaning):

*With Him are the keys of the unseen—no one knows them except Him. And He knows what is in the land and sea. Not even a leaf falls without His knowledge, nor a grain in the darkness of the earth or anything—green or dry—but is 'written' in a perfect Record. (Al-An'am Ch 6:59)*

Belief in the unseen is one of the requirements of faith out of other requirements mentioned in the Qur'an. Allah says (interpretation of meaning):

*"who believe in the unseen, establish prayer, and donate from what We have provided for them, and who believe in what has been revealed to you and what has been revealed before you; and they have faith in the Hereafter." (Al-Baqarah Ch 2:3-4)*

The companions believed the Prophet's (ﷺ) words blindly without any hesitation. Aisha (ra) reported: After the Prophet (ﷺ) was miraculously taken by night to the furthest mosque in Jerusalem, the people began to talk about it. Some of them renounced their faith and belief in him. They sought Abu Bakr (ra) and they said, "Have you heard that your friend imagined he was taken by night to the sacred house?" Abu Bakr (ra) said, "Did he (ﷺ) say that?" They said, "Yes." Abu Bakr (ra) said, "If he (ﷺ) said it, he (ﷺ) has spoken the truth." They said, "Do you believe he (ﷺ) went by night to the sacred house and returned before morning?" Abu Bakr (ra) said, "Yes. Verily, I believe what is even more astonishing than that. I believe he (ﷺ) has received messages from heaven for everything he (ﷺ) does." For this reason, Abu Bakr (ra) was named the Truthful, al-Siddiq. [Dala'il al-Nubuwwwah lil-Bayhaqi]

The Holy book spoke a great deal about unseen matters such as Lordship of Allah SWT, His attributes and actions, the seven heavens and what they contain, the angels, jinns, souls, other prophets, Paradise and Hell etc and the companions believed and we also believe.

## 3.1 Ilm al-Gaib of the Prophet (ﷺ)

Allah SWT says in the Qur'an (interpretation of the meaning):

*Say, "I am not the first messenger ever sent, nor do I know what will happen to me or you. I only follow what is revealed to me. And I am only sent with a clear warning." (Al Ahqaf Ch 46:9)*

*He is the ' Knower of the unseen, disclosing none of it to anyone, except a messenger whom He chooses (to inform through revelation), and then He appoints (angels as) watching guards before him and behind him, (so that devils may not tamper with the divine revelation,) (Al- Jinn Ch 72:26-27)*

*Say, "I have no power to benefit or protect myself, except by the Will of Allah. If I had known the unknown, I would have benefited myself enormously, and no harm would have ever touched me. I am only a warner and deliverer of good news for those who believe." (Al A'raf Ch 7: 188)*

The Qur'an clearly affirms that complete knowledge of the unseen (*al-Ghaib*) belongs solely to Allah (SWT), whose knowledge is absolute and all-encompassing. However, Allah may choose to reveal portions of this knowledge to certain messengers, according to His will. The Prophet Muhammad (ﷺ) was granted such revealed knowledge. Numerous hadiths confirm that he (ﷺ) was informed about various matters—including the story of creation, the lives of previous prophets and their nations, and future events such as the signs of the Hour, the emergence of the Dajjal, the return of 'Eesa (as), and the coming of Imam Mahdi. He (ﷺ) was also given vivid knowledge of the Hereafter: Doomsday, the life in the grave, resurrection, Judgment Day, Paradise, Hell, and more.

However, the Prophet's (ﷺ) knowledge of the unseen was not absolute— it was limited to what Allah had chosen to reveal to him. For example, he (ﷺ) did not know the exact time of Qiyamah. Allah's knowledge is absolute and boundless, while the Prophet's (ﷺ) knowledge of the unseen was a divine gift. Below are a few selected hadiths from among the many that highlight this.

### i. The Prophet (ﷺ) had the knowledge of unseen

**Hadith**: Narrated Huzaifa (ra): Prophet Muhammad (ﷺ) stood up in one meeting and he started to tell us about events from the beginning of this world to the end and he told us about Heaven and Hell and about the people who were going to Hell and who were going to Heaven and what will be their places in Heaven and Hell. Of course, some people remember what he told us and some people have forgotten. [Bukhari]

**Hadith**: The Prophet (ﷺ) stated, "Allah put the earth before me and I saw it from the East to the West." [Muslim]

**Hadith**: The Prophet (ﷺ) stood on the pulpit and said, "Ask me what you will." One person stood up and asked, "What will be my place in the Hereafter?" The Prophet (ﷺ) replied, "Hell." Another person, whose name was 'Abdullah ibn Huzaifa (people doubted whether he was a legitimate child), stood up and asked, "Who is my father?" The Prophet (ﷺ) replied, "Your father is Huzaifa." [The accusation on 'Abdullah ibn Huzaifa (ra) was cleared]. The Prophet (ﷺ) repeated, "Ask me, ask me." [Bukhari]

**Hadith**: Aisha (ra) narrated: The Prophet (ﷺ) in his fatal illness, called his daughter Fatima (ra) and told her a secret because of which she started weeping. Then he (ﷺ) called her and told her another secret, and she started laughing. When I asked her about that, she replied, "The Prophet (ﷺ) told me that he (ﷺ) would die in his fatal illness, and so I wept, but then he (ﷺ) secretly told me that from amongst his family, I would be the first of the family of his house to join him, and so I laughed." [Bukhari]

**Hadith**: Narrated Jabir bin Abdullah (ra): On the day of the battle of Uhud, a man came to the Prophet (ﷺ) and said, "Can you tell me where I will be if I should get martyred?" The Prophet (ﷺ) replied, "In Paradise." The man threw away some dates he was carrying in his hand, and fought till he was martyred. [Bukhari]

**Hadith**: Narrated 'Ikrima: that Ibn 'Abbas (ra) told him and 'Ali bin 'Abdullah to go to Abu Sa'id (ra) and listen to some of his narrations; So they both went (and saw) Abu Sa'id (ra) and his brother irrigating a garden belonging to them. When he saw them, he came up to them and sat down with his legs drawn up and wrapped in his garment and said, "(During the construction of the mosque of the Prophet ﷺ) we carried the adobe of the mosque, one brick at a time while 'Ammar (ra) used to carry two at a time. The Prophet (ﷺ) passed by 'Ammar (ra) and removed the dust off his head and said, "May Allah be merciful to 'Ammar (ra). He will be killed by a rebellious aggressive group. 'Ammar (ra) will invite them to (obey) Allah and they will invite him to the (Hell) fire." [Bukhari]

**Note**: Ammar ibn Yasir (ra) was martyred during the **Battle of Ṣiffin**, fighting on the side of Khalifa Ali ibn Abi Ṭalib (ra).

**Hadith**: Abdullah bin Najjay, son of Abdullah narrated from his father who would carry vessels of wudu of Ali (ra), when he reached Neenawa on his way to Siffin, he called out, "O Abdullah (surname of Hussain ra)! Be Patient on the banks of the Euphrates! Be Patient on the banks of the Euphrates!" I said: "What happened O Chief of Believers?" Ali (ra) said: I entered upon the Prophet (ﷺ) one day and his eyes were flowing with tears. I said: "Has someone upset you? Why are your eyes flowing with tears?" Messenger of Allah (ﷺ) said: "No. But Jibril left me a while ago and he gave me this news that Hussain (ra) would be killed on the banks of the Euphrates. Then he (Jibril) asked: Would you see the dust of the place where Hussain (ra) will fall? I said: Yes, show me. He gave a handful of dust and I could not but weep." [Musnad Ahmad]

**Hadith**: Narrated Said Al-Umawi: I was with Marwan and Abu Huraira (ra) and heard Abu Huraira (ra) saying: I heard the trustworthy, truly inspired one (i.e. the Prophet ﷺ) saying, "The destruction of my followers will be brought about by the hands of some youngsters from Quraish." Marwan asked, "Youngsters?" Abu Huraira (ra) said, "If you wish, I would name them: They are the children of so-and-so and the children of so-and-so." [Bukhari]

**Hadith**: It was narrated that Anas (ra) said: We were with Umar (ra) between Makkah and Madinah, and we looked for the new crescent moon. I was sharp sighted and I saw it, and I started saying to Umar (ra), don't you see it? He said: I will see it when I am lying in my bed. Then he started telling us about the people of Badr. He said: The Messenger of Allah (ﷺ) was showing us the places where they would fall (in battle), saying: "This is where so and so will fall in battle tomorrow, if Allah Wills; this is where so and so will fall in battle tomorrow, if Allah Wills." And they started to fall in those places, I said: By the One who sent you with the truth, they did not miss those places; they fell in those places. Then he ordered that they be thrown into a well, and he went to them and said: `O so and so, O so and so, did you find what Allah promised you to be true? For I found what Allah promised me to be true. 'Umar (ra) said: "O Messenger of Allah (ﷺ), are you speaking to people who are now dead?" He (ﷺ) said: "You do not hear what I am saying any better than they do, but they cannot answer." [Muslim]

**Hadith**: It was narrated from Abdullah Ibn 'Umar (ra) that the Messenger of Allah (ﷺ) said: This is the one at whose death the Throne shook, the gates of Heaven were opened of him and seventy thousand angles attended his funeral. It squeezed him once then released him." [Sunan an-Nasai]

**Note**: The particular Companion was Sa'd bin Mu'aj (ra) whose judgment regarding the Banu Qurayẓah was accepted by Allah SWT. The incident happened **after the Battle of the Trench (Khandaq)**.

**Hadith**: Narrated Abu Huraira (ra): We were in the company of Allah's Messenger (ﷺ) that we heard a terrible sound. Thereupon Allah's Apostle (ﷺ) said: Do you know what (sound) is this? We said: Allah and His Messenger (ﷺ) know the best. Thereupon he (ﷺ) said: That is a stone which was thrown seventy years before in Hell and it has been constantly slipping down and aired in Hell now it has reached its base. [Muslim]

**Hadith**: Narrated Anas bin Malik (ra): The Prophet (ﷺ) ascended the mountain of Uhud and he (ﷺ) was accompanied by Abu Bakr (ra), `Umar (ra) and `Usman (ra). The mountain shook beneath them. The Prophet (ﷺ) hit it with his foot and said, "O Uhud! Be firm, for on you there is none but a Prophet (ﷺ), a Siddiq and two martyrs." [Bukhari]

**Hadith**: Abu Bakrah (ra) reported: The Messenger of Allah, (ﷺ) said, **"This grandson of mine is a master. Perhaps Allah will reconcile two groups of Muslims through him."** [Bukhari]

**Note:** After 'Ali (ra) was martyred, the Muslims swore allegiance to his son Al-Hassan (ra), who afterwards gave up the caliphate to Muawiyah (ra) in order to unite the Muslims behind one ruler, sparing them bloodshed and disunity.

**Hadith:** Narrated Anas (ra): The Prophet (ﷺ) had informed the people of the martyrdom of Zaid (ra), Ja`far (ra) and Ibn Rawaha (ra) before the news of their death reached. The Prophet (ﷺ) said, "Zaid (ra) took the flag (as the commander of the army) and was martyred, then Ja`far (ra) took it and was martyred, and then Ibn Rawaha (ra) took it and was martyred." At that time the Prophet's (ﷺ) eyes were shedding tears. He (ﷺ) added, "Then the flag was taken by a Sword amongst the Swords of Allah (i.e. Khalid) and Allah made them (i.e. the Muslims) victorious." [Bukhari]

**Note:** The above incident refers to the Battle of Mutah that was fought in 8th year of Hijri, near the village of Mutah (currently located near the city of Karak in Jordan), between Muslims and the army of Byzantine Empire (Roman Empire).

**Hadith**: Narrated `Urwa: When those (Muslims) at Bir Ma'una were martyred and `Amr bin Umaiya Ad- Damri (ra) was taken prisoner, 'Amir bin at-Tufail, pointing at a killed person, asked `Amr, "Who is this?" `Amr bin Umaiya (ra) said to him, "He is 'Amir bin Fuhaira (ra)." 'Amir bin at-Tufail said, "I saw him lifted to the sky after he was killed till I saw the sky between him and the earth, and then he was brought down upon the earth. Then the news of the killed Muslims reached the Prophet (ﷺ) and he (ﷺ) announced the news of their death saying, "Your companions (of Bir Ma'una) have been killed, and they have asked their Lord saying, *'O our Lord! Inform our brothers about us as we are pleased with You and You are pleased with us.*" So Allah informed them (i.e. the Prophet (ﷺ) and his companions) about them (i.e. martyrs of Bir Mauna). On that day, `Urwa bin Asma bin As-Salt who was one of them, was killed, and `Urwa (bin Az- Zubair) was named after `Urwa bin Asma and Munjir (bin Az-Zubair) was named after Munjir bin `Amr (who had also been martyred on that day). [Bukhari]

**Note:** The Massacre of Bi'r Ma'una is a significant event in early Islamic history, where seventy of the Prophet's (ﷺ) companions, known for their deep knowledge and memorization of the Qur᾽an, were martyred. These companions were referred to as "Qurra" (reciters), indicating their status as Hafiz of the Qur'an.

### iii. Cases Allah SWT did not inform the Prophet (ﷺ)

**Hadith**: Narrated Ibn `Umar (ra): The Prophet (ﷺ) said, "The keys of the unseen are five and none knows them but Allah:

1. None knows (the sex) what is in the womb, but Allah:

2. None knows what will happen tomorrow, but Allah;

3. None knows when it will rain, but Allah;

4. None knows where he will die, but Allah (knows that);

5. None knows when the Hour will be established, but Allah." [Bukhari]

**Hadith**: Narrated Abu Huraira (ra): A black man or a black woman used to sweep the mosque and she died. The Prophet (ﷺ) asked about her. He was told that she had died. He said, "Why did you not inform me? Show me her grave." So, he (ﷺ) went to her grave and offered her funeral prayer." [Bukhari]

**Note**: The woman's death was not known to him (ﷺ).

**Hadith**: Narrated Ibn Abbas (ra): A person died and Allah's Messenger (ﷺ) used to visit him. He died at night and (the people) buried him at night. In the morning they informed the Prophet ﷺ (about his death). He (ﷺ) said, "What prevented you from informing me?" They replied, "It was night and it was a dark night and so we disliked to trouble you." The Prophet (ﷺ) went to his grave and offered the (funeral) prayer. [Bukhari]

**Hadith**: Narrated Um Salama (ra): The Prophet (ﷺ) said, "I am only a human being, and you people have disputes. May be someone amongst you can present his case in a more eloquent and convincing manner than the other, and I give my judgment in his favour according to what I hear. Beware! If ever I give (by error) somebody something of his brother's right then he should not take it as I have only, given him a piece of Fire." [Bukhari]

**Note**: Prophet (ﷺ) sometimes used to judge as he (ﷺ) used to hear the witness.

### iii. Ilmul gaib of other Prophets

As mentioned earlier, all Prophets had ilmul gaib as much as Allah Willed. Stories of other Prophets reported in the Qur'an establish that ilmul gaib of other Prophets were not absolute.

### Prophet Musa (as)

*"Now, throw down your staff!" But when he saw it slithering like a snake, he ran away without looking back. Allah reassured him, "O Musa! Do not be afraid! Messengers should have no fear in My presence. (An-Naml Ch 27: 10)*

Prophet Musa (as) did not know that a staff would become a snake. In fact, he (as) was afraid and ran away.

*We divided them into twelve tribes—each as a community. And We revealed to Moses, when his people asked for water, "Strike the rock with your staff." Then twelve springs gushed out. Each tribe knew its drinking place. We shaded them with clouds and sent down to them manna and quails, 'saying', "Eat from the good things We have provided for you."*

*They 'certainly' did not wrong Us, but wronged themselves. (Al A'raf Ch 7:160)*

*So We inspired Musa: "Strike the sea with your staff," and the sea was split, each part was like a huge mountain. (Ash Shu'arah Ch 26:63)*

Prophet Musa (as) knew that the staff could become a snake and it was one of his Mu'jizas. He did not know that the staff would disintegrate a rock to form springs. Allah had to send revelation.

Ch 26:63 is the story when Fir'awn and his people caught up with Musa (as) and children of Israel on the shores of the Red Sea, so the sea was ahead of them and Fir'awn and his troops were behind them. Hence, they said, "We are sure to be overtaken." Then Fir'awn and his troops drew near and were very close indeed. At that point Allah commanded Prophet Musa (as) to strike the sea with his staff, so he struck it, and it parted, by the will of Allah. Prophet Musa (as) did not know that the staff would be used for splitting the sea.

**Prophet Sulaiman (as)**

*And (when) he (Nabi Sulaiman) inspected the birds, he exclaimed: 'Why do I not see Hud-Hud, or is he among the absentees? Either he brings to me a valid proof (explanation) or I shall most certainly give him a severe punishment or slaughter him. The Hud-Hud stayed away for just a short time. (Upon his return) he said: 'I have discovered what you have not discovered and I come to you from (the land of) Saba' with reliable information. Verily, I found a woman ruling over people. She has been given everything (of worldly wealth) and she has a wonderful throne. I have found her and her people prostrating to the sun besides Allah.*

*Shaitan has adorned for them their deeds and has prevented them from the Path of Allah, hence they do not derive guidance.* " (An- Namal, Ch ٢٤ – ٢٠ :٢٧)

These are the Qur'anic verses commencing the story of Prophet Sulaiman (as) and Queen of Yemen at that time. After his father's death, Sulaiman (as) became emperor. He begged Allah for a kingdom such as none after him would have, and Allah granted his wish. Besides wisdom, Allah had blessed Sulaiman (as) with many abilities. He could command the winds and understand and talk to birds and animals. Allah directed him to teach both men and jinns to mine the earth and extract its minerals to make tools and weapons. Prophet Sulaiman (as) did not know the existence of the empire of the Queen of Yemen (Saba).

## 3.2 Does the Prophet (ﷺ) know about the happenings on earth after his death?

There is a strong belief among a large group of Ummah that *"those who visit the Prophet (ﷺ) should believe that he (ﷺ) is alive and they are present before him because there is no difference between his life and demise in that he (ﷺ) sees the Ummah and knows their states, intentions and thoughts. All of this is apparent to him and none of it is hidden."* The examination and cross-examination of the above belief are presented here—not to defame or triumph over others, but to accept the truth wherever it is found. The objective is sincere inquiry and adherence to what is correct. The following aḥadith, though already discussed from the perspective of *bid'ah* in Chapter 1, may now be revisited from a different angle for further reflection.

## i. Evidence in hadiths

**Hadith**: Narrated Ibn `Abbas (ra): Allah's Messenger (ﷺ) said, "You will be resurrected (and assembled) bare-footed, naked and uncircumcised." The Prophet (ﷺ) then recited the Divine Verse (that means): "*As We began the first creation, We shall repeat it: A promise We have undertaken. Truly we shall do it.*" (Ch 21:104) He (ﷺ) added, "The first to be dressed will be Ibrahim (as). Then some of my companions will take to the right and to the left. I will say: 'أَصْحَابِي My **companions**! 'It will be said, 'They had been renegaded since you left them.' I will then say what the Pious Slave Issa (as), the son of Mary said: 'And I was a witness over them while I dwelt amongst them; when You did take me up, You were the Watcher over them, and You are a Witness to all things. If You punish them, they are Your slaves, and if you forgive them, You, only You are the All-Mighty the All-Wise.' (Ch 5:117-118) Narrated Quaggas, "Those were the apostates who renegaded from Islam during the Caliphate of Abu Bakr (ra) who fought them." [Bukhari]

**Hadith**: It was narrated that Abu Hurairah (ra) said: The Messenger of Allah (ﷺ) said: 'My **Ummah** will come to me at the Cistern *(Hawd)*, and I will be driving the people away from it as a man drives another man's camels away from his own camels." They said: "O Prophet of Allah (ﷺ), will you recognize us?" He (ﷺ) said: "Yes. You will have a feature that no one else will have. You will come to me with glimmering faces and limbs because of the traces of w*udu*. But a group of you will be prevented from reaching me. I will say: 'O Lord, these are from among my followers.' An angel will reply and say to me: 'Do you know what they innovated after you were gone?' [Muslim]

**Hadith**: Narrated Asma (ra): The Prophet (ﷺ) said: I will be at my Lake-Fount (Kausar) waiting for whoever will come to me. Then some people will be taken away from me whereupon I will say, 'أُمَّتِي (**my followers**)!' It will be said, 'You do not know they turned Apostates as renegades (deserted their religion).' (Ibn Abi Mulaika said, "Allah, we seek refuge with You from turning on our heels from the (Islamic) religion and from being put to trial"). [Bukhari]

The above hadiths are descriptions about the difficult days of people after resurrection during al-Mahshar. People will run towards the Hawd to quench their thirst. Narrated `Abdullah (ra): The Prophet (ﷺ) said: I am your predecessor at the Lake-Fount (Kausar) and some men amongst you will be brought to me, and when I will try to hand them some water, they will be pulled away from me by force whereupon I will say, 'O Lord, my companions!' Then the **Almighty will say**, *"You do not know what they did after you left*, they introduced new things into the religion after you." [Bukhari]

The people who will be driven away include some Companions of the Prophet (ﷺ). The Prophet (ﷺ) will not recognise those who renegaded just after his death. Similarly, the Prophet (ﷺ) will not identify innovators of later generation among his followers. Thus, *all generations* of his followers are covered in the hadiths and infomations about their activities will be missing to him on the Day of Judgement. It is only salaam and durood which are sent to him, and details are discussed in **Section 2.8** 'Seeing the Prophet (ﷺ) when awake.'

## ii. Evidence in the Qur'an

The proof that the prophets are not given the information about their nations after their death can be interpreted from the Qur'an. Specifically, Allah mentions how He will ask Issa Ibn Maryam (as) about the Shirk activities of his followers on the Day of Judgement. Allah SWT says (interpretation of meaning):

*And 'on Judgment Day' Allah will say, "O Issa, son of Maryam! Did you ever ask the people to worship you and your mother as gods besides Allah?" (Al Ma'idah Ch 5:116)*

At the same time, Allah SWT tells us how Issa Ibn Maryam (as) will respond to His question in next verses 116-117 of Ch 5. All Prophets are free from sins. Their answers on the Day of Judgement are known to Allah SWT. Allah SWT says (interpretation of meaning):

*He will answer, "Glory be to You! How could I ever say what I had no right to say? If I had said such a thing, you would have certainly known it. You know what is 'hidden' within me, but I do not know what is within You. Indeed, You 'alone' are the Knower of all unseen. (Al-Ma'idah Ch 5:116)*

*I never told them anything except what You ordered me to say: "Worship Allah—my Lord and your Lord!" And I was witness over them as long as I remained among them. But when You took me, You were the Witness over them—and You are a Witness over all things. (Al Ma'idah Ch 5:117)*

Ibn Kasir writes in his Tafseer: "In fact, the purpose is to admonish his people who call them Christians that the one they are taking to be god is himself confessing to his servitude quite contrary to the belief they hold - and that he is free of all their accusations."

"On the day of Qiyamah, the prophets and their communities will be summoned. Then, Sayyidna Isa (عليه السلام) will be called. Then, Allah Ta' ala will remind him of His blessings and drawing him closer, He will say, 'O Isa son of Maryam: اذْكُرْ نِعْمَتِي عَلَيْكَ وَعَلَىٰ وَالِدَتِكَ Remember My blessing upon you and upon your mother.' Then, in the end, He would say: يَا عِيسَى ابْنَ مَرْيَمَ أَأَنتَ قُلْتَ لِلنَّاسِ اتَّخِذُونِي وَأُمِّيَ إِلَـٰهَيْنِ مِن دُونِ اللَّـهِ) (O Isa son of Maryam, did you say to the people: Take me and my mother as gods beside Allah?). Sayyidna Isa (عليه السلام) will deny it saying that he did not. Then, the question will be asked from the Christians. They will say: Yes, this is what he had ordered us to do. After that, they will be driven towards Hell."

In addition to the interpretation provided by Tafsir Ibn Kasir, another understanding of the verse **(Qur'an 5:117)** — *"And I was a witness over them as long as I remained among them. But when You took me, You were the Witness over them"* — is that Prophet 'Isa (peace be upon him) no longer bears witness to the actions of the Christians after Allah (SWT) raised him to the heavens. This suggests that he is not aware of the widespread acts of Shirk committed by them. Consequently, it becomes difficult to establish that other Prophets who have passed away are receiving knowledge of the actions of their respective nations after their deaths.

## 3.3 Companions had no knowledge of unseen

There is no evidence that companions possessed independent knowledge of the unseen. The present section illustrates that the companions did not acquire such knowledge on their own.

**Hadith**: Qays narrated that when Ummul Mu'minin Aisha (ra) reached Banu Amir's water with her army, dogs started barking there. She asked, "What is the name of this water?" They said, "The water of Hawab." Hearing this, she replied, "Then I must go back." Someone of her companions advised on this decision, "No, but we should continue going. Maybe when Muslims will see you, Allah will make peace between them." Aisha (ra) said, "Allah's Messenger (ﷺ) once said to me: How will be the situation of one (wife) of you when the dogs of Hawab will bark at her." [Musnad Ahmad]

**Note**: The incident refers to Battle of Jamal. The Prophet (ﷺ) said it to Aisha (ra) but she did not know the 'one wife' was herself.

**Hadith**: Narrated Hisham's father: Aisha (ra) said, "I went to Abu Bakr (ra) (during his fatal illness) and he asked me: In how many garments was the Prophet (ﷺ) shrouded? She replied: 'In three Suhuliya pieces of white cloth of cotton, and there was neither a shirt nor a turban among them.' Abu Bakr (ra) further asked her, 'On which day did the Prophet (ﷺ) die?' She replied, 'He (ﷺ) died on Monday.' He asked, 'What is today?' She replied, 'Today is Monday.' He added, 'I hope I shall die sometime between this morning and tonight.' Then he looked at a garment that he was wearing during his illness and it had some stains of saffron. Then he said, 'Wash this garment of mine and add two more garments and shroud me in them.' I said, 'This is worn out.' He said, 'A living person has more right to wear new clothes than a dead one; the shroud is only for the body's pus.' He did not die till it was the night of Tuesday and was buried before the morning." [Bukhari]

**Note**: Abu Bakr (ra) was the most virtuous person among all the companions and were among the 'Ashra Mubashara' (the ten who were promised Paradise). His guess did not come true.

**Hadith:** Narrated Kharija bin Zaid bin Sabit: Um Al-`Ala, an Ansari woman who had given a pledge of allegiance to Allah's Messenger (ﷺ) told me: "The Muhajirin (emigrants) were distributed amongst us by drawing lots, and we got `Usman bin Maz'un in our share. We made him stay with us in our house. Then he suffered from a disease which proved fatal. When he died, he was given a bath and was shrouded in his clothes. Allah's Messenger (ﷺ) came and I said, (addressing the dead body), 'O Aba As-Sa'ib! May Allah be Merciful to you! I testify that Allah has honoured you.' Allah's Messenger (ﷺ) said, 'How do you know that Allah has honoured him?" I replied, 'Let my father be sacrificed for you, O Allah's Messenger (ﷺ)! On whom else shall Allah bestow His honour?' Allah's Messenger (ﷺ) said, 'As for him, by Allah, death has come to him. By Allah, I wish him all good (from Allah). By Allah, in spite of the fact that I am Allah's Messenger (ﷺ), I do not know what Allah will do to me.", Um Al-`Ala added, "By Allah, I will never attest the righteousness of anybody after that." [Bukhari]

**Note**: Prophet (ﷺ) did not allow attestation of righteousness of a Companion by Um Al- 'Ala (ra).

**Hadith:** Narrated Sa'id bin Al-Musaiyab: 'Umar (ra) came to the Mosque while Hassan (a companion other than Prophet's (ﷺ) grandson) was reciting a poem. ('Umar (ra) disapproved of that). On that Hassan ibn Sabit (ra) said, "I used to recite poetry in this very Mosque in the presence of one (i.e. the Prophet ﷺ) who was better than you." Then he (Umar ra) turned towards Abu Huraira (ra) and said (to him), "I ask you by Allah, did you hear Allah's Messenger (ﷺ) saying (to me), "Retort on my behalf. O Allah! Support him (i.e. Hassan) with the Holy Spirit?" Abu Huraira said, "Yes." [Bukhari]

**Note**: Umar ibn Khattab (ra) did not know that Hassan (ra) recited poem in the Mosque in presence of the Prophet (ﷺ).

**Hadith:** Abd Sa'id Khudri (ra) reported: We were in the company of Ubayy bin Ka'b that Abu Musa Ash'ari came there in a state of anger. He stood (before us) and said: I ask you to bear witness in the name of Allah whether anyone amongst you heard Allah's Messenger (ﷺ) as saying: Permission (for entering the house) should be sought three times and if permission is granted to you (then get in) otherwise go back. Ubayy b. Ka'b (ra) said: What is the matter? He said: I sought permission yesterday from 'Umar b. Khattab (ra) three times but he did not permit me, so I came back; then I went to him today and visited him and informed him that I had come to him yesterday and greeted him thrice, then came back, whereupon he said: Yes, we did hear you but be were at that time busy, but why did you not seek permission (further and you must have never gone back until you were permitted to do so). He said: I sought permission (in the manner) that I heard Allah's Messenger (ﷺ) having said (in connection 'With the seeking of permission for entering the house of a stranger). Thereupon he (Umar) said: By Allah, I shall torture your back and your stomach unless you bring one who may bear witness to what you state. 'Ubayy b. Ka'b (ra) said: By Allah, none should stand with you (to bear testimony) but the youngest amongst us. And he therefore, said to Abu Sa'id (ra): Stand up. So, I stood up until I came to Umar (ra) and said: "I heard Allah's Messenger (ﷺ) say this." [Muslim]

**Note**: Umar (ra) was not aware of matters related to permission for entering others' house.

**Hadith:** It was narrated that Ibn 'Abbas (ra) said: "The Messenger of Allah (ﷺ) passed by two graves, and he (ﷺ) said: "They are being punished, but they are not being punished for anything grave (i.e., it was not difficult to avoid). One of them used to walk around spreading malicious gossip, and the other did not protect himself from his urine." He (ﷺ) called for a palm branch, split it in two, then planted one piece on one grave and the other on the other grave. Then he (ﷺ) said: "Perhaps it (the punishment) will be reduced for them so long as this does not dry out." [Bukhari, Muslim, Sunan an-Nasai]

**Note**: Companions of the Prophet (ﷺ) could not see or hear the punishment in the grave but the Prophet (ﷺ) could.

**Hadith:** Narrated Sahl bin Sa`d As Saidi (ra): Allah's Messenger (ﷺ) (and his army) encountered the pagans and the two armies, fought and then Allah's Apostle (ﷺ) returned to his army camps and the others (i.e. the enemy) returned to their army camps. Amongst the companions of the Prophet (ﷺ), there was a man who could not help pursuing any single isolated pagan to strike him with his sword. Somebody said, "None has benefited the Muslims today more than so-and-so." On that Allah's

Messenger (ﷺ) said, "He is from the people of the Hell-Fire certainly." A man amongst the people (i.e. Muslims) said, "I will accompany him (to know the fact)." So he went along with him, and whenever he stopped he stopped with him, and whenever he hastened, he hastened with him. The (brave) man then got wounded severely, and seeking to die at once, he planted his sword into the ground and put its point against his chest in between his breasts, and then threw himself on it and committed suicide. On that the person (who was accompanying the deceased all the time) came to Allah's Messenger (ﷺ) and said, "I testify that you are the Messenger of Allah." The Prophet (ﷺ) said, "Why is that (what makes you say so)?" He said "It is concerning the man whom you have already mentioned as one of the dwellers of the Hell-Fire. The people were surprised by your statement, and I said to them, "I will try to find out the truth about him for you." So I went out after him and he was then inflicted with a severe wound and because of that, he hurried to bring death upon himself by planting the handle of his sword into the ground and directing its tip towards his chest between his breasts, and then he threw himself over it and committed suicide." Allah's Messenger (ﷺ) then said, "A man may do what seem to the people as the deeds of the dwellers of Paradise but he is from the dwellers of the Hell-Fire and another may do what seem to the people as the deeds of the dwellers of the Hell- Fire, but he is from the dwellers of Paradise." [Bukhari]

**Note**: This incident happened during Battle of Khaibar. Allah's Apostle (ﷺ) knew in advance by the will of Allah whereas the companions did not know about the particular warrior.

**Hadith**: Narrated Salim's father: The Prophet (ﷺ) sent Khalid bin Al-Walid (ra) to the tribe of Jazima and Khalid (ra) invited them to Islam but they could not express themselves by saying, "Aslamna أَسْلَمْنَا (i.e. we have embraced Islam)," but they started saying "Saba'na! Saba'na صَبَأْنَا، صَبَأْنَا (i.e. we have come out of one religion to another)." Khalid (ra) kept on killing (some of) them and taking (some of) them as captives and gave every one of us his Captive. When there came the day then Khalid (ra) ordered that each man (i.e. Muslim soldier) should kill his captive, I said, "By Allah, I will not kill my captive, and none of my companions will kill his captive." When we reached the Prophet (ﷺ), we mentioned to him the whole story. On that, the Prophet (ﷺ) raised both his hands and said twice, "O Allah! I am free from what Khalid has done." [Bukhari]

**Note**: Khalid bin Walid (ra) did not know that they were already Muslims nor he could read their mind that by 'Saba'na' they meant 'Aslama'.

**Hadith**: Narrated Jabir ibn Abdullah: Ibn Shihab said: Jabir ibn Abdullah (ra) used to say that a Jewess from the inhabitants of Khaibar poisoned a roasted sheep and presented it to the Apostle of Allah (ﷺ) who took its foreleg and ate from it. A group of his companions also ate with him. The Apostle of Allah (ﷺ) then said: Take your hands away (from the food). The Apostle of Allah (ﷺ) then sent someone to the Jewess and he called her. He (ﷺ) said to her: Have you poisoned this sheep? The Jewess replied: Who has informed you? He (ﷺ) said: This foreleg which I have in my hand has informed me. She said: Yes. He (ﷺ) said: What did you intend by it? She said: I thought if you were a prophet, it would not harm you; if you were not a prophet, we should rid ourselves of him (i.e. the Prophet ﷺ). The Apostle of Allah (ﷺ) then forgave her, and did not punish her. But some of his companions who ate it, died. The Apostle of Allah (ﷺ) had himself cupped on his shoulder on account of that which he had eaten from the sheep. Abu Hind cupped him with the horn and knife. He was a client of Banu Bayadah from the Ansar. [Sunan Abu Dawud]

**Note**: The Companions died because they did not know that meat was poisoned.

**Hadith:** It was narrated that Abu Hurairah (ra) said: We were with the Messenger of Allah (ﷺ) in the year of Khaibar, and we did not get any spoils of war except for wealth, goods and clothes. Then a man from Banu Ad-Dubaib, who was called Rifa'ah bin Zaid, gave the Messenger of Allah (ﷺ) a black slave who was called Mid'am (ra). The Messenger of Allah (ﷺ) set out for Wadi Al-Qura. When we were in Wadi Al-Qura, while Mid'am (ra) was unloading the luggage of the Messenger of Allah (ﷺ), an arrow came and killed him. The people said: 'Congratulations! You will go to Paradise,' but the Messenger of Allah (ﷺ) said: 'No, by the One in Whose hand is my soul! The cloak that he took from the spoils of war on the Day of Khaibar is burning him with fire.' When the people heard that, a man brought one or two shoelaces to the Messenger of Allah (ﷺ) and the Messenger of Allah (ﷺ) said: 'One or two shoelaces of fire.' [Sunan an Nasai]

**Note:** The Prophet (ﷺ) had this knowledge of the Gaib by the will of Allah but the companions' predictions were wrong.

**Hadith:** It was reported that Abu'l-Darda' (ra) said: The Prophet (ﷺ) sat on the minbar and addressed the people, and recited an aayat. Ubayy ibn Ka'b (ra) was beside me and I said to him, 'O Ubayy, when was this verse revealed?' He refused to answer me. I asked him again and he ignored me, and I asked him again and he still ignored me, refusing to speak to me until the Messenger of Allah (ﷺ) had come down from the minbar. Then Ubayy said to me, 'All you got from your Jumu'ah was speaking *idle talk*.' When the Messenger of Allah (ﷺ) left, I went to him and told him what had happened. He said, 'Ubayy spoke the truth. If you hear your Imam speaking, then listen to him until he finishes.' [Sunan Ibn Majah, Musnad Ahmad]

**Note**: Abu'l-Darda' (ra) did not know that by the time particular verse of the Qur'an was revealed.

**Hadith**: Narrated Jabir (ra): When Negus (Najashi) died, the Prophet (ﷺ) said, "Today a pious man has died. So, get up and offer the funeral prayer for your brother As'hama." [Bukhari]

**Note**: The Prophet (ﷺ) knew but compnaions did not. Najashi was a king of Abyssinia, a Christian county known today to be in Ethiopia.

**Hadith**: Abu Huraira (ra) reported: The Messenger of Allah (ﷺ) entrusted me to protect the charity of Ramadan. Someone came to me and began taking from the food. I took hold of him, and I said, "I will certainly take you to the Messenger of Allah (ﷺ)!" Abu Huraira (ra) told the story to the Prophet (ﷺ), saying, "The man told me that when I go to bed, I should recite the Verse of the Throne (Ayatul Kursi). Allah will appoint a protector over me, and no devil will come near me until morning." The Prophet (ﷺ) said, **"He told you the truth, although he is a liar. That was Satan."** [Bukhari]

**Note**: Abu Huraira (ra) could not recognise Satan.

**Hadith**: Narrated `Aisha (ra): Two old ladies from among the Jewish ladies entered upon me and said, "The dead are punished in their graves," but I thought they were telling a lie and did not believe them in the beginning. When they went away and the Prophet (ﷺ) entered upon me, I said, "O Allah's Messenger (ﷺ)! Two old ladies…." and told him the whole story. He (ﷺ) said, "They told the truth; the dead are really punished, to the extent that all the animals hear (the sound resulting from) their punishment." Since then I always saw him seeking refuge with Allah from the punishment of the grave in his prayers. [Bukhari]

**Note**: Aisha (ra) did not know about punishment in grave before confirmation from the Prphet (ﷺ).

**Hadith: Narrated by Abu Hurairah (ra):** "A man was insulting Abu Bakr (ra) while the Prophet ﷺ was sitting, and Abu Bakr (ra) was restraining himself (i.e., he remained silent). The man kept insulting him, and Abu Bakr (ra) replied back harshly. Then the Prophet ﷺ got up and left. Abu Bakr (ra) went after him and said: 'O Messenger of Allah ﷺ, he was insulting me and you were sitting there. But when I responded harshly, you got up and left.' The Prophet ﷺ said: **'There was an angel with you replying on your behalf. But when you started replying, the Shaytan came. I do not sit with Shaytan.'** Then he ﷺ said: 'O Abu Bakr (ra), there are three things that are always true: No one is wronged and then forgives it, but Allah increases him in honor; no one opens the door of giving, but Allah will increase him in wealth; and no one opens the door of begging, but Allah will increase him in poverty.'" [Musnad Ahmad; al-Mu'jam al-Kabir of al-Tabarani with some variations in wording]

**Note**: The Prophet ﷺ saw the Angel and Satan but Abu Bakr (ra) did not.

Since Companions of the Prophet (ﷺ) had no ilmul gaib, discussion on the knowledge of unseen of other people among this Ummah including virtuous people is insignificant and irrelevant. A famous hadith is reproduced here regarding the knowledge of unseen and miracle from the people of Bani Israel.

**Hadith**: Narrated Abu Huraira (ra): The Prophet (ﷺ) said, "None spoke in cradle but three: (The first was) Easa (as), (the second was), there a man from Bani Israel called Juraij. While he was offering his prayers, his mother came and called him. He said (to himself), 'Shall I answer her or keep on praying?" (He went on praying) and did not answer her, his mother said, "O Allah! Do not let him die till he sees the faces of prostitutes." So while he was in his hermitage, a lady came and sought to seduce him, but he refused. So she went to a shepherd and presented herself to him to commit illegal sexual intercourse with her and then later she gave birth to a child and claimed that it belonged to Juraij. The people, therefore, came to him and dismantled his hermitage and expelled him out of it and abused him. Juraij performed the ablution and offered prayer, and then came to the child and said, 'O child! Who is your father?' The child replied, 'The shepherd.' (After hearing this) the people said, 'We shall rebuild your hermitage of gold,' but he said, 'No, of nothing but mud.'(The third was the hero of the following story) A lady from Bani Israel was nursing her child at her breast when a handsome rider passed by her. She said, 'O Allah! Make my child like him.' On that the child left her breast, and facing the rider said, 'O Allah! Do not make me like him.' The child then started to suck her breast again. (Abu Huraira further said, "As if I were now looking at the Prophet (ﷺ) sucking his finger (in way of demonstration.") After a while the people passed by, with a lady slave and she (i.e. the child's mother) said, 'O Allah! Do not make my child like this (slave girl)!, On that the child left her breast and said, 'O Allah! Make me like her.' When she asked why, the child replied, 'The rider is one of the tyrants while this slave girl is falsely accused of theft and illegal sexual intercourse." [Bukhari and Muslim]

Easa (as) was a Prophet and the Mujija and knowledge of unseen are discussed in preceeding section of the book. This particular incident is also recorded in the Qur'an (interpretation of meaning):

*Indeed, I am the servant of Allah. He has given me the Scripture and made me a Prophet" (Surah Maryam Ch 19:30)*

Allah may grant portions of this hidden knowledge to His Prophets to serve a divine wisdom. The infants' speech is not evidence that they themselves possessed the unseen nor the miracle, but that Allah, the All-Knowing, disclosed it to them for a specific purpose. It must also be noted that among the Ummah of the Prophet Muhammad ﷺ no such incident of an infant speaking in the cradle has ever occurred. Furthermore, the Prophet ﷺ himself explicitly stated that only three such cases took place. This declaration restricts the matter to those instances alone, and therefore it cannot be generalized or extended to others. Any later claim of similar occurrences must be rejected, for it contradicts the authentic statement of the Messenger of Allah ﷺ.

## 3.4 Knowing another person's mind

Allah SWT says in the Qur'an:

*Whether you speak secretly or openly—He surely Knows the best what is hidden in the heart. (Al-Mulk, Ch 67:13; interpretation of meaning)*

The Prophet (ﷺ) could know what was in a person's mind through divine revelation. However, there is no evidence to suggest that the companions had the ability to read the thoughts of others.

**Hadith**: It was narrated that Usamah bin Zaid (ra) and this is the Hadith of ibn Abi Shaibah said: "The Messenger of Allah (ﷺ) sent us on a campaign, and in the morning, we attacked Al-Huruqat of Juhainah. I caught up with a man and he said: *'La ilaha illallah,'* but I stabbed him. Then I felt troubled by that, and I told the Prophet (ﷺ) about it. The Messenger of Allah (ﷺ) said: 'Did *he say La ilaha illallah* and you killed him?' I said: 'O Messenger of Allah (ﷺ), he only said it for fear of the weapon.' He (ﷺ) said: 'Did you open his heart to find out whether he said it (out of fear) or not?' And he (ﷺ) kept repeating it until I wished that I had become Muslim on that day." Sa'd said: "By Allah, I will not kill a Muslim until the one with the belly - meaning Usamah approves of killing him." A man said: "Doesn't Allah say: "And fight them until there is no more Fitnah and the religion will all be for Allah. Sa'd said: "We fought them so that there would be no Fitnah but you and your companions want to fight them so that there will be Fitnah. " [Muslim, similar Hadith in Bukhari]

**Note**: Usama Bin Zaid (ra) failed to read the heart of whom he killed.

**Hadith**: Narrated 'Umar bin Al-Khattab (ra): People were (sometimes) judged by the revealing of a Divine Inspiration during the lifetime of Allah's Apostle (ﷺ) but now there is no longer any more (new revelation). Now we judge you by the deeds you practice publicly, so we will trust and favour the one who does good deeds in front of us, and we will not call him to account about what he is really doing in secret, for Allah will judge him for that; but we will not trust or believe the one who presents to us with an evil deed even if he claims that his intentions were good. [Bukhari]

**Note**: Umar (ra) clearly explained that he had no ilmul gaib. Umar (ra) propagated the message of finality of prophethood that in absence of the Prophet (ﷺ), communication to human being on earth by Allah SWT is stopped for ever (except Mubasshirat). Mubasshirat is described in Chapter 3.

**Hadith**: Abd al-Rahman bin Abu Bakra reported on the authority of his father that a person praised another person in the presence of Allah's Apostle (ﷺ), whereupon he (ﷺ) said: "Woe be to thee, you have broken the neck of your friend, you have broken the neck of your friend; he (ﷺ) said this twice. If one of you has to praise his friend at all, he should say: I think (him to be) so and Allah knows it well and **I do not know the secret of the heart** and Allah Knows the destined end, and I cannot testify his purity against Allah but (he appears) to be so and so." [Muslim]

This single hadith settles the matter of 'knowing another person's thoughts or minds.' The Prophet (ﷺ) himself clearly stated that only Allah (SWT) knows what lies within a person's heart. We are not granted access to such hidden knowledge.

### 3.5 Guess, Intuition, Inspiration, Karamaah and Mu'jiza

**i. Guess**

A guess is an uncertain or random assumption made with little or no reliable information, and there is no assurance that the outcome will be correct. For example, imagine an urn containing two identical balls—one black and one white. If you're asked to draw the black ball without any means to distinguish between them, whatever choice you make is purely a guess, with no logical basis behind it. In Islam, conjecture/inherited assumption is not accepted as a reliable basis, especially when it comes to making religious decisions. The Qur'an and Hadith have clearly instructed us that conjecture can never replace the truth.

*"And most of them follow nothing but conjecture. Indeed, conjecture can never take the place of the truth." — (Surah Yunus, 10:36)*

## ii. Intuition or Kashf

Intuition or spiritual intuition (Kashf) is that inner sense or feeling where a person instinctively knows whether something they are doing is right or wrong, even if the outcome may be negative.

Unlike a guess, intuition carries less uncertainty because it is rooted in deep, subconscious knowledge. The brain processes patterns based on previous experiences and uses them to make immediate judgments. Essentially, intuition is the best possible guess. Psychologists believe that intuition involves pattern recognition, as the mind searches through long-term memory for similar situations and then provides judgments in the moment. However, *intuition* is not considered valid legal evidence, as it remains speculative and carries inherent uncertainty. (Uncertainty refers to a situation when chance of happening an event is less than 100%.)

Making decisions based on intuition is a common practice in everyone's daily life, regardless of faith—whether believers or non-believers. It is simply a natural part of being human and holds no particular distinction. This kind of decision-making has evolved into a computational technique known as Artificial Neural Networks (ANN), which is a subset of Artificial Intelligence (AI). ANN is a machine learning method designed to replicate the human brain's learning processes. It uses mathematical computations to simulate how the human brain works, drawing on a 'trained database' of data similar to our own experiences. In this sense, intuition can be understood as computational mathematics. The idea that intuition is a unique attribute of *friends of Allah* is not substantiated. Professors John Hopfield from Princeton University (USA) and Geoffrey Hinton from the University of Toronto (Canada) were awarded the Nobel Prize in Physics in 2024 for their contributions to the development of ANN.

*Kashf* is regarded as a spiritual state granted to a wali (friend) of Allah. It is believed to be a form of spiritual unveiling— generally regarded as occurring during wakefulness to perceive realities that are normally hidden from ordinary senses (gaib). While it is described by some as a means of receiving divine insight, affirming it as a form of direct divine communication poses theological challenges. Specifically, it conflicts with the principle of *Khatm al-Nubuwwah*, which affirms that direct communication from Allah SWT ceased for ever with the Prophet Muhammad (ﷺ). Moreover, there is no evidence of unveiling of *gaib* among the Companions.

Intuition can be influenced by Satan. Abdullah Ibn 'Umar (ra) informed that 'Umar (ra) set out with the Prophet (ﷺ) to look for Ibn Sayyaad, and they found him playing with some boys near the battlement of Banu Maghalah. At that time Ibn Sayyaad was on the threshold of adolescence. He did not notice anything until the Messenger of Allah (ﷺ) struck him on the back with his hand. Then he said to Ibn Sayyaad, "Do you bear witness that I am the Messenger of Allah (ﷺ)?" Ibn Sayyaad looked at him and said, "I bear witness that you are the Messenger (ﷺ) of the unlettered." Ibn Sayyaad said to the Prophet (ﷺ), "Do you bear witness that I am the messenger of Allah (ﷺ)?" He ignored that and said, "I believe in Allah and His Messengers." Then he asked him, "What do you see?" Ibn Sayyaad said, "(Sometimes) a truthful one comes to me and (sometimes) a liar comes." The Prophet (ﷺ) said, "You have been confounded." Then the Prophet (ﷺ) said to him, "I am concealing something from you." Ibn Sayyaad said, "It is al-dukh." [Referring to Surah al-Dukhaan]. The Prophet (ﷺ) said to him, "Be off with you! You will never go beyond your rank." 'Umar (ra) said, "Permit me to strike his neck (kill him), O Messenger of Allah (ﷺ)." The Prophet (ﷺ) said, "If he is he (the Dajjaal), then you will not be able to overpower him, and if he is not (the Dajjaal), then your killing him will not do any good."Saalim said, I heard Ibn 'Umar (ra) say: After that the Messenger of Allah (ﷺ) and Ubayy ibn Ka'b set off to go to some date-palm trees where Ibn Sayyaad was. The Prophet (ﷺ) concealed himself in order to hear something from Ibn Sayyaad before Ibn Sayyaad saw him. The Prophet (ﷺ) saw him lying on his bed with a blanket around him from which was coming a murmuring sound. The mother of Ibn Sayyaad saw the Messenger of Allah (ﷺ) hiding behind the trunk of the palm-tree and said, "O Saaf!" – which was his name – "Here is Muhammad ﷺ)!" Then Ibn Sayyaad jumped up and the Prophet (ﷺ) said, "If she had left him alone, things would have been made clear." [Bukhari]

## Kashf al-Qabr

Kashf al-Qabr is a practice aimed at communicating with souls in the grave. This practice is already prevalent in other religions. In Islam, some individuals believe that Kashf al-Qabr allows a person to determine whether a particular soul is in a state of torment or blessing.

**Hadith**: Anas (ra) reported Allah's Apostle (ﷺ) as saying: If you were not (to abandon) the burying of the dead (in the grave), I would have certainly supplicated Allah that He should make you listen the torment of the grave. [Muslim]

**Hadith**: Abdullah (ra) reported: The Prophet (ﷺ) said, "Verily, the dead are surely punished in their graves, such that even the beasts can hear their cries." [al-Mu'jam al-Kabir Tabarani]

**Hadith**: Narrated Abu Sa`id Al-Khudri (ra): Allah's Messenger (ﷺ) said: When the funeral is ready and the men carry it on their shoulders, if the deceased was righteous it will say, "Present me (hurriedly)," and if he was not righteous, it will say, "Woe to it (me)! Where are they taking it (me)?" Its voice is heard by everything except man and if he heard it he would fall unconscious." [Bukhari]

**Hadith**: It was narrated from Anas (ra) that the Prophet (ﷺ) said: "When a person is placed in his grave and his companions leave him, ……But as for the kaafir or hypocrite, he says, 'I do not know, I used to say what the people said.' It is said, 'You did not know and you did not follow those who knew.' Then he is struck a blow with an iron hammer between his ears and he screams a scream which everything around him can hear apart from the two races of mankind and the jinn." [Bukhari]

**Hadith**: Zayd ibn Sabit (ra) reported: The Prophet (ﷺ) said, "Verily, this nation will be put to trial in their graves. Were it not that you would stop burying each other, I would have called upon Allah to make you hear the punishment of the grave as I hear it." Then, the Prophet (ﷺ) turned to face us, saying, "Seek refuge in Allah from the torment of the Hellfire." They said, "We seek refuge in Allah from the torment of the Hellfire." The Prophet (ﷺ) said, "Seek refuge in Allah from the torment of the grave." They said, "We seek refuge in Allah from the torment of the grave." The Prophet (ﷺ) said, "Seek refuge in Allah from tribulations, the evident of them and the hidden." They said, "We seek refuge in Allah from tribulations, the evident of them and the hidden." The Prophet (ﷺ) said, "Seek refuge in Allah from the tribulation of the False Messiah." They said, "We seek refuge in Allah from the tribulation of the False Messiah." [Muslim]

The following conclusions can be derived from the hadiths above:

- There are punishments in the graves;

- The animals can hear the cries of the punished;

- Humans and Jinns cannot hear the punishment;

- If humans could hear the screams, they would be fainted and would abandon the burying people in the grave.

Since those claiming *Kashf al-Qabr* are human beings—not animals—and are neither unconscious nor detached from the burial process, their claim of knowing the conditions of the deceased in the grave is unfounded. The life of *Barzakh* belongs to the realm of the unseen, knowledge of which is solely with Allah (SWT). Moreover, making such claims—

especially when the Prophet (ﷺ) has given clear guidance—is considered a transgression for any believer.

At times, people also claim to have seen fire in graves. However, in Islamic tradition, the punishment of the grave — including fire — is part of the unseen realm and not something visible in the physical world. The fire of Hell, as described in an authentic Hadith, is far more intense than any earthly fire. Abu Hurairah (ra) narrated that the Prophet Muhammad (ﷺ) said: "This fire of yours, which the children of Adam ignite, is only one part out of seventy parts of the heat of Hell." The companions asked, "By Allah, would this not have been enough, O Messenger of Allah ﷺ?" He ﷺ replied, "It is sixty-nine parts more — all of them equally severe." [Tirmizi]

To give perspective, the temperature of an ordinary fire made from kindled firewood typically ranges from 600°C to 1,100°C, depending on the type of wood, oxygen levels, and burning conditions. The actual reference temperature of fire mentioned in Tirmizi, is only known with certainty by Allah (SWT). However, using the Hadith's 70-fold comparison, Hellfire could be estimated at 42,000°C to 77,000°C, vastly beyond human experience. If a temperature of just 1,100°C were present in a grave, the surrounding soil would be transformed into solid brick due to extreme heat— yet we find no evidence of such transformation in actual graves.

In the Hadith of Al-Isra' wal-Mi'raj (The Night Journey), the Prophet ﷺ was shown various punishments in the Barzakh. One scene depicted a man whose head was being crushed with a rock, representing those who spread lies. [*Sahih Bukhari*] In another narration, also in *Sahih Bukhari*, it is said: "A man is struck with a hammer made of iron, and he lets out a scream that is heard by all creation—except humans and jinn."

Despite these descriptions, historical evidence from exhumed graves — such as in cases where resurrectionists (body snatchers) stole human remains to sell to medical institutions — shows intact skeletons. The skulls were not crushed, nor were the remains reduced to ash, despite what the Hadith metaphorically describe.

This clearly affirms a foundational Islamic belief: the punishment in the grave is part of the unseen (Ghayb). It belongs to the realm of the Hereafter (Barzakh), and Allah (SWT) has placed a veil between this world and the next. If all graves were opened today, we would only find physical remains (except fresh bodies of the Prophets and fortunate people), not fire or punishment visible to the human eye. That is because the fire in the grave is not a worldly, material fire — it is part of the unseen torment that becomes real only after death. Fire of the torment is beyond the domain of *space-time continuum* of Physics.

When the wall of 'A'ishah's (ra) house collapsed, exposing the feet of 'Umar ibn al-Khaṭṭab (ra) in his grave, the people of Madinah did not witness any signs of the blessings of Paradise, despite the fact that he was among the *Asharah Mubasharah*—the ten companions promised Paradise. Similarly, when a companion exhumed the grave of his father, who had been martyred in the Battle of Uḥud and whose body remained miraculously fresh, no visible signs of Paradise were observed. Installing a *load-cell* in a grave will not reveal the squeezing pressure experienced within. Placing a *spy camera* inside will not capture footage of the angels' interrogation. Inserting a *thermometer* will not record the heat of any torment that may occur. The realities of the grave—its comforts or punishments—belong to the unseen realm and lie beyond the reach of human senses. Their truth is affirmed through divine revelation, not though empirical or sensory observation.

Thus, the lack of visible signs in such cases does not negate the promised blessings or punishments. Rather, it reaffirms our belief that such matters belong to the knowledge and domain of the unseen, known only to Allah (SWT), and should be accepted with conviction through the guidance of Qur'an and authentic Sunnah.

**Hadith**: Narrated Hishaam ibn 'Urwah, from his father [Zubair (ra)]: When the wall fell on them during the caliphate of Al-Waleed ibn 'Abdul Malik, the people started repairing it. A foot appeared to them from it and the people panicked and thought that it was the foot of the Prophet ﷺ. No one could be found who could tell them about it till I ('Urwah) said to them, "By Allah, this is not the foot of the Prophet ﷺ but it is the foot of 'Umar (ra)." [Bukhari]

**Note**: It happened during the caliphate of **Al-Waleed ibn Abdul Malik**, who ruled from **86 AH to 96 AH.** According to historical accounts, the repairs and expansions of Masjid al-Nabawi in Madinah were carried out during Al-Waleed's caliphate, approximately 65 years after the death of Umar (ra).

**Hadith**: Jabir ibn 'Abdullah (ra) narrated: "At the time of the Battle of Uhud, my father called me at night and said: 'I have a feeling that I will be the first to be killed among the Prophet's Companions. I am going to leave none behind dearer to me than you, except the Messenger of Allah

(ﷺ). Indeed, there is a debt that I have to pay off, so pay it off on my behalf, and take good care of your sisters.' In the morning, he was the first to be killed. I buried him along with another man in the same grave. I did not feel good about leaving him buried with another. So, I got him out of his grave six months later, and found him the same as the day I put him therein, except for his ear. Then, I placed him in a grave where he was buried alone." [Bukhari]

### iii. Inspiration or Ilham

In Islam, *ilham* (الهام) refers to divine inspiration. In psychology, inspiration is understood as a motivational response to a stimulus that leads to new ideas or creative solutions to problems. In the Islamic context, *ilham* is the knowledge or guidance placed directly into the heart of a man or woman by Allah (SWT). It serves as a form of communication between Allah (SWT) and humans, distinct from *wahi*. This mode of communication is known only to Allah. We do not know how the persons receiving the divine communication recognized it as Ilham. When *ilham* was granted in response to a specific situation, it became a source of *ilm al-ghaib* (knowledge of the unseen) for that individual in that context. As such, *ilham* is both accurate and authentic. Being divine in nature, it transcends the laws of physical phenomena of nature.

### Existence of ilham before the Prophet (ﷺ)

The example of ilham and consequent action is the story of the mother of Prophet Musa (as) in the Qur'an. Allah SWT says:

*We inspired the mother of Musa: "Nurse him, but when you fear for him, put him then into the river, and do not fear or grieve. We will certainly return him to you, and make him one of the messengers." (Al-Qasas Ch 28:7; interpretation of meaning)*

The incident refers to catastrophe period when Musa (as) was born and all new born male children were killed by Fir'awn. Thus, belief in ilham prior to the Prophet (ﷺ) is a part of faith since it is recorded in the Quran.

**Existence of ilham after the Prophet (ﷺ)**

Abu Huraira (ra) reported: The Messenger of Allah (ﷺ) said, "Before you, were nations with divinely inspired people (مُحَدَّثُونَ). If such a person were in my nation, it would surely be 'Umar (ra)." [Bukhari; this hadith is also narrated from Aisha (ra) in Muslim]

Look at the first sentence '*Before you were nations with divinely inspired people.*' This again confirms existence of ilham prior to our Prophet (ﷺ).

The next sentence is '*If such a person were in my nation, it would surely be 'Umar (ra).*' There is a clear declaration of the Prophet (ﷺ) that there is no chance of any occurrence of ilham among this Ummah. Hadith of al-Bukhari in preceeding section discusses the status of Umar (ra) regarding his ilmul gaib. That means, among the nation of the Prophet (ﷺ) till the Doomsday, nobody will receive any sort of direct communication from Allah SWT nor anybody will receive any sort of divine instruction except Mubasshirat. Any claim of ilham by anybody during any generation among this nation will directly contradict the finality of Prophethood, which is presented in Chapter 1.

Sometimes the second sentence in the hadith is phrased in the present tense by some people, such as: "If there is any of such among my followers, then it is 'Umar (ra)." It would still conflict with the concept of knowledge of the unseen and contradict the finality of Prophethood. Umar (ra) himself clarified that he had no knowledge of the unseen. Therefore, even if the sentence is expressed in the present tense, its meaning should be understood in the past tense.

There is mention of ilham in the Qur'an regarding the honey bee: *And your Lord inspired the bees: "Make ˹your˺ homes in the mountains, the trees, and in what people construct, (An-Nahl Ch 16:68)*. Ibn Kasir writes: What is meant by inspiration here is guidance. Honey bee has a prominent status among other life forms by virtue of its intelligence, sense and functional insight. So unique is their system and so established are their rules and regulations that human mind has but to marvel at their system of governance. It is to be mentioned here that in engineering, an optimization algorithm called the Bees Algorithm have been developed, inspired from the natural foraging behaviour of honey bees, to find the optimal solution.

## iv. Karamaah

Karamaah is the miraculous act that happens to righteous Ummah which defies laws of nature. Karamaah is not related to the will of any person, rather it is by Allah's Will. Karamaah of Maryam (as) is mentioned in the Qur'an. Allah SWT says (interpretation of meaning):

*So her Lord accepted her graciously and blessed her with a pleasant upbringing—entrusting her to the care of Zakariyya. Whenever Zakariyya*

*visited her in the sanctuary, he found her supplied with provisions. He exclaimed, "O Maryam! Where did this come from?" She replied, "It is from Allah. Surely Allah provides for whoever He wills without limit."*
*(Ali Imran Ch 3:37)*

Story of people of cave is a miracle mentioned in the Qur'an. Allah SWT says (interpretation of meaning):

*They had remained in their cave for three hundred years, adding nine. (Al-Kahf Ch 18:25)*

**Hadith**: Abu Hurayrah (ra) narrated: ...that Bint al-Haris said, when Khubayb bin 'Udayy was a prisoner of the Quraysh in Makkah: "...By Allah, one day, I saw him eating from a bunch of grapes in his hand while he was locked in a steel cage, and there were no crops growing in Makkah at the time." [Bukhari]

**Hadith**: Anas bin Malik (ra) narrated: "One night, 'Ubad bin Bishr (ra) and Usayd bin Hudayr (ra) left the residence of the Prophet (ﷺ) on a very dark night. Suddenly, a light appeared that lit their way for them. When they parted ways, the light disappeared." [Bukhari]

**Hadith**: Anas ibn Malik (ra) **reported: My uncle Anas ibn An-Nadr** (ra) **did not take part in the battle of Badr; so, he said: "O** Messenger of Allah (ﷺ), I was absent from the first battle you fought against the polytheists. If Allah give me a chance to fight them, no doubt, Allah will show how (bravely) **I will fight." So, on the day of the battle of Uhud, when the Muslims left their posts and were defeated, he said: "O** Allah, I apologize to You for what these (i.e. his companions) **have done, and I denounce what these** (i.e. the polytheists) **have done." Then he**

**advanced with his sword and met Sa'd ibn Mu'az (ra) passing in front of him so he said to him: 'O Sa'd ibn Mu'az (ra), the Paradise, by the Lord of the Ka'bah, I smell the fragrance of Paradise near Mount Uhud.'** Sa'd later said: 'O Messenger of Allah (ﷺ), what he did was beyond my power.' Anas (ra) said: 'We found on his body over eighty wounds caused by swords, spears, and arrows. He was killed and mutilated by the polytheists to the extent that no one was able to recognize him except his sister, from his fingertips. **We believe that the Qur'anic verse:** {Among the believers are men true to what they promised Allah. Among them is he who has fulfilled his vow [to the death], and among them is he who awaits [his chance]. And they did not alter [the terms of their commitment] **by any alteration}** [Surat al-Ahzab: ٢٣] **refers to him and the likes of him."** [Bukhari & Muslim]

**Note**: Getting smell of the Paradise was the karamaah here.

**Hadith**: Narrated Anas (ra): Whenever drought threatened them, Umar bin Al-Khattab (ra) used to ask Al-Abbas bin Abdul Muttalib (ra) to invoke Allah for rain. He (Umar) used to say, "O Allah! We used to ask our Prophet (ﷺ) to invoke You for rain, and You would bless us with rain, and now we ask his uncle to invoke You for rain. O Allah! Bless us with rain." And so, it would rain. [Bukhari]

Karamah is one of the ways in which Allah SWT shows mercy to His slaves and is part of his reward in this world. However, many stories of famous personalities that have been narrated in this regard may not be sound. It is essential therefore, to verify reports of this nature before taking them seriously or quoting them. Following are some examples:

*Illustration 1: The person offered prayer on air/water (as if floating).*

This act defies laws of Physics and is a karamaah. The Companions of the Prophet (ﷺ) have no record of such activity. Prophet Yunus (as) boarded a ship to flee his people (without divine permission). "When he ran away to the laden ship..." *(As-Saffat Ch 37:140)* Allah commanded Nuh (as) to build a **large ark** before the coming flood. "So We saved him and those with him in the laden ship." *(Ash-Shu'ara Ch 26:119)* Hence such claim is fabricated.

*Illustration 2: The person could see the Heavens and Throne of Allah in meditation.*

This act requires ilmul gaib which Companions of the Prophet (ﷺ) did not have (discussed in Chapter 2). The Companions have no record of such activity in hadiths. The Prophet of Allah (ﷺ) saw Heaven and Hell during Eclipse Prayer. Narrated Abdullah Ibn Abbas (ra): They (his Companions) said: "Messenger of Allah (ﷺ), we saw you reach out to something, while you were standing here, then we saw you restrain yourself." He (ﷺ) said: "I saw Paradise and reached out to a bunch of its grapes; and had I taken it you would have eaten of it as long as the world endured. I saw Hell also. No such (abominable) sight have I ever seen as that which I saw today;" [A part of the hadith from Muslim] If this act of the person is believed, one is placing him above the rank of the Companions and making him at the same level of the Prophet (ﷺ) (Nauzubillah). Hence this claim is false.

*Illustration 3: Making a chicken alive from its post-lunch left-over bones.*

Giving life to a dead (by Will of Allah) was a Mujiza of Eassa (as) only mentioned in the Qur'an.

*"and make him a messenger to the Children of Israel to proclaim, 'I have come to you with a sign from your Lord: I will make for you a bird from clay, breathe into it, and it will become a 'real' bird—by Allah's Will. I will heal the blind and the leper and raise the dead to life—by Allah's Will. And I will prophesize what you eat and store in your houses. Surely in this is a sign for you if you 'truly' believe." (Surah Ali Imran Ch 3:49; interpretation of meaning)*

A person cannot be at the level of Prophet Eassa (as) and such claim is fabricated. It is only Dajjal who will have super acts.

*Illustration 4: A lady fell from the fort in Egypt and the man caught her flying from a Bukhara 3500 kM away.*

The Prophet (ﷺ) migrated from Makkah to Madina on a camel named al-Qaswaa (in a worldly manner), while many of his Companions made the journey even on foot, not by flying. The Companions were martyred in battles and did not evade the swords of the disbelievers by flying. Furhter, the Prophet of Allah (ﷺ) never touched any non-Mahram women. Therefore, this claim is false. Narrated Anas (ra): (The people of) Bani Salama intended to shift near the mosque (of the Prophet (ﷺ) but Allah's Apostle (ﷺ) disliked to see Madina vacated and said, "O the people of Bani Salama! Don't you think that you will be rewarded for your footsteps which you take towards the mosque?" So, they stayed at their old places. [Bukhari] The Companions (The people of Bani Salama) could not attend the prayer by flying.

*Illustration 5: The Ka'ba advanced by traversing to welcome a lady on the occasion of Hajj.*

The Prophet of Allah (ﷺ) and his 1400 Companions had to go back without performing Umra as per the Treaty of Hudaybiyya. The Companions were very much depressed and grieved. The Ka'ba did not move towards Hudaybiyyah for Allah's Messenger (ﷺ) and his Companions. When the Prophet (ﷺ) performed his Farewell Hajj with over one lakh Companions, the Ka'ba did not move to greet them. This indicates that the story of the Ka'ba moving is fabricated.

*Illustration 6: The man looked at his desciple in anger and the person died on the spot.*

There is no evidence to suggest that a gaze filled with anger from the Prophet (ﷺ) or his companions caused anyone to drop dead. Moreover, killing an innocent is a major sin in Islam.

It is worth to mention here that there are possibilities that exaggerated stories of the people were added by followers of later generations.

If any supernatural act—such as those described above or similar occurrences—takes place, it is essential to examine and evaluate it in light of the Qur'an and the Sunnah, for they are the ultimate and final criteria for truth. Islam teaches that no matter how extraordinary or awe-inspiring an act may appear, if it contradicts the guidance of the Qur'an and Sunnah, it must be rejected. Such acts should not be taken at face value, as they may be illusions or deceptions from Satan intended to mislead. Therefore, believers must remain cautious and grounded in authentic Islamic teachings when encountering anything that appears to be supernatural.

## v. Mu'jizah

The mu'jizah is only for the Prophets. The mu'jizah is the extraordinary sign with which Allah supports His Prophets and Messengers, and challenges people. Allah SWT says (that means):

*They have sworn forceful oaths by Allah that if a sign comes to them, they will surely believe in it. Say, "Signs are in Allah's power alone." What will make you realize that even when they (the signs) come, they will not believe? (Al-An'am Ch 6:109)*

The Prophet (ﷺ) had innumerable mu'jizah and only few are presented here. The extraordinary mu'jizah of the Prophet (ﷺ) reported in the Qur'an are: splitting of the moon in Ch 54:1, Isra (night journey of the Prophet (ﷺ) from Makkah to Jerusalem revealed in Ch 17:1) and Mi'raj (ascension into heaven) in Surah An-Najm Ch 53.

**Hadith**: Narrated Anas bin Malik (ra) that the people of Makkah asked Allah's Messenger (ﷺ) to show them a miracle. So, he (ﷺ) showed them the moon split in two halves between which they saw the Hira' mountain. [Bukhari]

**Hadith**: Narrated Salim bin Abi Aj-Jad: Jabir bin Abdullah (ra) said: The people became very thirsty on the day of Al-Hudaibiya (Treaty). A small pot containing some water was in front of the Prophet (ﷺ) and when he (ﷺ) had finished the ablution, the people rushed towards him. He (ﷺ) asked, "What is wrong with you?" They replied, "We have no water either for performing ablution or for drinking except what is present in front of you." So, he (ﷺ) placed his hand in that pot and the water started flowing among his fingers like springs. We all drank and performed ablution (from it). I asked Jabir (ra), "How many were you?" He replied, "Even if we had been one-hundred-thousand, it would have been sufficient for us, but we were fifteen-hundred." [Bukhari]

**Hadith**: Narrated by Abu Huraira (ra): One day the Messenger of Allah (ﷺ) led the prayer. Then turning (towards his Companions) he (ﷺ) said: "O you man, why don't you say your prayer well? Does the observer of prayer not see how he is performing the prayer, for he performs it for himself? By Allah, I see behind me as I see in front of me." [Muslim]

**Hadith**: Narrated Yazid bin Abi Ubaid: I saw the trace of a wound in Salama's (ra) leg. I said to him, "O Abu Muslim! What is this wound?" He said, "This was inflicted on me on the day of Khaibar and the people said, 'Salama (ra) has been wounded.' Then I went to the Prophet (ﷺ) and he (ﷺ) puffed his saliva in it (i.e. the wound) thrice and since then I have not had any pain in it till this hour." [Bukhari]

A question may arise: Does this mean that decisions based on intuition (*kashf*) or guesswork are not blessed by Allah (SWT)? The answer is: Allah (SWT) certainly blesses and shows mercy to His servants. He guides them as a gift, knowing exactly when and how to assist them. In some situations, a person's intuition may lead him to a certain outcome by the Will of Allah, and later he may realize that his decision was indeed correct. However, at the moment of making the decision, he will not always be aware or feel that Allah (SWT) is guiding them in that instance.

Is karamaah non-existent today? The occurrence of karamaat among the righteous individuals of this ummah is firmly established and is beyond doubt. These miracles serve as a way for Allah to strengthen and reward

His believing servants in this world. However, it is essential to approach karamaah with caution and a correct understanding. Sometimes, it so happens that a righteous and pious individual fall into the deception of Shaytan—that is, he perceives an extraordinary event he is experiencing as a *karamah*, while in reality, it may be a cunning trap laid by Shaytan. Shaytan can bring about occurrences that appear outwardly miraculous, but in essence, they lead a person away from the guidance of the Qur'an and Sunnah. As a result, the individual may fall into self-delusion, thinking that Allah is pleased with him and that he has attained a special spiritual status, even though he is gradually deviating from the straight path. Therefore, in order to discern a true *karamah*, it is essential to examine it in the light of *Tawhid*, the Sunnah, and the Shari'ah. Only then can we protect ourselves from Shaytan's deceptive and crafty manipulations. An important point is that **karamah** can only be confirmed **after** it occurs — not before.

A well-known incident from the life of 'Abd al-Qadir Jilani (raḥimahullah) provides a profound lesson regarding the distinction between a genuine *karamah* and Shaytanic deception. Once, Shaytan appeared before him in the sky in the form of a massive beam of radiant light and declared, "O 'Abd al-Qadir! I am your Lord. I have made the forbidden lawful for you." Immediately, 'Abd al-Qadir Jilani (raḥimahullah) responded by saying: "*La ḥawla wa la quwwata illa billah*". By saying this, he made it clear that Allah can never declare anything lawful that contradicts the Shari'ah. Witnessing this reaction, Shaytan exposed his trickery and admitted, "Through this kind of deception, I have misled seventy *awliya*'." Shaykh 'Abd al-Qadir replied: "My Lord never commands anything that contradicts His Book and the Shari'ah of His Messenger."

Although the narration is not authenticated through chains of transmission like a ḥadith and does not meet the criteria of *ṣaḥīḥ* according to traditional ḥadith sciences, it nonetheless contains an important lesson. It illustrates that the deception of Shayṭan can reach levels beyond our imagination—even pious and God-fearing individuals can become spellbound in his traps. It is worth to mention here that Among this Ummah, the one who will display the most extraordinary and supernatural feats will be the Dajjal. He will possess the ability to bring down rain, cause vegetation to grow, and even appear to raise the dead. These miraculous signs will deceive many, leading them to believe he is divine. However, those whom Allah wills to protect will be safeguarded from his trial. Following hadith may be referred in this context.

**Hadith**: An-Nawwas b. Sam'an (ra) reported that Allah's Messenger (ﷺ) made a mention of the Dajjal one day in the morning. He (ﷺ) sometimes described him to be insignificant and sometimes described (his turmoil) as very significant (and we felt) as if he were in the cluster of the date-palm trees. When we went to him (to the Holy Prophet ﷺ) in the evening and he read (the signs of fear) in our faces, he (ﷺ) said: ……….. We said: Allah's Messenger (ﷺ), how long would he stay on the earth? He (ﷺ) said: For forty days, one day like a year and one day like a month and one day like a week and the rest of the days would be like your days (Total: 13 months 42 days). We said: Allah's Messenger, would one day's prayer suffice for the prayers of day equal to one year? Thereupon he (ﷺ) said: No, but you must make an estimate of time (and then observe prayer). We said: Allah's Messenger, how quickly would he walk upon the earth? Thereupon he (ﷺ) said: Like cloud driven by the wind. He would come to the people and invite them (to a wrong religion) and they would affirm their faith in him and respond to him. He would then give command to the sky and there would be rainfall upon the earth and it would grow crops. Then in the evening, their pasturing animals would come to them with their humps very high and their udders full of milk and their flanks stretched. He would then come to another people and invite them. But they would reject him and he would go away from them and there would be drought for them and nothing would be left with them in the form of wealth. He would then walk through the waste land and say to it: Bring forth your treasures, and the treasures would come out and collect (themselves) before him like the swarm of bees. He would then call a person brimming with youth and strike him with the sword and cut him into two pieces and (make these pieces lie at a distance which is generally) between the archer and his target. He would then call (that young man) and he will come forward laughing with his face gleaming (with happiness) and it would be at this very time that Allah would send Eassa (as), son of Mary, and he will descend at the white minaret in the eastern side of Damascus wearing two garments lightly dyed with saffron and placing his hands on the wings of two Angels………[A part of the hadith from Muslim]

It is important to understand that karamaah is not a continuous attribute of any individual, nor it is like a certification that enables someone to perform miracles continuously and consistently, day after day and year after year. Instead, karamaat are exceptional acts granted by Allah, manifesting at specific instances according to His divine Will.

## vi. Relics and Tabarruk

Tabarruk means to seek barakah (بركة) from Allah SWT through left-over items (relics) of the Prophets. Barakah means getting something more than expectation by the grace of Allah. It refers to a divine blessing, abundance and prosperity. The Qur'an refers to how the relics of Harun and Musa (peace be upon them) were preserved by the angels, and how they descended from Heaven.

*Their prophet further told them, "The sign of Talut's kingship is that the Ark (Tabut) will come to you—containing reassurance from your Lord and relics of the family of Musa and the family of Harun, which will be carried by the angels. Surely in this is a sign for you, if you 'truly' believe." (Al-Baqarah Ch 2: 248; interpretation of meaning)*

In the commentary of this verse, Imam al-Tabari writes: '[the relics were] the staff, the remains of the Tablet, parts of the Tawrah and shoes of Musa (as). Other commentators add that also included was Manna* and some clothes of Musa and Harun (peace upon them).' So special were these relics that Banu Isra'il would seek victory over their enemies through the means of these sacred relics. Similar was the tabrruk of the shirt of Prophet Yusuf (as) as recorded in the Qur'an:

*But when the bearer of the good news arrived, he cast the shirt over Yaqub's face, so he regained his sight. Yaqub then said 'to his children', "Did I not tell you that I truly know from Allah what you do not know?" (Surah Yusuf Ch 12: 96; interpretation of meaning)*

*Manna: The word manna appears in the Quran three times, in verses 2:57, 7:160, and 20:80. It is a kind of sweet of Jannah which was sent down by Allah Almighty for the people of Bani Israel during Prophet Musa (as).

Some hadiths related to **tabarruk** and **relics** are presented below. From the examples of blessings gained through the signs of the Prophet Muhammad (ﷺ) among the companions, we will learn the correct and Islamic usage of relics and **tabarruk** and its proper boundaries.

**Hadith**: Anas b. Malik (ra) reported: When Allah's Messenger (ﷺ) had thrown pebbles at the Jamrat and had sacrificed the animal, he ﷺ turned (the right side) of his head towards the barber, and i.e shaved it. He then called Abu Talha al-Ansari (ra) and gave it to him. He ﷺ then turned his left side and asked him (the barber) to shave. And he (the barber) shaved and gave it to Abu Talha (ra) and told him to distribute it amongst the people. [Muslim]

**Hadith**: Asma (ra), daughter of Abu Bakr (ra), brought out a mantle of royal Persian quality with a gore of brocade and hemmed front and back with brocade, and said: This was Allah's messenger's (ﷺ) mantle which was with 'A'isha (ra), which I inherited when she died. The Prophet (ﷺ) used to wear it, and we washed it for the sick and sought a cure by means of it. (The water in which it was washed would be given to the sick to drink, or the garment itself was placed on them, or given to them to touch or kiss, and so receive a blessing) [Muslim]

**Hadith**: Narrated Abu Juhaifa (ra): I came to the Prophet (ﷺ) while he was inside a red leather tent, and I saw Bilal (ra) taking the remaining water of the ablution of the Prophet (ﷺ), and the people were taking of that water and rubbing it on their faces; and whoever could not get anything of it, would share the moisture of the hand of his companion (and then rub it on his face). [Bukhari]

**Hadith**: Narrated Ibn Hazyam that he went with his grandfather, Hazyam, to the Prophet (ﷺ). Hazyam (ra) said to the Messenger of Allah (ﷺ): "I have sons and grandsons, some of whom are pubescent and others still children." Motioning to the young child next to him, he said: "This is the youngest." The Prophet (ﷺ) brought this young child whose name was Hanzalah next to him, wiped on his head, and told him, May Allah bless you.' After that, people started to bring Hanzalah a person with a swollen face or a sheep with a swollen udder (udder is the organ of a cow or sheep that produces milk and hangs like a bag between legs). Hanzalah would place his hand on that part of his head the Prophet (ﷺ) wiped, then touch the swollen part and say "Bismillah," and the swelling would be cured. [Musnad Ahmad]

**Hadith**: Ibn Abi Shaybah narrated with a sahih chain that it was the practice of the Companions in the masjid of the Prophet (ﷺ) to place their hands on the knob of the hand rail of the Minbar where the Prophet (ﷺ) used to place his hand. There they would supplicate to Allah hoping Allah would answer their supplication because they were placing their hands where the Prophet (ﷺ) placed his while making their supplication. [Musannaf Ibn Abi Shaybah]

**Hadith**: Sahl ibn Sa'd (ra) narrated that he heard the Prophet (ﷺ) on the day of (the battle of) Khaybar say, "I will give the flag to a person at whose hands Allah will grant victory." So the Companions got up, wishing eagerly to see to whom the flag would be given, and every one of them wished to be given the flag. But the Prophet (ﷺ) asked for 'Ali (ra).

Someone informed him that he was suffering from eye-trouble. So, he (ﷺ) ordered them to bring 'Ali (ra) in front of him. Then the Prophet (ﷺ) spat in his eyes, and his eyes were cured immediately, as if he had never had any eye-trouble." [Bukhari and Muslim]

**Hadith**: Anas ibn Malik (ra) narrated: The Prophet (ﷺ) *once came to our house and took a nap, and he* (ﷺ) *was sweating (in his sleep). My mother brought a little bottle and began to collect the sweat in it. The Prophet* (ﷺ) *woke up and said, 'O Umm Sulaym (ra), what is this that you are doing?' Thereupon, she said, 'This is your sweat, which we mix in our perfume, and it becomes the most fragrant perfume.'* [Muslim]

**Hadith**: 'A'ishah (ra) said: "When the Prophet ﷺ would become ill, he would recite the *Mu'awwidhat* (Surah al-Falaq and al-Nas) and blow over himself. But when his illness became severe, I would recite these surahs and blow over him, then wipe his body using his own hand, seeking the blessing of his noble hand." [Bukhari]

**Note**: A'ishah (ra) clearly understood that wiping with the Prophet's ﷺ hand was not the same as wiping with her own.

**Hadith**: Anas (ra) reported: When they liberated Tastar, they found a (dead) man with a long nose in a coffin. The people were seeking victory and seeking rain through him. Abu Musa (ra) wrote to Umar ibn al-Khattab (ra) about that. Umar (ra) wrote back, saying, "Indeed, this man is one of the Prophets. Fire and earth do not consume the bodies of the Prophets." Umar (ra) wrote further, "Look for him, you and your companion, and bury him in a place no one knows but the two of you."

Anas (ra) said, "Then I went with Abu Musa (ra) and we reburied him." [Muṣannaf Ibn Abi Shaybah]

**Note**: Taśtar is a city in south-weśt of Iran and the body was of Prophet Daniel (as). The incident took place during caliphate of Umar (ra).

Some people claim it is permissible to seek tabarruk from the relics of the scholars and righteous people such as pond water — from which that person used to perform **wudu**, keeping śtaff and clothes, eating left-over food/drinks, licking saliva, preserving soil/pebbles after urinating (iśtinja) and so on. However, there is no proof in the Quran, the Sunnah, or the actions of the companions and righteous anceśtors for seeking blessings from relics other than those of the Prophet (ﷺ) himself. None of them ever said to seek blessings from the relics of Abu Bakr (ra), although he is the beśt of the Ummah of the Prophet (ﷺ), nor with the relics of Umar (ra), nor Usman (ra), nor Ali (ra). Rather, seeking blessings from the relics of anyone other than the Prophet (ﷺ) is considered Bid'ah (innovation), and it has led to significant exaggeration regarding the śtatus of pious scholars. Such practices in many places have led **grave worship, exaggerated reverence,** and **misguidance** like praying to others besides Allah. Such belief in barakah from the relics of anyone other the Prophets means persons are given the śtatus of a Prophet that contradicts the finality of prophethood.

### 3.6 Jinns have no Ilmul gaib

Allah SWT śtates in Surah Saba that Jinns have no ilmul gaib in context with Prophet Sulaiman's (as) death. Allah SWT subjugated jinns for him. Allah says (interpretation of the meaning):

*And from the jinns, (We subjugated for him) those who dived in water for him and did jobs other than that. And We were the One who kept watch over them.* (Al Anbiya Ch 21: 82)

Prophet Sulaiman (as) was seated, holding his staff, while some jinn were busy working. The jinn were focused on their task when Allah took Sulaiman's (as) life, but they remained unaware of his death until the staff broke and his body, which had been leaning on it, collapsed. It was then revealed to everyone that the jinns do not have knowledge of the unseen. Allah SWT says (interpretation of meaning): *And when We decreed for Solomon death, nothing indicated to the jinn his death except a creature of the earth eating his staff. But when he fell, it became clear to the jinn that if they had known the unseen, they would not have remained in humiliating punishment."* (Surah Saba, Ch 34:14)

## 3.7 Seeing (virtuous) dead persons when awake

Allah SWT says in the Book (interpretation of meaning):

وَٱلنَّٰزِعَٰتِ غَرْقًا

وَٱلنَّٰشِطَٰتِ نَشْطًا

*By those ʾangelsʾ stripping out ʾevil soulsʾ harshly,*

*and those pulling out ʾgood soulsʾ gently, (An-Nazi'at Ch 79: 1-2)*

**Hadith**: It was narrated from Abu Hurairah (ra) that the Prophet (ﷺ) said: "When the believer is dying, the angels of mercy come to him with white silk and say: Come out content and with the pleasure of Allah upon you to the mercy of Allah, fragrance and a Lord Who is not angry; so it comes out like the best fragrance of musk. They pass him from one to another until they bring him to the gate of heaven, where they say: How good is this fragrance that has come to you from the Earth! Then the souls of the believers come to him and they rejoice more over him than any one of you rejoices when his absent loved one comes to him. They ask him: 'What happened to so-and-so, what happened to so-and-so?' They say: 'Let him be, for he was in the hardship of the world. When he says, 'Did he not come here?' They say: 'He was taken to the pit (of Hell).' Come out discontent, subject of Divine wrath, to the punishment of Allah, the Mighty and Sublime; So, it comes out like the foulest stench of a corpse. They bring him to the gates of the Earth, where they say: 'How foul is this stench!' Then they bring him to the souls of the disbelievers." [Sunan an-Nasai]

Thus, death in Islam means separation of soul from the body. It is a transition from this world to the life of grave, called life in barzakh. Since final announcement and allocation of Heaven and Hell will be done by Allah SWT after resurrection, life in barzakh is an intermediate life between worldly life and eternal life in heaven or hell. Life of barzakh is described in several hadiths. Narrated `Abdullah bin `Umar (ra): Allah's Messenger (saws) said, "When anyone of you dies, he is shown his place both in the morning and in the evening. If he is one of the people of Paradise, he is shown his place in it, and if he is from the people of the Hell-Fire, he is shown his place there-in. Then it is said to him, "This is your place till Allah resurrect you on the Day of Resurrection." [Bukhari]

The claim of seeing or meeting deceased virtuous individuals while awake is a highly sensitive and debated topic in the Indian subcontinent.

Some individuals assert that they have encountered such persons and even received advice from them during wakeful state. However, according to Islamic teachings, once a person dies, they enter the state of **Barzakh**, where all forms of communication with the worldly realm come to an end. The nature of life in the grave falls entirely within the realm of the **unseen ('ilm al-ghayb)**, known only to Allah (SWT).

It is established that the deceased are shown their eventual place in Paradise or Hell on a daily basis, but they do not have the ability to leave their graves or interact with the living. Such beliefs also contradict clear statements in the Qur'an. Among the many relevant verses, the following may be particularly pertinent:

ثُمَّ إِنَّكُم بَعْدَ ذَٰلِكَ لَمَيِّتُونَ

ثُمَّ إِنَّكُمْ يَوْمَ ٱلْقِيَٰمَةِ تُبْعَثُونَ

*After that you will surely die, then on the Day of Judgment you will be resurrected. (Al-Mu'minun Ch 23:15-16; interpretation of the meaning)*

## 3.8 Seeing the Prophet (ﷺ) when awake

It is possible for a person to see the Prophet (ﷺ) in a dream, and that Shaitan cannot appear in the actual image of the Prophet (ﷺ), but he could appear in another form and claim that he is the Prophet (ﷺ). Abu Hurayrah (ra) said: I heard the Prophet (ﷺ) say: "Whoever sees me in a dream will see me when he is awake; the Shaitan cannot take my shape." [Bukhari; Muslim]

Asim ibn Kulayb (who said), my father told me: I said to Ibn 'Abbas (ra): "I saw the Prophet (ﷺ) in a dream." He said, "Describe him to me." He said, "I mentioned al-Hasan ibn 'Ali (ra) and said that he (ﷺ) looked like him." He (Ibn Abbas) said: "You indeed saw him." [Mustadrak al-Hakim]

If a person claims that he has seen the Prophet (ﷺ) in a dream in shape of another person, then he has not seen the Prophet (ﷺ). The correct view of the scholars is that he (ﷺ) may be seen at any age or in any condition, so long as he (ﷺ) appears as he (ﷺ) really looked at any time, whether as a youth, in the prime of manhood, in later age or any other time of his life. However, if someone sees a figure claiming to be the Prophet (ﷺ) in a form that does not match his authentic description, then this is not the Prophet (ﷺ); rather, it is possible that Shaytan has appeared in disguise.

Seeing the Prophet (ﷺ) when awake is another topic of the highest controversy on which Ummah has been divided. This topic has done the most severe damage to Muslims today in the subcontinent. Justification and counter-justification of the groups have been summarized below.

One group of scholars claim the Prophet (ﷺ) did not pass away. He (ﷺ) is the way he (ﷺ) was alive before death and he (ﷺ) can hear us. As per this concept, *'the Prophet (ﷺ) is alive in his grave, in a worldly manner. He (ﷺ) is nourished by Allah in his grave, and he (ﷺ) engages in the performance of Salaah. He (ﷺ) also hears directly the greetings/blessings (durood) sent to him by one who stands close to his grave'*. Many prominent religious leaders, preachers, famous scholars and personalities claimed that they used to see the Prophet (ﷺ) when awake. The other claims are as follows:

- He (ﷺ) remains present in religious gatherings and people leave one vacant seat on the stage/dias for him in some places.

- The Prophet (ﷺ) sometimes gives suggestions to resolve contemporary issues.

- He (ﷺ) joins the supplications on various religious occasions and du'as during Night of Qadr in particular.

- Virtuous people could hear the reply of the Salam by the Prophet (ﷺ).

- There are claims that the Prophet (ﷺ) exposes his holy hand out of the holy grave upon request for kissing.

- It is also reported that all Prophets come out from their graves as and when they wish and virtuous men can only see them.

These claims are available in recorded form in numerous popular Islamic books. Various hadiths and the Qur'anic verses are put forward to justify their view. Some of the supportive references of these views are listed below.

1. **The verse of the Qur'an**: *"Think not of those as dead who are killed in the way of Allah. Nay, they are alive, with their Lord, and they have provision," (Ali 'Imran Ch 3:169; interpretation of meaning)*

2. **Hadith**: Prophet (ﷺ) said: "The Prophets are alive and they pray in their graves." [Sunan al-Kubra lil Bayhaqi]

3. **Hadith:** Anas ibn Malik (ra) reported: The Messenger of Allah (ﷺ) said, "I passed by Musa (as) during my night journey (Isra') near the red mound; he was praying in his grave." [Muslim]

4.  **Hadith**: Narrated Anas (ra): The Prophet (ﷺ) said, "When a human being is laid in his grave and his companions return and he even **hears their footsteps**, two angels come to him and make him sit and ask him: What did you use to say about this man, Muhammad (ﷺ)? He will say: I testify that he is Allah's slave and His Apostle. Then it will be said to him, 'Look at your place in the Hell-Fire. Allah has given you a place in Paradise instead of it.' The Prophet (ﷺ) added: The dead person will see both his places. But a non-believer or a hypocrite will say to the angels, 'I do not know, but I used to say what the people used to say!' It will be said to him, 'Neither did you know nor did you take the guidance (by reciting the Qur'an).' Then he will be hit with an iron hammer between his two ears, and he will cry and that cry will be heard by whatever approaches him except human beings and jinns." [Bukhari]

5.  **Hadith**: It was narrated that Anas (ra) said: "During the night, the Muslims heard the Messenger of Allah (ﷺ) standing and calling out at the well of Badr; 'O Abu Jahl bin Hisham! O Shaaibh bin Rabiah! O 'Utbah bin Rabiah! O Umayyah bin Khalaf! Have you found what your Lord promised to be true? For I have found what my Lord promised me to be true.' They (companions) said: 'O Messenger of Allah (ﷺ), are you calling out to people who have turned into rotten corpses?' He (ﷺ) said: 'You do not hear what I say any better than they do, but they cannot answer.' [Sunan an-Nasai]

6.  **Hadith**: Aws ibn Abi Aws (ra) who said: The Messenger of Allah (ﷺ) said: "One of the best of your days is Friday. On it, Adam was created, on it he died, on it the Trumpet will be sounded, and

on it all creation will swoon. So, send a great deal of blessings upon me on this day, for your blessings will be shown to me." They said, "O Messenger of Allah (ﷺ), how will our blessings be shown to you when your body has disintegrated?" He (ﷺ) said, "Allah has forbidden the earth to consume the bodies of the Prophets." [Musnad Ahmad]

Straightforward interpretation of the above references leads to the conclusion that if martyrs are not dead and they get their provisions, the Prophets are also alive in graves (in a worldly manner) and they are getting their provisions because their ranks are higher. Secondly, the prophets pray in their graves. Thirdly, communication between the alive and dead is available in the hadith of Sunan an-Nasai.

With reference to the Qur'anic verse 3:169, there is a clear explanation in authentic hadith. It was narrated from 'Abdullah (ra) concerning the Verse: *"Think not of those as dead who are killed in the way of Allah. Nay, they are alive, with their Lord, and they have provision,"* [Ch 3:169] that he (Abdullah) said: We asked about that, and the Prophet (ﷺ) said: Their souls are like green birds that fly wherever they wish in Paradise, then they come back to lamps suspended from the Throne. While they were like that, your Lord looked at them and said, "Ask me for whatever you want." They said: "O Lord, what should we ask You for when we can fly wherever we wish in Paradise?" When they saw that they would not be left alone until they had asked for something, they said: "We ask You to return our souls to our bodies in the world so that we may fight for Your sake (again)." When He saw that they would not ask for anything but that, they were left alone. [Sunan Ibn Majah]

Abdur-Rahman bin Ka`b bin Malik narrated from his father that Allah's Messenger (ﷺ) said: "The believer's soul is a bird that feeds on the trees of Paradise until Allah sends it back to its body when the person is resurrected." [Musnad Ahmad]

Interpretation of the verse 3:169 in the hadith is self-explanatory that the souls are like birds in Paradise. Note the phrases 'to return our souls to our bodies in the world' and 'until Allah sends it back to its body.' Therefore, the bodies are in the grave while souls are in Paradise and thus it is a life in barzakh and they will be resurrected like others.

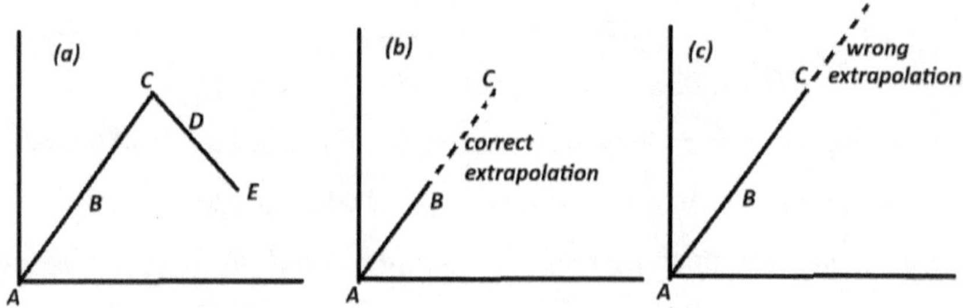


**Fig 4**: *Extrapolation explained*

[Note: Extrapolation is a method in Mathematics that involves predicting the trend beyond study range where complete behaviour is known. Fig (a) is the complete trend of a parameter. If the trend in Fig (b) is determined upto B, we can estimate or predict the trend upto C by extrapolation since Fig (a) is available. Suppose trend upto C is only studied instead of complete behaviour as in Fig (a), and if inferences are made, then it is a wrong extrapolation because entire range was not studied and trend CDE is not captured.]

It is narrated in the hadith of al-Bukhari that the dead hears the footsteps of the persons. This hadith does not go beyond footsteps. Not a single source is available that proves that communication of the dead with the earth continues beyond the footstep. Since, barzakh is a matter of ilmul gaib, '**extrapolation**' cannot be applied to draw conclusion. (Even, in case of knowledge of seen, extrapolation cannot be applied arbitrarily.)

The incident of Badr holds a unique place in Islamic history for clear reasons. Among those who perished, such as Abu Jahl, Utbah, and others, were some of the fiercest enemies of Islam who had rejected the Prophet (ﷺ). The event where the Prophet (ﷺ) spoke to the dead was a one-time occurrence during his lifetime. It was a miracle granted by Allah (SWT), allowing him to address the deceased pagans from the battle of Badr, who were able to hear him. This miraculous event falls under the realm of *ilmul gaib* and should not be extended to the Prophet's followers. As previously discussed in section 2.4, the companions did not possess *ilmul gaib*. Therefore, cases involving divine revelation or the knowledge of the unseen granted to Prophets should not be generalized to others. The Prophet (ﷺ) witnessed the burning cloak in Mid'am's (ra) grave, the squeezing of Saaad bin Mua'z's (ra) grave, the prayer of Musa (as) in his grave, and the punishment of other people in their graves. However, this does not imply that his followers, including the Companions, possessed the ability to see these unseens.

Moreover, the Prophet (ﷺ) did not address deceased pagans by name in other battles, as it was not a common practice of his. Bringing dead to life was a unique mu'jiza granted to Prophet Issa (as) [although there is no evidence to suggest that those who returned to life after death continued living afterward]. Only Allah SWT knows which miracles/mu'jizas are to be bestowed upon each Prophet and when they will be bestowed. Allah says (interpretation of the meaning):

*and ʿmake himʾ a messenger to the Children of Israel ʿto proclaim, ʾ 'I have come to you with a sign from your Lord: I will make for you a bird from clay, breathe into it, and it will become a ʿrealʾ bird—by Allah's Will. I will heal the blind and the leper and raise the dead to life—by Allah's Will. And I will prophesize what you eat and store in your houses. Surely in this is a sign for you if you ʿtrulyʾ believe. (Ali- Imran Ch 3:49)*

The Prophet (ﷺ) left us for ever and he (ﷺ) was buried. On the day of demise of the holy Prophet (ﷺ), Abu Bakr (ra) delivered a Khutba which is as follows. This hadith is presented in Chapter 1 and reproduced here again for continuity of reading.

Narrated 'Aisha (ra): Allah's Messenger (ﷺ) died while Abu Bakr (ra) was at a place called As-Sunah (Al-'Aliya) 'Umar (ra) stood up and said, "By Allah! Allah's Messenger (ﷺ) is not dead!" 'Umar (ra) (later on) said, "By Allah! Nothing occurred to my mind except that." He said, "Verily! Allah will resurrect him and he will cut the hands and legs of some men." Then Abu Bakr (ra) came and uncovered the face of Allah's Messenger (ﷺ), kissed him and said, "Let my mother and father be sacrificed for you, (O Allah's Messenger ﷺ), you are good in life and in death. By Allah in Whose Hands my life is, Allah will never make you taste death twice." Then he went out and said, "O oath-taker! Don't be hasty." When Abu Bakr (ra) spoke, 'Umar (ra) sat down. Abu Bakr (ra) praised and glorified Allah and said, No doubt! Whoever worshipped Muhammad, then Muhammad is dead, but whoever worshipped Allah, then Allah is Alive and shall never die." Then he recited Allah's Statement.: *"(O*

*Muhammad) Verily you will die, and they also will die."* (Ch 39:30) He also recited: *"Muhammad is no more than an Apostle; and indeed, many Apostles have passed away, before him, if he dies or is killed, will you then turn back on your heels? And he who turns back on his heels, not the least harm will he do to Allah And Allah will give reward to those who are grateful." Ch 3:144)*

The people wept loudly, and the Ansar were assembled with Sad bin 'Ubada (ra) in the shed of Bani Saida. They said (to the emigrants). "There should be one 'Amir from us and one from you." Then Abu Bakr (ra), Umar bin Al-Khattab (ra) and Abu 'Baida bin Al-Jarrah (ra) went to them. 'Umar (ra) wanted to speak but Abu Bakr (ra) stopped him. 'Umar (ra) later on used to say, "By Allah, I intended only to say something that appealed to me and I was afraid that Abu Bakr (ra) would not speak so well." Then Abu Bakr (ra) spoke and his speech was very eloquent. He said in his statement, "We are the rulers and you (Ansars) are the ministers (i.e. advisers)," Hubab bin Al-Mundhir (ra) said, "No, by Allah we won't accept this. But there must be a ruler from us and a ruler from you." Abu Bakr (ra) said, "No, we will be the rulers and you will be the ministers, for they (i.e. Quarish) are the best family amongst the 'Arabs and of the best origin. So, you should elect either 'Umar (ra) or Abu 'Ubaida bin Al-Jarrah (ra) as your ruler." 'Umar (ra) said (to Abu Bakr), "No but we elect you, for you are our chief and the best amongst us and the most beloved of all of us to Allah's Messenger (ﷺ)." So 'Umar (ra) took Abu Bakr's (ra) hand and gave the pledge of allegiance and the people too gave the pledge of allegiance to Abu Bakr (ra). Someone said, "You have killed Sad bin Ubada." 'Umar (ra) said, "Allah has killed him." [Bukhari]

The sentences *'Allah will never make you taste death twice'* (in the Hereafter, there is no death and life is eternal), *'Whoever worshipped Muhammad* ﷺ*, then Muhammad* ﷺ *is dead'*, verses 39:30 and 3:144 lead to a conclusion that the Prophet (ﷺ) is no more with us. He (ﷺ) will not come to the world again. In fact, he (ﷺ) will be the first person for whom holy grave will be opened on the day of Resurrection.

Narrated Abu Hurairah (ra): The Messenger of Allah (ﷺ) said: "I will be the leader of the sons of Adam (as) on the Day of Resurrection, and the first one for whom the grave is opened, and the first one to intercede and the first one whose intercession will be accepted." [Muslim]

Narrated `Aisha (ra): The Prophet (ﷺ) expired in my house and on the day of my turn, leaning against my chest. One of us (i.e. the Prophet's wives) used to recite a prayer asking Allah to protect him from all evils when he (ﷺ) became sick. So, I started asking Allah to protect him from all evils (by reciting a prayer). He (ﷺ) raised his head towards the sky and said, "With the highest companions, with the highest companions فِي الرَّفِيقِ الأَعْلَى فِي الرَّفِيقِ الأَعْلَى." ` Abdur- Rahman bin Abu Bakr (ra) passed carrying a fresh leaf-stalk of a date-palm and the Prophet (ﷺ) looked at it and I thought that the Prophet (ﷺ) was in need of it (for cleaning his teeth). So, I took it (from `Abdur Rahman) and chewed its head and shook it and gave it to the Prophet (ﷺ) who cleaned his teeth with it, in the best way he (ﷺ) had ever cleaned his teeth, and then he gave it to me, and suddenly his hand dropped down or it fell from his hand [i.e. he (ﷺ) expired] So, Allah made my saliva mix with his saliva **on his last day on earth** and **his first day in the Hereafter.** [Bukhari]

The above hadith of al-Bukhari is highly relevant here and self explanatory that states that mother of beleivers, Aisha (ra) clearly stated that the Prophet (ﷺ) is in the eternal life of Hereafter.

The Prophet (ﷺ) was made to go forward to lead the other prophets in prayer in Al-Masjid Al-Aqsa during Isra' and Mi'raj. But when he (ﷺ) reached heavens and the gates of heavens were opened one by one, he (ﷺ) found that the Prophets Adam (as), Musa (as), Harun (as), Idris (as), Yusuf (as), Issa (as), Yahya (as) and Ibrahim (as) were already present there to greet him. It is quite astonishing that how other prophets could reach the heavens (at an infinite distance beyond our perception) after performing salat in congregation behind our Prophet (ﷺ) in Jerusalem. Even if they travelled at the speed of light (speed of light is 3 lakhs kilometre in one second and is the fastest entity in the universe), it is not possible by laws of Physics, because sunlight from the sun at finite distance takes 8 minutes 20 sec to reach the earth. Light takes one lakh years to cross our galaxy, the *Milky Way*. Actually, it is not surprising that other prophets had reached earlier because they already died and they are in the life of barzakh. It is not the worldly life and **'space-time continuum'** of Modern Physics is not applicable to them.

Based on the above discussion, it is clear that the Prophets and Messengers were also human beings (not in honour and rank*) and their worldly life also ended, that is, they left us for ever. They will not come to this world again. However, they are alive in their holy graves, offering prayers and are enjoying a special and honourable life in the graves. This life is not like the life of this world and is different from the life of ordinary dead people. It is different from the afterlife of Siddiqin, Shuhada and Salehin. Our beloved Prophet Muhammad ﷺ is also alive in his holy grave and is enjoying the special blessings and blessings that Allah Almighty has reserved for him. Only Allah knows the nature of the life of Prophets in their holy graves.

There is no authentic hadith reporting that the Companions of the Prophet (ﷺ) ever saw him when awake including the most beloved Companions of the Prophet (ﷺ). Narrated Amr bin Al-As (ra): The Prophet (ﷺ) deputed me to command the Army of Jat-as-Salasil. I came to him and said, "Who is the most beloved person to you?" He (ﷺ) said, "Aisha (ra)." I asked, "Among the men?" He (ﷺ) said, "Her father." I said, "Who then?" He (ﷺ) said, "Then Umar bin Al-Khattab (ra)." He (ﷺ) then named other men. [Bukhari]

Scholars point out that Aisha (ra), the Mother of the Believers, lived beside the Prophet's (ﷺ) holy grave for 12 years and continued to live for about 44 years after his demise. Yet, there is no authentic narration from Aisha (ra) claiming to have seen the Prophet (ﷺ) while awake after his death. During the caliphate of Usman (ra), when the challenges greatly increased, he could have benefitted from the Prophet's (ﷺ) guidance, but this did not occur. Similarly, during the caliphate of Ali (ra), in critical moments like the Battles of Jamal, Nahrawan, and Siffin, he would have needed consultation from the Prophet (ﷺ), but this did not happen. Aisha (ra) herself faced a difficult decision regarding her participation in the Battle of Jamal, but she received no direct guidance from the Prophet (ﷺ). The same can be said for the needs of Hassan (ra) and Hussayin (ra). Given that none of these beloved and closest companions, including Aisha (ra), Abu Bakr (ra), Umar (ra), Usman (ra), Ali (ra), Hassan (ra), and Hussayin (ra) saw the Prophet (ﷺ) while awake after his death, claims by others of seeing him (ﷺ) in such a state are highly questionable.

While the Prophet Muhammad (ﷺ) is no longer physically among us, *durud* **serves as a living spiritual link** between him (ﷺ) and the Ummah. Durud is delivered to him by angels and is responded by the Prophet (ﷺ). Abdullah bin Mas'ud narrated that the Messenger of Allah (ﷺ) said, **"Indeed, Allah (Most High) has angels who travel the Earth conveying to me the Salam of my Ummah".** [Sunan an-Nasai, Musnad Ahmad] Narrated Abu Hurairah (ra): The Prophet (ﷺ) said: If any one of you greets me, Allah returns my soul to me and I respond to the greeting. [Abu Dawud, Musnad Ahmad]

The confusion about the possibility of direct communication between the Prophet ﷺ and his Ummah has been caused by the misinterpretation of some hadiths by some individuals, and one such is follows.

**Hadith**: Nafi' reported: Abdullah Ibn Umar (ra) when he arrived on his journey, he would enter the mosque of Madina and then go to the graves. Ibn Umar (ra) would say, "Peace be upon you, O Messenger of Allah ﷺ. Peace be upon you, O Abu Bakr. Peace be upon you, O my father." [al-Sunan al-Kubraa lil-Bayhaqi]

Above hadith is labelled Sahih and it affirms the legitimacy of visiting the Prophet's ﷺ grave and greeting him with peace. However, it does not imply any form of direct communication, as some may claim. Because, in every prayer during the Tashahhud, we say: *"As-salamu 'alaika ayyuhan-nabiyyu wa raḥmatullahi wa barakatuh"* (Peace be upon you, O Prophet, and the mercy of Allah and His blessings). This greeting is not based on the belief that the Prophet ﷺ hears it directly; rather, it is a form of sending salutations with the understanding that the angels convey it to him. Had Ibn 'Umar (ra) intended his greeting to signify direct communication, it would be inconsistent for him to address Abu Bakr (ra) and his own father, 'Umar ibn al-Khaṭṭab (ra), in the same manner. This suggests that his salutations were not premised on the assumption of an ongoing, conscious dialogue, but rather constituted formal expressions of respect and supplication, in accordance with established prophetic tradition.

When visiting the graves of the believers—even those who were not particularly known to us—we are taught to say: "As-salamu 'alaykum ahla al-diyari min al-mu'minin wa al-muslimin, ………" (Peace be upon you, O inhabitants of the dwellings, from among the believers and the Muslims. …….." [Sahih Muslim] At first glance, this salam may seem as though we are addressing the deceased directly—as if speaking to them in conversation. The purpose of this greeting is not to *call upon* the deceased, but rather to offer peace upon them and make du'a for them, as instructed by the Prophet ﷺ. While the language uses the second person (upon *you*), it does not imply that we are seeking anything from the dead or engaging them in direct dialogue.

While some scholars have inferred that the Prophet ﷺ hears greetings directly from those near his grave, this is not based on a specific sahih hadith. There is nothing in the Quran or in the authentic Sunnah to indicate that the Prophet (ﷺ) can hear every Du'a or call from human beings. Rather it is proven that the only thing that reaches him (ﷺ) is salaam and durud.

**Hadith**: Narrated 'Urwa: When those (Muslims) at Bir Ma'una were martyred and 'Amr bin Umaiya Ad-Damri (ra) was taken prisoner, 'Amir bin at-Tufail, pointing at a killed person, asked 'Amr, "Who is this?" 'Amr bin Umaiya (ra) said to him, "He is 'Amir bin Fuhaira (ra)." 'Amir bin at-Tufail said, "I saw him lifted to the sky after he was killed till I saw the sky between him and the earth, and then he was brought down upon the earth. Then the news of the killed Muslims reached the Prophet (ﷺ) and he (ﷺ) announced the news of their death saying, "Your companions (of Bir Ma'una) have been killed, and they have asked their Lord saying, *'O our Lord! Inform our brothers about us as we are pleased with You and You are pleased with us.*" So Allah informed them (i.e. the Prophet (ﷺ) and his companions) about them (i.e. martyrs of Bir Mauna). On that day, `Urwa bin Asma bin As-Salt who was one of them, was killed, and `Urwa (bin Az- Zubair) was named after `Urwa bin Asma and Munjir (bin Az-Zubair) was named after Munjir bin `Amr (who had also been martyred on that day). [Bukhari]

The invocation of the martyrs is indeed noteworthy. It is significant to observe that the noble Companions (رضي الله عنهم), even during the lifetime of the Prophet ﷺ, did not address him in their supplications by saying, "O our Prophet (ﷺ)..." This reflects their clear understanding of the concept of *Tawheed* — that supplication (*du'a*) is an act of worship directed solely to Allah. They understood that the Prophet ﷺ does not hear the calls of others directly unless Allah permits him to do so.

The basic principle concerning the dead is that they do not hear the words of living because Allah says: "but you cannot make hear those who are in graves" (Surah Fatir Ch 35: 22).

The arguments and advocacy supporting the belief that the Prophet (ﷺ) did not expire seem to stem from a concern that denying this would diminish his rank and honor (نَعُوْذُ بِالله). If this is the sole basis for the belief, the argument is quite weak for two reasons:

i.   There is no doubt among the entire Ummah that the Prophet (ﷺ) occupies the highest rank and honour here and Hereafter. All love him with due respect and he (ﷺ) is always within Ummah's hearts.

ii.  The arguments also imply that as if worldly life is better than the eternal life. There are indications in the hadiths that the Prophet (ﷺ) was desirous of the eternal life once the mission was complete. Because he (ﷺ) knew that Paradise is a place described as a "garden of everlasting bliss" and a "home of peace." The Prophet (ﷺ) saw the Paradise during his M'iraj. The Messenger of Allah (ﷺ) said: Allah has said: "I have prepared for My righteous servants what no eye has seen, what no ear has heard, and what no heart has conceived." (Tirmizi).

Narrated Abu Said Al-Khudri (ra): Allah's Messenger (ﷺ) addressed the people saying, "Allah has given option to a slave to choose this world or what is with Him. The slave has chosen what is with Allah." Abu Bakr (ra) wept, and we were astonished at his weeping caused by what the Prophet (ﷺ) mentioned as to a slave (of Allah) who had been offered a choice, (we learned later on) that Allah's Messenger (ﷺ) himself was the person who was given the choice, and that Abu Bakr (ra) knew the best of all of us. Allah's Messenger (ﷺ) added, "The person who has favoured me most of all both with his company and wealth, is Abu Bakr (ra). If I were to take a Khalil other than my Lord, I would have taken Abu Bakr (ra) as such, but (what relates us) is the Islamic brotherhood and friendliness. All the gates of the Mosque (Mosque of the Prophet ﷺ) should be closed except the gate of Abu Bakr (ra)." [Bukhari]

A'ishah (ra) said that Allah's Messenger (ﷺ) would say, **"No prophet dies until he sees his place in Jannah and then he is given the option [to choose this life or the Hereafter]."** So when he (ﷺ) suffered from illness on his death-bed, he (ﷺ) became unconscious. When he (ﷺ) regained consciousness, he (ﷺ) looked up into the sky and said: **"With those upon whom Allah has bestowed His Favour from among the Prophets, the truthful who aided the truth, the martyrs and the righteous—how excellent these companions are!** (Ch 4:69) O Allah forgive me, have mercy on me, and unite me with the highest companionship." So, from that, I knew he (ﷺ) had chosen the Hereafter. [Bukhari, Muslim]

Similar hadith is reported about Prophet Musa (as) in al-Bukhari. Narrated Abu Huraira (ra): The angel of death was sent to Musa (as) and when he went to him, Musa slapped him severely, spoiling one of his eyes. The angel went back to his Lord, and said, "You sent me to a slave who does not want to die." Allah restored his eye and said, "Go back and tell him (i.e. Musa) to place his hand over the back of an ox, for he will be allowed to live for a number of years equal to the number of hairs coming under his hand." (So, the angel came to him and told him the same). Then Musa (as) asked, "O my Lord! What will be then?" He said, "Death will be then." He said, "(Let it be) now." He asked Allah that He bring him near the Sacred Land (Jerusalem) at a distance of a stone's throw. Allah's Messenger (ﷺ) said, "Were I there I would show you the grave of Musa (as) by the way near the red sand hill." [Bukhari]

Even a common Muslim desires eternal life as a place of eternal bliss, luxury and pleasure. Narrated Abu Sa'id Al-Khudri (ra): Allah's Messenger (ﷺ) said: When the funeral is ready and the men carry it on their shoulders, if the deceased was righteous it will say, "Present me (hurriedly)," and if he was not righteous, it will say, "Woe to it (me)! Where are they taking it (me)?" Its voice is heard by everything except man and if he heard it he would fall unconscious." [Bukhari]

Note the phrase *"it will say"*. Means, the dead will say when it is still on the earth and not yet buried. People carrying it do not hear. So, the transition of life starts after death.

Abu Huraira (ra) reported Allah's Apostle (ﷺ) as saying: "Make haste at a funeral; if the dead person was good, it is a good state to which you are sending him on; but if he was otherwise it is an evil of which you are clearing-out yourselves." [Muslim]

The above discussion may be summarized as follows:

- The Prophet Muhammad ﷺ, like all other Prophets, has passed away from this worldly life.

- All Prophets are really alive in their graves- the reality of which is known only to Allah ﷻ.

- In graves, the Prophets continue to perform **prayer**.

- Prophets' life in grave are different from Siddiqin, Shuhada and Salehin.

- **Angels** convey the **Durud (salutations)** to the Prophet ﷺ.

- On the **Day of Resurrection**, the holy grave of the Prophet ﷺ will be the first to be opened.

- There is no authentic evidence of **direct communication** between the Prophet ﷺ and his companions after his passing.

Direct communication is not possible after death, as the Prophet ﷺ has left the realm of worldly life.

- There is no authentic narration or reliable source that confirms any of the companions of the Prophet ﷺ saw him in a wakeful state after his demise.

For a more detailed discussion on this topic, readers are encouraged to refer to the renowned work *Hayat al-Anbiya* by the eminent scholar and muhaddis, Imam al-Bayhaqi (رحمه الله), which addresses the subject of the Prophets' life in the grave with scholarly depth. Ibn Ḥajar al-ʿAsqalani (d. 852 AH / 1449 CE), one of the foremost hadith scholars and commentators, addressed the issue of the **life of the prophets in their graves** in "*Fath al-Bari*", his commentary on Sahih **al-Bukhari**.

***Honour and rank of the Prophet ﷺ**: The prophet ﷺ was sent to all mankind as messenger of "*a bearer of glad tidings and a warner*" and he ﷺ was therefore a human being. Allah says:

قُلْ إِنَّمَا أَنَا بَشَرٌ مِّثْلُكُمْ يُوحَىٰ إِلَىَّ أَنَّمَآ إِلَٰهُكُمْ إِلَٰهٌ وُٰحِدٌ

*"Say, 'I am only a man like you, to whom has been revealed that your god is one God.'"* (Surah Al-Kahf, Ch 18:110; interpretation of meaning)

**Although the Prophet ﷺ was a human being, he ﷺ was not like other human beings.** The Qur'an clearly affirms his humanity, yet it also distinguishes him by the greatest of honours: **he ﷺ received divine revelation (waḥi)** from Allah SWT. This connection to the Divine sets him apart from all others. Moreover, **he ﷺ was granted countless miracles,** both physical and spiritual, that no ordinary person could perform—such as the splitting of the moon, water flowing from his fingers, and being greeted by trees and stones. His entire life was a living miracle, a sign for all of creation. In terms of **rank, character, and honour**, he ﷺ is beyond comparison. Allah Himself praised him in the Qur'an (interpretation of meaning):

- وَإِنَّكَ لَعَلَىٰ خُلُقٍ عَظِيمٍ

  *And you are truly ˹a man˺ of outstanding character. (Surah Al-Qalam, 68:4)*

- وَمَآ أَرْسَلْنَٰكَ إِلَّا رَحْمَةً لِّلْعَٰلَمِينَ

  *We have not sent you but as a mercy to the worlds. (Surah Al-Anbiya, 21:107)*

Thus, while the Prophet ﷺ was a human being in form, **his reality, status, and nearness to Allah** elevate him far beyond the ordinary.

## 3.9 The Prophet (ﷺ) is the last

Allah SWT says in the Quran (that means):

*Muḥammad is not the father of any of your men, but is the Messenger of Allah and the seal of the prophets. And Allah has 'perfect' knowledge of all things. (Ch 33:40)*

**Hadith**: Isma'il bin Abu Khalid said: "I said to 'Abdullah bin Abi Awfa: 'Did you see Ibrahim, the son of the Messenger of Allah (ﷺ)?' He said: 'He died when he was small, and if it had been decreed that there should be any Prophet after Muhammad (ﷺ), his son would have lived. But there is no Prophet after him.' [Sunan Ibn Majah]

**Hadith**: Sawban (ra) narrated that the Messenger of Allah (ﷺ) said: "The Hour shall not be established until tribes of my Ummah unite with the idolaters, and until they worship idols. And indeed, there shall be thirty imposters in my Ummah, each of them claiming that he is a Prophet. And I am the last of the Prophets, there is no Prophet after me." [Tirmizi]

**Hadith**: Narrated Abu Hurairah (ra): The Prophet (ﷺ) said: The Last Hour will not come before there come forth thirty liar Dajjals (fraudulents) lying on Allah and His Apostle (ﷺ). [Abu Dawud]

**Hadith**: Abu Musa Ash'ari (ra) reported that Allah's Messenger (ﷺ) mentioned many names of his and said: I am Muhammad, Ahmad, Muqaffi (the last in succession), Hashir, the Prophet of repentance, and the Prophet of Mercy. [Muslim]

**Hadith**: The Prophet (ﷺ) has himself said, 'You must know that there will come no Prophet after me and no faith after my faith of Islam...' [Al-Mustadrak Hakim: a part of the hadith].

**Hadith**: Anas (ra) reported that after the death of Allah's Messenger (ﷺ), Abu Bakr (ra) said to 'Umar (ra): Let us visit Umm Aiman (ra) as Allah's Messenger (ﷺ) used to visit her. As we came to her, she wept. They (Abu Bakr and Umar) said to her: "What makes you weep? What is in store (in the next world) for Allah's-Messenger (ﷺ) is better than (this worldly life)." She said: "I weep not because I am ignorant of the fact that what is in store for Allah's Messenger (ﷺ) (in the next world) is better than (this world), but I weep because the revelation which came from the Heaven has ceased to come. This moved both of them to tears and they began to weep along with her." [Muslim]

Note the saying *'the revelation which came from the Heaven has ceased to come.'* That means there is no Prophet after Prophet Muhammad (ﷺ) and after the demise of the Holy Prophet (ﷺ), any kind of divine communication viz. *wahi, ilham* or *kashf* between any person on the earth and Allah SWT is not possible (of course, except good dreams).

**Hadith**: Narrated Abu Huraira (ra) that Allah's Messenger (ﷺ) said, "My similitude in comparison with the other prophets before me, is that of a man who has built a house nicely and beautifully, except for a place of **one brick** in a corner. The people go about it and wonder at its beauty, but say: 'Would that this brick be put in its place!' So, I am that brick, and I am the last of the Prophets." [Bukhari]

**Note**: This hadith is already mentioned in Chapter 1. The Prophet (ﷺ) mentioned about one brick only. This confirms the declaration of finality of Prophethood.

### 3.10 Wali of Allah (Plural: Awliya)

Wali of Allah means 'ally' of Allah. It is a status granted by Allah SWT that is to be attained and not inherited. Allah SWT says (interpretation of meaning):

*There will certainly be no fear for **awliya** of Allah, nor will they grieve.*

*They are those who are faithful and are mindful of Him.*

*For them is good news in this worldly life and the Hereafter. There is no change in the promise of Allah. That is truly the ultimate triumph. (Surah Yunus Ch 10:62-64)*

Ibn Kasir said in his Tafsir: "Here Allah, may He be exalted, tells us that His awliya are those who believe and fear Him, as their Lord describes them. So, everyone who fears Allah and is mindful of Him is a wali. {There will be no fear concerning them} regarding what awaits in the future of the terrors of the resurrection, {nor will they grieve} for what they have left behind in this world."

**Hadith**: It was narrated that Abu Hurairah (ra) said: The Messenger of Allah (ﷺ) said: Among the slaves of Allah are some whom the prophets and martyrs will envy. It was said: Who are they, O Messenger of Allah (ﷺ), so that we may love them? He (ﷺ) said: They are people who love one another for the sake of Allah, not because of ties of trade or kindred. Their faces will be light on thrones of light. They will not fear when the people fear and they will not grieve when the people grieve. Then he recited the words, *There will certainly be no fear for **awliya** of Allah, nor will they grieve.* [Ch 10:62]. [Abu Dawud]

**Hadith**: Narrated Abu Hurairah (ra) from the Prophet (ﷺ) who said: Allah says: "Whosoever shows enmity to a wali of Mine has declared war on Me. My slave draws not close to Me with anything more loved by Me than the obligatory religious duties I have enjoined upon him, and My slave continues to draw close to Me with supererogatory deeds so that I will love him. So, when I love him, I will be his hearing with which he hears, his vision with which he sees, his hand with which he strikes, and his foot with which he walks. So, by My help and guidance he will hear, by My help and guidance he will see, by My help and guidance he will strike, and by My help and guidance he will walk. Were he to ask [something] of Me, I would surely give it to him, and were he to seek refuge in Me, I would surely grant him it. I do not hesitate to do anything as I hesitate to take the soul of My believing slave, for he hates death and I hate to hurt him, but there is no escaping it." [Bukhari]

We should not declare a particular person 'wali' because achieving true faith and piousness are matters of the heart that requires ilmul gaib. Hadith from sahih al-Bukhari of Um Al- 'Ala and narration from Abd al-Rahman of sahih al-Muslim is highly relevant here.

**Hadith**: Abd al-Rahman b. Abu Bakra reported on the authority of his father that a person praised another person in the presence of Allah's Apostle (ﷺ), whereupon he (ﷺ) said: "Woe be to thee, you have broken the neck of your friend, you have broken the neck of your friend; he (ﷺ) said this twice. If one of you has to praise his friend at all, he should say: I think (him to be) so and Allah knows it well and I do not know the secret of the heart and Allah Knows the destined end, and I cannot testify his purity against Allah but (he appears) to be so and so." [Muslim]

**Hadith**: Narrated Kharija bin Zaid bin Sabit: Um Al- 'Ala (ra), an Ansari woman who had given the Pledge of allegiance to Allah's Messenger (ﷺ) said, "Usman bin Maz'un (ra) came in our share when the Ansars drew lots to distribute the emigrants (to dwell) among themselves, he became sick and we looked after (nursed) him till he died. Then we shrouded him in his clothes. Allah's Messenger (ﷺ) came to us, I (addressing the dead body) said, "May Allah's Mercy be on you, O Aba As-Sa'ib! I testify that Allah has honoured you." The Prophet (ﷺ) said, 'How do you know that?' I replied, 'I do not know, by Allah.' He said, 'As for him, death has come to him and I wish him all good from Allah. *By Allah, though I am Allah's Messenger (ﷺ), I neither know what will happen to me, nor to you.*' Um Al-'Ala said, "By Allah, I will never attest the righteousness of anybody after that." She added, "Later I saw in a dream, a flowing spring for `Usman. So, I went to Allah's Messenger (ﷺ) and mentioned that to him. He said: That is (the symbol of) his good deeds (the reward for) which is going on for him." [Bukhari]

The Prophet (ﷺ) forbade declaring someone as definitively righteous, as this is a matter that falls within Allah's knowledge of the unseen (ilmul gaib). The Prophet (ﷺ) prohibited the attestation of righteousness of a Companion [Usman bin Maz'un (ra)] by a Companion [Um Al-'Ala (ra)]. Whereas, Allah SWT says about the Companions:

*It is from these people that We will accept the good they did, and overlook their misdeeds— along with the residents of Paradise, in fulfilment of the true promise they have been given. (Al-Ahqaf Ch 46:16; interpretation of meaning)*

Note the wordings of the Prophet (ﷺ): *"By Allah, though I am Allah's Messenger (ﷺ), I neither know what will happen to me, nor to you."* Let us look at the hadiths about the status of the Prophet (ﷺ) among many hadiths.

**Hadith**: Narrated Abu Hurairah (ra) that the Messenger of Allah (ﷺ) said, "Ask Allah to grant me Al-Wasilah." They said, "O Messenger of Allah (ﷺ)! And what is Al-Wasilah?" He (ﷺ) said, "The highest level of Paradise. No one will attain it except for one man, and I hope that is I." [Tirmizi]

**Hadith**: Narrated Abu Huraira (ra): Allah's Messenger (ﷺ) said, "I have been sent (as an Apostle) in the best of all the generations of Adam's offspring since their Creation." [Bukhari]

**Hadith**: Narrated Abu Hurairah (ra) that the Messenger of Allah (ﷺ) said, "I am the first for whom the earth will be split, and then I will be adorned with garments from the garments of Paradise. Then I will stand at the right of the Throne. No one from the creation will be in that place other than I." [Tirmizi]

The highest status of the Prophet (ﷺ) is beyond doubt among the Ummah. Possibly, the message conveyed by this sentence is that granting Paradise or Hell is within the Jurisdiction of Allah SWT and it is His Domain. It is an audacity on our part to interfere within Allah's Dominion. Secondly, the Prophet of Allah (ﷺ) wanted to make people afraid of Hereafter so that they take the religion seriously. Sometimes Allah's Apostle (ﷺ) used to warn people by saying similar sentences. Narrated Abu Hurairah (ra): Messenger of Allah (ﷺ) got up when the Verse: *And warn your tribe of near kindred.... (Ch 26: 214)* was revealed and said, "O Quraish people! (or he said a similar word) Buy yourselves! I cannot save you from Allah (if you disobey Him) O Bani Abu Manaf! I cannot save you from Allah (if you disobey Him). O Abbas! The son of Abdul Muttalib! I cannot save you from Allah (if you disobey Him) O Safiya, (the aunt of Messenger of Allah ﷺ) I cannot save you from Allah (if you disobey Him). O Fatima, the daughter of Muhammad! Ask what you wish from my property, but I cannot save you from Allah (if you disobey Him)." [Bukhari]

Contrary to wali of Allah SWT, there is another type 'wali' reported in the Qur'an: *wali of Shaitan.* Allah SWT says:

وَإِنَّ ٱلشَّيَـٰطِينَ لَيُوحُونَ إِلَىٰٓ أَوْلِيَآئِهِمْ لِيُجَـٰدِلُوكُمْ ۖ وَإِنْ أَطَعْتُمُوهُمْ إِنَّكُمْ لَمُشْرِكُونَ

*The satans inspire their friends to dispute with you. If you were to obey them, you would be Mushriks. (Al-An'am Ch 6:121; interpretation of meaning)*

Ibn Kasir writes: There are two types of revelation, one from Allah and one from the devil. Allah's revelation came to Prophet Muhammad (ﷺ), while the Shaytan's revelation (i.e. inspiration) comes to his friends.

## 3.11 Can anyone see Allah SWT in dreams and when awake?

Some scholars are of the opinion that the Prophet (ﷺ) saw Allah SWT during Mi'raj. It is mentioned in the Qur'an that nobody can see Allah because our eyes are not designed and fabricated for this. Our vision is much inferior to animal. No one will see Him in this world, because seeing Allah in Paradise is the greatest blessing, that will happen only to the people of Paradise. *Many faces, that day, will be glowing, looking towards their Lord,* (Ch 75: 22-23). So, Allah SWT has kept it for His believers in the abode of honour after the Day of Judgement. The Prophet (ﷺ) said (in connection with fitna of Dajjal) that no one will see Allah SWT until he dies. This is reported in Sahih Muslim. Allah SWT says in the Qur'an (that means):

- *When Musa came at the appointed time and his Lord spoke to him, he asked, "My Lord! Reveal Yourself to me so I may see You." Allah answered, "You cannot see Me! But look at the mountain. If it remains firm in its place, only then will you see Me." When his Lord appeared to the mountain, He levelled it to dust and Moses collapsed unconscious. When he recovered, he cried, "Glory be to You! I turn to You in repentance and I am the first of the believers."* (Al A'raf Ch 7: 143)

- No vision can encompass Him, but He encompasses all vision. For He is the Most Subtle, All-Aware. (Al An'am Ch 6:103)

**Hadith**: Narrated Abu 'Ishaq-Ash-Shaibani: I asked Zir bin Hubaish regarding the Statement of Allah (that means): *And was at a distance of but two bow lengths or (even) nearer; So did (Allah) convey The Inspiration to His slave (Jibril) and then he (Jibril) Conveyed (that to Muhammad).* (An- Najm Ch 53:9-10) On that, Zir said, "Ibn Mas`ud (ra) informed us that the Prophet (ﷺ) had seen Jibril having 600 wings." [Bukhari]

**Hadith**: Narrated `Abdullah (ra): Regarding the Verse (that means): "Indeed he (Muhammad) did see. Of the Signs of his Lord, The Greatest!" (Ch 53:18) That the Prophet (ﷺ) had seen a green carpet spread all over the horizon of the sky. [Bukhari]

**Hadith**: Narrated Aisha (ra): Whoever claimed that (the Prophet) Muhammad (ﷺ) saw his Lord, is committing a great fault, for he (ﷺ) only saw Jibril in his genuine shape in which he was created covering the whole horizon. [Bukhari]

**Hadith**: Narrated Masruq: I asked Aisha (ra): What about His Statement: (that means) *"Then he approached And came closer, And was at a distance of but two bow-lengths or (even) nearer?"* (Ch 53:8-9) She replied: It was Jibril who used to come to the Prophet (ﷺ) in the figure of a man, but on that occasion, he came in his actual and real figure and (he was so huge) that he covered the whole horizon. [Bukhari]

**Hadith**: Narrated Masruq: `Aisha (ra) said, "If anyone tells you that Muhammad (ﷺ) has seen his Lord, he is a liar, for Allah says (that means): *'No vision can grasp Him.'* (Al-An'am Ch 6:103) And if anyone tells you that Muhammad (ﷺ) has seen the Unseen, he is a liar, for Allah says (that means): *"None has the knowledge of the Unseen but Allah."* [Bukhari]

**Hadith**: It was narrated that Masruq said: I was reclining at 'Aishah's (ra) and she said: 'O Abu 'Aishah, there are three things, whoever speaks of one of them has fabricated a great lie against Allah.' I said: 'What are they?' She said: "Whoever claims that Muhammad (ﷺ) saw his Lord, has fabricated a great lie against Allah." He said: "I was reclining, but I sat up and said: 'O Mother of the Believers, wait for me and do not rush me. Didn't Allah say (that means): *"And indeed he saw him in the clear horizon."* and: *"And indeed he saw him at a second descent."*? She said: "I was the first one of this Ummah to ask the Messenger of Allah (ﷺ) about that, and he (ﷺ) said: That was only Jibril, I did not see him in his form which he was created in except on these two occasions. I saw him descending from heaven, the greatness of his form filling the space between heaven and earth. She said: "Have you not heard the saying of Allah, the Mighty and Sublime (that means): *No vision can grasp Him, but He grasps all vision. He is Al-Lad (the Most Subtle and Courteous), Well-Acquainted with all things.*? And have you not heard Allah's saying (that means): *It is not given to any human being that Allah should speak to him unless (it be) by Revelation, or from behind a veil, or (that) He sends a Messenger to reveal what He wills by His Leave. Verily, He is Most High, Most Wise.*? She said: "Whoever claims that the Messenger of Allah (ﷺ) concealed anything of the Book of Allah has fabricated a great lie against Allah, for Allah says (that means): *O Messenger! Proclaim* *(the Message) which has been sent down to you from your Lord. And if you do not, then you have not conveyed His Message....* And she said: "And whoever claims to have been told what will happen tomorrow, he has fabricated a great lie against Allah, for Allah says (that means): *Say: None in the heavens and the earth knows the Ghaib (unseen) except Allah.*" [Muslim]

**Hadith**: It was narrated that Abu Zarr (ra) said: I asked the Messenger of Allah (ﷺ), 'Did you see your Lord?' He (ﷺ) said, "He is veiled by Light, how could I see Him?" [Muslim]

**Hadith**: Narrated Jarir (ra): We were sitting with the Prophet (ﷺ) and he looked at the moon on the night of the full-moon and said, "You people will see your Lord as you see this full moon, and you will have no trouble in seeing Him, so if you can avoid missing (through sleep or business, etc.) a prayer before sunrise (Fajr) and a prayer before sunset (Asr) you must do so." [Bukhari]

Above hadiths are the proof that the Prophet (ﷺ) did not see Allah SWT during Mi'raj. On the other hand, Abdullah Ibn Abbas (ra) is of the view that the Prophet of Allah (ﷺ) saw Allah on the night of Miraj. [Sunan Tirimizi] Scholars are of the opinion that by vision, Ibn Abbas (ra) meant the eyes of the heart and not the eyes of his head. This is established by Ibn Abbas' (ra) other narration in Sahih Muslim.

**Hadith**: The Meaning of the Saying of Allah, The Mighty and Sublime: *And indeed, he saw him at a second descent (another time)"* (Ch 53:13); And did the prophet (saws) see his lord on the night of the Isra? It is narrated on the authority of Ibn 'Abbas that he (the Holy Prophet ﷺ) saw (Allah) with his heart. [Muslim]

Is it possible to see Allah in a dream? No authentic hadith proves that other Prophets and companions of the Prophet (ﷺ) saw Allah SWT in dreams. It is only our Prophet (ﷺ) who saw Allah SWT in a dream. Abdullah Ibn Abbas (ra) said: The Messenger of Allah (ﷺ) said, My Lord came to me tonight in the most beautiful form. I think he (ﷺ) said, in a dream. He said, O Muhammad (ﷺ), do you know what the chiefs on high disputed about? I said, No. He put His hand between my shoulder-blades and I could feel its coolness on my chest (or just beneath my throat), then I knew everything that is in the heavens and on earth. He said, O Muhammad (ﷺ), do you know what the chiefs on high disputed about? I said, Yes. He said, about expiation, and expiation is staying in the mosque after prayers, walking to join congregational prayers, and doing wudu properly in adverse conditions. Whoever does that will live a good life and die a good death, and will be as sinless as the day his mother bore him. He said, O Muhammad (ﷺ), when you pray, say *Allahumma innee asaluka fal al-khayraat wa tark al-munkaraat wa hubb al-masaakeen, wa idha aradta bi ibaadika fitnatan faqbudni ilayka ghayra maftoon* (O Allah, I ask you to make me do good deeds and avoid evil deeds, and to make me love the poor and wretched. If You want to test Your slaves, then take me unto You without subjecting me to the trial). One's status in Paradise may be raised by spreading the greeting of salaam, feeding others, and praying at night when people are sleeping. [Musnad Ahmad, Tirmizi]

## 3.12 Glorification by inanimate objects

The sun, moon, stars, mountains, trees, animals, and even shadows prostrate or glorify Allah. Inanimate objects and animals have awareness and obedience to Allah's will, though it is unseen to us. Allah SWT says (interpretation of meaning):

- *Do you not see that to Allah **prostrates** whoever is in the heavens and whoever is on the earth—the sun, the moon, the stars, the mountains, the trees, the animals, and many of the people? But many are deserving of punishment. (Surah Al-Hajj Ch 22:18)*

- *And to Allah **prostrates** whoever is within the heavens and the earth, willingly or by compulsion, and their shadows as well in the mornings and the afternoons. (Surah Ar-Ra'd Ch 13:15)*

- *We subjugated the mountains with him which used to **glorify** Allah, evening and morning – (Surah Swad Ch 88:18).*

- *The seven heavens and the earth and all that is in them **glorify** Him. There is not a thing but glorifies His praise, but you do not understand their glorification. (Al Isra Ch 17:44)*

**Hadith**: Abu Huraira reported Allah's Messenger (ﷺ) as saying: An ant had bitten a Prophet (one amongst the earlier Prophets) and he ordered that the colony of the ants should be burnt. And Allah revealed to him:" Because of an ant's bite you have burnt a community from amongst the communities which sings My glory." [Muslim]

These verses of the Qur'an and hadiths highlight that the entire universe glorifies and submits to Allah. The form of glorification done by inanimate objects is not verbal or audible in the way we speak or hear.

It may be expressed in a language only Allah understands, or in a state of being—total submission to divine order. In verse 22:18, Allah says *"Do you not see that to Allah prostrates"* whereas in verse 17:44, it is said that *"but you do not understand their glorification"*. These verses are not contradictory. Instead, they refer to different aspects of creation's relationship with Allah. Surah 17:44 emphasizes universal glorification (tasbih) that we cannot perceive. Surah 22:18 emphasizes submission and prostration (sujud)—some of which we can witness, especially among humans. These verses together form a comprehensive picture: All creation glorifies and submits to Allah, but in ways that vary—and some of those ways are beyond human comprehension.

Among the most remarkable miracles of the Prophet ﷺ were those in which inanimate objects—trees, rocks, and even food—responded to him, greeted him, or obeyed his command. These signs not only astonished the Companions (ra) but also served as powerful proofs of his divine mission. There are also reports that the Companions heard the tasbih of inanimate objects during the holy life of the Prophet ﷺ.

**Hadith:** Narrated Abu Zar (ra): The Prophet (ﷺ) asked me at sunset, "Do you know where the sun goes (at the time of sunset)?" I replied, "Allah and His Apostle (ﷺ) know the best." He (ﷺ) said, "It goes (i.e. travels) till it prostrates itself underneath the Throne and takes the permission to rise again, and it is permitted and then (a time will come when) it will be about to prostrate itself but its prostration will not be accepted, and it will ask permission to go on its course but it will not be permitted, but it will be ordered to return whence it has come and so it will rise in the west. And that is the interpretation of the Statement of Allah: "And the sun runs its fixed course for a term (decreed). That is the Decree of (Allah) the Exalted in Might, the All- Knowing." (Ch 36.38) [Bukhari]

**Hadith**: Narrated `Abdullah ibn Mas'ud (ra): We used to consider miracles as Allah's Blessings, but you people consider them to be a warning. Once we were with Allah's Messenger (ﷺ) on a journey, and we ran short of water. He (ﷺ) said, "Bring the water remaining with you." The people brought a utensil containing a little water. He (ﷺ) placed his hand in it and said, "Come to the blessed water, and the Blessing is from Allah." I saw the water flowing from among the fingers of Allah's Messenger (ﷺ), and no doubt, we heard the meal glorifying Allah, when it was being eaten (by him). [Bukhari]

**Hadith**: Narrated Jabir bin `Abdullah (ra): The Prophet (ﷺ) used to stand by a stem of a date-palm tree (while delivering a sermon). When the pulpit was placed for him we heard that stem crying like a pregnant she-camel till the Prophet (ﷺ) got down from the pulpit and placed his hand over it. [Bukhari]

**Hadith**: Narrated by Jabir ibn Samurah (ra): The Messenger of Allah ﷺ said: "Indeed I recognize a stone in Makkah that used to greet me before I was commissioned as a Prophet. I still recognize it now." [Muslim; Tirmizi]

**Hadith**: Jabir (ra) narrated: "'We travelled with the Messenger of Allah (ﷺ) until we halted in a spacious valley. The Messenger of Allah (ﷺ) went to relieve himself, and I followed him, bringing a bucket of water. The Messenger of Allah (ﷺ) looked, but he did not see anything with which to conceal himself, then he saw two trees at the end of the valley.

The Messenger of Allah (ﷺ) went to one of them and took hold of one of its branches, and said: "Follow me, by Allah's Leave," and it came with him like a camel with a nose ring that follows its driver. Then he (ﷺ) went to the second tree and took hold of one of its branches and said: "Follow me, by Allah's Leave," and it came with him in a similar manner. Then when he (ﷺ) reached the middle of the space between them, he (ﷺ) joined them together and said: "Come together and (conceal) me, by Allah's Leave," and they joined together.' "Jabir (ra) said: 'I went away, lest the Messenger of Allah (ﷺ) realize that I was nearby, and go even further away. I sat down, thinking to myself. Then I saw the Messenger of Allah (ﷺ) coming, and the two trees had parted and each one was standing in its own place. [Muslim]

Is it possible to see trees prostrating or to hear tasbih of inanimate? Yes, but only under extraordinary circumstances, such as: a miracle (mu'jizah) for Prophets and the companions who were then present. From the authentic sources, no well-established or sound hadith confirms that the Companions—after the death of the Prophet ﷺ—continued to hear or witness inanimate objects glorifying Allah or giving salaam as they did during the Prophet's ﷺ lifetime.

Can Satan deceive someone into believing they saw this? Yes, definitely by delusion. Satan can exploit pride (I am more special than others and I have become a *wali*), credulity (quick to believe the extraordinary), and spiritual misguidance (wanting to experience hidden knowledge without proper grounding in the Sunnah). This is established by the Quranic verses about magicians of Firwan. In **Surah Ta-Ha (20:66-69)** and **Surah al-A'raf (7:116-117)**, Allah mentions the story of the magicians who challenged Prophet Musa (as). Magicians **did not** turn ropes into real living snakes. Rather, it was **a delusion created by magic. Giving life** is **solely Allah's attribute**, and never within the capacity of human magic or satanic power.

### 3.13 Mubashshirat

Throughout this chapter, the term *mubashshirat* has been frequently mentioned in the context of divine communication. Therefore, a brief explanation of its meaning is provided below.

In Islamic tradition, *mubashshirat* refers to visions or dreams that convey glad tidings, often considered as a form of divine communication, especially after the cessation of formal revelation with the death of Prophet Muhammad (ﷺ).

**Hadith**: Anas bin Malik (ra) narrated: The Messenger of Allah (ﷺ) said: 'Indeed Messenger-ship and Prophethood have been terminated, so there shall be no Messenger after me, nor a Prophet.' He (Anas) said: The people were concerned about that, so he (ﷺ) said: 'But there will be Mubash-shirat.' So, they said: 'O Messenger of Allah (ﷺ)! What is Mubash-shirat?' He (ﷺ) said: 'The Muslim's dreams, for it is a portion of the portions of Prophethood.' [Tirmizi]

This hadith clarifies that after the finality of prophethood, true dreams experienced by believers remain as a remnant of divine communication. Mubashshirat are not considered a source of legislation (shari'ah) but may serve as personal encouragement, spiritual reinforcement, or even warnings. They occur to believers as a gift from Allah, and can sometimes foreshadow future events or provide consolation during hardship.

However, the interpretation of dreams—especially those considered *mubashshirat*—should be approached with great care and caution. Not every dream carries divine significance. The Prophet (ﷺ) said: "Dreams are of three types: a dream from Allah, a dream which causes distress and which comes from the Satan, and a dream which comes from what a person thinks about when he is awake, and he sees it when he is asleep." [Bukhari; Muslim] Misinterpreting dreams can result in confusion, incorrect assumptions, or even misguidance. In fact, determining whether a dream qualifies as *mubashshirat* in absence of the Prophet ﷺ is inherently difficult, as the Prophet ﷺ classified dreams into three types— one from Allah, one from the self, and one from Shayṭan—each with an equal likelihood (probability of each outcome is only 33.3%). Due to the inherent uncertainty and complexity of dreams, scholars emphasize that their interpretation should be entrusted only to those who possess sound Islamic knowledge, deep insight, and wisdom. Narrated Abu Huraira (ra): The Prophet ﷺ used to say, "Do not interpret dreams except by a knowledgeable person or an advisor." [Sunan al-Darimi] This ensures that interpretations remain aligned with the principles of the Shari'ah and are not misrepresented. It must also be acknowledged that the interpretations offered by any individual cannot carry absolute certainty in the absence of Prophets—particularly the Prophet Muhammad ﷺ— whose understanding was divinely guided. Secondly, identical dreams seen by different individuals may bear distinct meanings, as interpretation is influenced by personal context and spiritual state. This underscores the intricacy of dream interpretation and the need for caution when relying on generalized *decodings* commonly found in popular books. The complexity of dream interpretation can be examined under three key aspects:

i. **The Companion's ability to interprete dreams**: There are authentic narrations (hadiths) that demonstrate that the Companions of the Prophet ﷺ could interpret dreams.

**Hadith**: Narrated Ibn `Abbas (ra): A man came to Allah's Messenger (ﷺ) and said, "I saw in a dream, a cloud having shade. Butter and honey were dropping from it and I saw the people gathering it in their hands, some gathering much and some a little. And behold, there was a rope extending from the earth to the sky, and I saw that you (the Prophet ﷺ) held it and went up, and then another man held it and went up and (after that) another (third) held it and went up, and then after another (fourth) man held it, but it broke and then got connected again." Abu Bakr (ra) said, "O Allah's Messenger (ﷺ)! Let my father be sacrificed for you! Allow me to interpret this dream." The Prophet (ﷺ) said to him, "Interpret it." Abu Bakr (ra) said, "The cloud with shade symbolizes Islam, and the butter and honey dropping from it, symbolizes the Qur'an, its sweetness dropping and some people learning much of the Qur'an and some a little. The rope which is extended from the sky to the earth is the Truth which you (the Prophet ﷺ) are following. You follow it and Allah will raise you high with it, and then another man will follow it and will rise up with it and another person will follow it and then another man will follow it but it will break and then it will be connected for him and he will rise up with it. O Allah's Messenger (ﷺ)! Let my father be sacrificed for you! Am I right or wrong?" The Prophet ﷺ replied, "You are right in some of it and wrong in some." Abu Bakr (ra) said,

"O Allah's Prophet ﷺ! By Allah, you must tell me in what I was wrong." The Prophet (ﷺ) said, "Do not swear." [Bukhari]

ii. **The Companions' inability to classify dreams**: Even the noble Companions of the Prophet ﷺ—despite their piety and closeness to revelation—were at times unable to determine the true nature or category of a dream. This highlights the inherent difficulty in discerning whether a dream is divinely inspired, self-generated, or from Shayṭan.

**Hadith**: Jabir (ra) bin Abdullah reported that there came to Allah's Apostle (ﷺ) a desert Arab and said: Allah's Messenger (ﷺ), I saw in the state of sleep as if my head had been cut off and I had been moving on haltingly after it. Thereupon Allah's Messenger (ﷺ) said to that desert Arab: Do not narrate to the people the vain sporting of Satan with you in your sleep and (the narrator) also said: I heard Allah's Messenger (ﷺ) in his subsequent address: None amongst you should narrate the vain sporting of devil with him in the dream. [Muslim]

iii. **True Dreams Experienced by Disbelievers**: Another layer of complexity arises from the fact that even disbelievers have occasionally experienced dreams that later proved to be true. The Qur'an itself mentions such instances (Ch 12:46-49), as in the case of the Egyptian king's dream interpreted by Prophet Yusuf ('alayhis-salam). This demonstrates that truthful dreams are not exclusive to believers, making interpretation more intricate. Some of the most groundbreaking and civilization-shaping inventions in history were inspired by the dreams of non-Muslims. These visionary ideas, born in the subconscious, have left a lasting impact on science and technology. A few notable examples include:

- **The Periodic Table** – Russian chemist Dmitri Mendeleev reportedly saw the complete arrangement of chemical elements in a dream, which led to the development of the modern periodic table.

- **The Sewing Machine** – Elias Howe invented the lockstitch sewing machine after dreaming of a tribe with spears that had holes near the tips—this inspired the placement of the needle's eye.

- **Atomic Structure** – Niels Bohr (Nobel Prize in Physics in 1922) conceived the model of the atom, with electrons orbiting the nucleus, after a dreamlike vision.

- **Aromatic Chemistry** – In 1865, August Kekulé dreamt of a snake biting its own tail, which led to his discovery of the ring structure of benzene, revolutionizing organic chemistry.

- **Neuroscience Breakthrough** – Otto Loewi (Nobel Prize in Medicine in 1936) dreamt of an experiment that would prove the chemical transmission of nerve impulses. Upon waking, he conducted the experiment and confirmed his theory, a landmark discovery in neuroscience.

These examples reflect how powerful and mysterious the realm of dreams can be—even outside the sphere of divine communication.

In conclusion, the essence of the chapter on "Knowledge of the Unseen" can be aptly summarized by a single verse from the Qur'an, which states (interpretation of meaning):

*Say (O Prophet), "I have no power to benefit or protect myself, except by the Will of Allah. If I had known the unknown, I would have benefited myself enormously, and no harm would have ever touched me. I am only a warner and deliverer of good news for those who believe." (Surah Al-A'raaf Ch 7:188)*

# Epilogue

The book begins by addressing the fundamental principle of Islam, monotheism, and provides a clear warning against Shirk. It proceeds to explore the dangers of innovations (Bid'ah), illustrating how Allah SWT and the Prophet (ﷺ) cautioned against them and drawing connections to contemporary innovations. At the end of the book, a critical analysis of the concept of the knowledge of unseen has been included to prevent misunderstandings or misuse. This is important because deceptive acts, such as jugglery or illusions, may originate from Satan to mislead people.

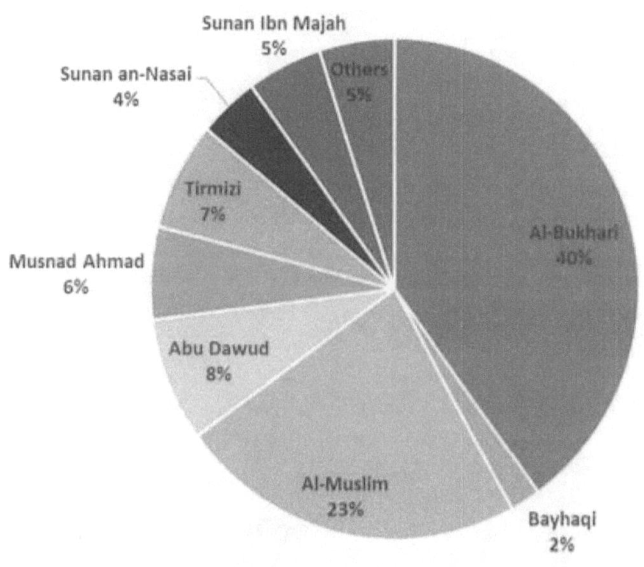


Attempt has been made to use high quality sources throughout the book, keeping in mind the significant responsibility associated with writing on religious matters. There are about 400 relevant hadiths included in this book. The sources of the hadiths are presented in the form of a pie chart, where others 5% include Musnad Abi Yaala, Darimi, Sagheer, Musannaf Ibn Abi Shaybah, Tabarani and Musannaf Abdur Razzaq.